Introdu

The series of books I have writte..., ..., the communications from various groups of spirits to the Rev. G. Vale Owen, are for the express purpose of explaining the reality – the organization, the process, the environment, the progression of spirits, the work, the daily life – of Heaven and the realms below to provide for those interested an understanding of why we are on earth, in our present physical form, and what is waiting for us when our dense shell is cast off and we return to the real world … the spirit world.

The books by the Rev. G. Vale Owen certainly stand on their own and I recommend anyone interested in further research to read his books. I suggest starting with *Beyond the Veil*, a compilation of four books. G. Vale Owen presented a rich commentary from spirits – starting from his own mother, to spirits who had roamed the higher levels of heaven around the earth to the depths of purgatory.

The information provided is revelatory, amazing, and disconcerting. Our status of independent life forms, living a life shaped by random events, beginning and ending on earth is irrevocably altered by what was exposed. It was to add weight to the view of the spirit realm presented in G. Vale Owen's books that I thought writing my own series of books about his was warranted.

The core reason is that in all of his writings the word Spiritism was never uttered. The word spirituality and spiritualism were used, but the tying back of the communications from the other side to the Doctrine of Spiritism was not expressly made. In the entire set of books, nothing said in the thousands of words brought to him from the spirit realm stood in disagreement to the Doctrine of Spiritism … in fact they expanded it. Explanations and glimpses into levels of heaven and its processes were all additive. The spirit world was more fully painted as a real working environment.

I firmly believe that G. Vale Owen was a Spiritist in belief, even though he didn't label himself as one. In the era he lived, with the active pushback from organized religion to the concepts of individual spirituality, reincarnation, and karma may have made a better choice to not make a stand on the Doctrine of Spiritism, or he wasn't aware of the books by Allan Kardec and Leon Denis during the time when the original fervor of Spiritism, spread by the French, had dimmed, and was mainly being revived in the distant shores of Brazil.

In Spiritist literature, published in Brazil, in Portuguese, his name is mentioned. In fact seeing his name in print, alongside a list of Spanish and Portuguese sounding names, who were gathered in the spirit world to help promote Spiritism on earth is what first brought his name to my attention. I had never heard of him before. From that first peek at an incongruent name in a list, I found his books and started my discovery.

In 2016, in a meeting of mediums in a Spiritist center in Rio de Janeiro, my wife and I were told that a spirit would be helping us who was a European; he had tried to spread Spiritists' concepts to America during his physical life and he was now part of a team of spirits who would help the effort to bring the Doctrine of Spiritism to North America. Subsequent communications have solidified my belief that G. Vale Owen is amongst us, assisting this great effort to bring knowledge to the English speaking world about the Third Revelation – Spiritism.

Since his series of books, which were published in the early Twentieth Century, more than four hundred and fifty books have been published in the middle to late 20th Century by the great Brazilian Spiritist medium Francisco (Chico) C. Xavier, all exposing and explaining more about the other side. Other Spiritist authors as well have psychographed (writing down communications from spirits) books; presenting a wealth of information about the unseen spheres around the earth. The vast majority of these have been in Portuguese, and only a fraction has been translated into English. And yet, the information contained in the messages to G. Vale Owen is still pertinent, in that they explore territory and concepts not heretofore mentioned.

2

Hence, I have taken each message, or group of messages – compared it to other Spiritist literature and attempted to explain what it means to us – here on earth. Earth, where each of us, believes at times that we are alone and cast-off from friends, society, and God. Nothing could be further from the truth.

Organization of Spiritism – As Revealed to an Anglican Vicar

I have taken the complete set of his works and categorized it according to the following classifications.

Heaven and Below – Book 1 of Spiritism as Revealed to an Anglican Vicar – Covers communications that pertain to three main themes:

- Life in heaven
- Lower regions
- Appearances of Jesus in the spirit realm

Spirits and the Spirit Universe - Book 2 of Spiritism as Revealed to an Anglican Vicar – Covers communications that pertain to five main themes:

- Spirit Education – Lower levels of heaven
- Spirit Education – Higher levels of heaven
- Spirit Attributes
- Power of Spirits
- Knowledge of the Universe(s)

How We are Guided by Spirits - Book 3 of Spiritism as Revealed to an Anglican Vicar – Covers communications that pertain to three main themes:

- Guiding humans on earth
- Spirit assistance
- Future events

My classifications are not perfect; they overlap at times and cover information that could have been spread to multiple themes.

But, I hope they suffice to broadly discuss the subject under which they were placed.

I have also used the numeric designation of the levels of heaven as originally presented in the books by the Rev. G. Vale Owen. The spirits quite plainly state they are using this numbering for convenience only and that other spirits may use other classifications. As an example, in the books psychographed by Francisco (Chico) C. Xavier, I have not detected this same numbering system, only references to higher or lower spheres.

The spirits communicating to G. Vale Owen, spoke about levels one to ten, with the eleventh level as a major dividing line between knowledge and aptitude for a spirit. The eleventh level is regarded as a major graduation point, where the act of creation begins. All levels below are involved in the process of learning and readying oneself.

In each book, I reproduce this introduction and the chapter covering the life of the Rev. G. Vale Owen. I also reused the Glossary and Bibliography. I wanted each to stand independently. Otherwise all content is original in the three books.

In summary, I have endeavored to gather the available Spiritist literature (in English) and combine it with thoughts coming from the spirit realm through G. Vale Owen to illustrate a small section of the vast spirit universe that awaits each one of us.

How we are Guided by Spirits – Book 3 of Spiritism as Revealed to an Anglican Vicar

By

Brian Foster

http://www.nwspiritism.com/

1st Edition

Table of Contents

The Reverend G. Vale Owen

The Rev. G. Vale Owen, or G.V.O. to his friends and congregation was a Church of England minister who psychographed messages from spirit world, starting in the 1910s. His works correspond with previous Spiritist writings by Allan Kardec and the future works by Francisco (Chico) C. Xavier. His books revealed many levels of heaven and the life of the spirits around us.

Helped by the Spirit World

One never knows what you will find when reading a Spiritist book. Sometimes I have to read a book twice to find a hidden meaning or a nugget of truth I didn't realize at first. When I see a name mentioned I often look it up, trying to find connections between what spirits say and my world.

I learned about Emanuel Swedenborg when his name was mentioned during a speech by a wise spirit in a lecture in the celestial city of Nosso Lar. It was an exciting personal discovery about a man who preceded Allan Kardec in his revelations about the spirit world. He brought the concept that we are the same after death to the courts of Europe in the 1700s. He introduced many Spiritist precepts before they were codified by Mr. Kardec.

I first heard the name of Rev. G. Vale Owen in an even more circuitous manner. I was sitting in my comfortable armchair reading, when my wife, who was sitting on her chair on the other side of a small table spoke to me about a book she had just finished.

She regularly reviews Spiritist books she had read because

there are many only in print in Portuguese. While I can speak the language a little, reading anything more complex than a quick newspaper article is beyond me. Therefore, she discusses any new ideas she has gathered with me.

She was at the end of the book *Voltei*, when she mentioned to me about a party of spirits who were meeting with the spirit author of the book, to let him know he should continue the work for Spiritism that he has had done while in a physical body. My wife read the list of participants, which included Emmanuel, the spirit mentor of Chico Xavier, Andre Luiz, the spirit author of many books, Dr. Bezzara De Menezes, considered to be the father of the Spiritist movement in Brazil.

At first I attempted to ignore her, so I could continue to finish putting my thoughts down on my laptop. She persisted, so I tried to satisfy her with a nod and a grunt. Evidently it wasn't enough, so she put the book in my view and told me to look at the list of invitees.

I quickly glanced at the parade of names and truthfully it was impressive. Many of the spirits who have either been leading the effort to establish Spiritism in Brazil while incarnate, since passed, or in spirit form were in attendance. Most had typical Brazilian names, except the last one; Vale Owen, Rev. G.[1]

Spotting that incongruent name intrigued me. Who was this reverend who attended an event with the leading proponents of Spiritism in the spheres above our planet? I dropped what I was doing and searched for his name.

I rapidly found out the basic facts from Wikipedia:

"Vale Owen was born in Birmingham, England, the eldest son of George Owen, a chemist and druggist, and his wife Emma. He was educated at the Midland Institute and Queen's College, Birmingham (a predecessor college of Birmingham University). In 1893 he was ordained by the Bishop of Liverpool as curate in the parish of Seaforth, in Liverpool. He became curate successively at Fairfield in 1895 and St

Matthew's, Scotland Road, in 1897, both also in Liverpool. In 1900 he became vicar of Orford, Warrington, where he created a new church, which was built in 1908, and worked there until 1922.

The death of his mother in 1909 awoke his psychic abilities and he began to receive psychic communication in 1913. He received messages via a process known as automatic writing, which can be defined as writing performed without conscious thought or deliberation, typically by means of spontaneous free association or as a medium for spirits or psychic forces.

Given the impact on him of the information he received in this way, he converted to Spiritualism."[2]

He converted to Spiritualism, no mention of Spiritism. While Spiritualism is similar in many respects, Spiritism consistently follows the lead of Allan Kardec in the basic messages. Subsequent Spiritist books are meant to supplement and provide us more information. Spiritism isn't meant to be static, but a dynamic supply of knowledge from the spirit realm to us, to be parceled out as we advance enough to comprehend the message.

Reading that I decided not to investigate further, since he didn't seem to be in the Spiritist mainstream while on earth. Then I picked up the book *Voltei* again and looked at the front page to see when the book was first written. I found a handwritten inscription from my wife's and I delightful mentor at the Seara Fraterna Spiritist center in Rio de Janeiro. Her name is Juraci and I had learned to follow her advice implicitly, since when I resisted, something always happened to me to get back on track and do what she had politely mentioned.

Over the years I had learned to read the signs given to me from the spirit plane. Seeing the insistence of my wife and the origin of the book, unmistakably told me to push forward and not to cease my research. If you would like to read about my personal experience with spirits guiding my life, it is all in my book, *7 Tenets of Spiritism – How They Impact Your Daily Life*.

13

The Beginning

Reverend G. Vale Owen (G.V.O. to his friends) was reluctant to believe what he felt coming from the spirit world was true. He tells us:

> "There is an opinion abroad that the clergy are very credulous beings. But our training in the exercise of the critical faculty places us among the most hard-to-convince when any new truth is in question. It took a quarter of a century to convince me - ten years that Spirit Communication was a fact, and fifteen that the fact was legitimate and good."[3]

G. Vale Owen contemplated carefully about speaking to spirits. As a Vicar in the Anglican Church comporting with the other side is not a regular order of business. However, spirits were busy in sending vibrations to G.V.O. to deliver positive feelings and thoughts so he could make his free-will choice to begin in earnest the job of educating humanity about the life which awaits them after death:

> "From the moment I had taken this decision, the answers began to appear. First my wife developed the power of automatic writing. Then through her I received requests that I would sit quietly, pencil in hand, and take down any thoughts which seemed to come into my mind projected there by some eternal personality and not consequence on the exercise of my own mentality. Reluctance lasted a long time, but at last I felt that friends were at hand who wished very earnestly to speak with me. They did not overrule or compel my will in any way - that would have settled the matter at once, so far as I was concerned - but their wishes were made ever more plain."[4]

Once he made his decision to begin psychographing, the process took some time to begin to make sense. G. Vale Owen tells us how he started:

> "I felt at last that I ought to give them an opportunity, for I was impressed with the feeling that the influence was a good one, so, at last, very doubtfully, I decided to sit in my cassock in the

Vestry after Evensong.

The first four or five messages wandered aimlessly from one subject to another. But gradually the sentences began to take consecutive form, and at last I got some which were understandable. From that time, development kept pace with practice. When the whole series of messages was finished I reckoned up and found that the speed had been maintained at an average of twenty-four words per minute."[5]

When the communications from the spirit realm started, there was no turning back. Reading *The Life Beyond the Veil*, I could feel the urge to proceed to the next and the next message. Each interesting in itself; the whole builds into a narrative of the wonders of life in the spirit world. If I was in Vale Owen's shoes, I doubt that after the first few nights of coherent communications, I could ever stop.

Being a Reverend for a small church in Orford, England brought no great compensation. Even though the money would have been welcomed to help his family, G. Vale Owen refused any payment, just like Chico Xavier did in Brazil.

His ideals in denying himself any monetary gain for automatic writing (Spiritist also use the term psychograph) impressed his fellow countrymen. An account of it is mentioned by G. Vale Owen's son, the Rev. Eustace Owen, in writing about his father to the Greater World Association:

"In the book HE LAUGHED IN FLEET STREET, Bernard Falk describes a meeting between Lord Northcliffe and my father, in 'The Times' office, when the former asked him to accept £1,000 for publishing extracts from the Script in the 'Weekly Dispatch.' He continues:

'Vale Owen shook his head. For this part of his writings, he said, he could not take any money. He had been well paid by the publicity given him, and by being able to carry out the sacred duty of placing his revelations before the world. Knowing well Vale Owen's poverty I was genuinely sorry to hear him refuse payment, but he was not to be dissuaded..."[6]

G. Vale Owen knew that if received any money from his efforts he would be accused of falsely creating messages from the spirit world just for the purpose of profit.

Later, in the 1930's the great Brazilian medium Chico Xavier was attacked by many as being one of a large legion of imposters, whose only aim was to increase his personal wealth. Chico said that he could never fall down, since he never stood up, meaning that he couldn't be charged as a person who only wants wealth because he never took money. All proceeds from his books were donated to charity. As a Spiritist, he knew that selling his services that he received as a gift from God is immoral.

Books by Rev. G. Vale Owen

Rev. G. Vale Owen's messages and writing can presently be found in eight books. His first four books were published and then compiled into one edition. Most were published in the 1920s.

1. The Life Beyond the Veil – is composed of the following four books.

    a. The Lowlands of Heaven

    b. The Highlands of Heaven

    c. The Ministry of Heaven

    d. The Battalions of Heaven

2. Outlands of Heaven – which actually contains two books, but were published in one edition.

    a. The Children of Heaven

    b. The Outlands of Heaven

3. Paul and Albert

4. The Kingdom of God – which is composed mainly of G. Vale Owen's interpretation of what the spirit realm

16

communicated to him.

I encourage everyone to read the books by G. Vale Owen, they are fascinating reading and you may have completely different interpretations of what you read than I.

The Lowlands of Heaven

The nightly writings that G. Vale Owen psychographed were first initiated by his deceased mother. She had died on June 8, 1909, at the age of sixty-three. During her life, she had never expressed interest in communicating with spirits.

The first entry in The Lowlands of Heaven is dated Tuesday, September 23, 1913. G.V.O.'s mother describes her home in heaven and her current occupation. Vale Owen asks her what her home is like:

"Earth made perfect. But of course what you call a fourth dimension does not exist here, in a way, and that hinders us in describing it adequately. We have hills and rivers and beautiful forests, and houses, too, and all the work of those who have come before us to make ready. We are at present at work, in our turn, building and ordering for those who must still for a little while continue their battle on earth, and when they come they will find all things ready and the feast prepared."[7]

Vale Owen's mother lived in one the first spheres of heaven. This is where souls who have recently died and who are allowed entry into the celestial spheres first arrive. A majority of the work accomplished is the direct assistance of spirits passing from life on earth or to those in the Lower Zones, or Umbral as the Brazilian Spiritist call it, who require help acclimatizing to the heavenly atmosphere.

The description of life in this sphere has many similarities with descriptions in the Andre Luiz series of books psychographed by Francisco C. Xavier. There is less information about the teams of people who journey to earth to help incarnates. On the other hand there are excursions to others parts of these first levels of heaven which tells us aspects not covered in other published accounts, by other Spiritist mediums.

For example, a series of halls were described, an Orange Hall which contained all permutations of that color, then the Red Hall, which had every hue and gradient of red imaginable. Next Vale Owen's mother told us the purpose of the halls:

> "You are wondering to what purpose these building of crystal are put. They are for studying the effect of colors as applied to different departments of life, animal, vegetable and even mineral life, but the two former chiefly, together with clothing. For both the texture and the hue of our garments take their quality from the spiritual state and character of the wearer. Our environment is part of us, just as with you, and light is one component, and an important one, of our environment. Therefore, it is very powerful in its application, under certain conditions, as we saw it in these halls.

> I am told the results of those studies are handed on to those who have charge of trees and other plant life on earth and other planets. But there are other results which are too rare in nature for such application to the grosser environment of earth and the other planets, so, of course, only a very small part of these studies is handed on in your direction."[8]

There is much more information and accounts that tug at your heart as you are led over the landscape of heaven and the rescuing of souls who had lost hope and need direction.

Sir Arthur Conan Doyle, who was a Spiritualist and fervently believed in the afterlife, wrote the introduction to *The Life Beyond the Veil*. Here is a short excerpt:

> "And is it subversive of old beliefs? A thousand times No. It broadens them, it defines them, it beautifies them, it fills in the empty voids which have bewildered us, but save to narrow pedants of the exact word who have lost touch with the spirit, it is infinitely reassuring and illuminating.

> How many fleeting phrases of the old Scriptures now take visible shape and meaning?

Do we not begin to understand that "House with many mansions," And realize Paul's "House not made with hands," even as we catch some fleeting glance of that glory which the mind of man has not conceived neither has his tongue spoken?"[9]

As Allan Kardec's books brought us an understanding of the spirit realm and our place within it, so has Reverend G. Vale Owen's books presented a picture from a different angle, the same place, the same universe composed of an unimaginable varied landscape and levels. But an account with a different tone more like many of the books which would come after with the advent of the flood of information about ourselves and the spirit world by Chico Xavier.

The Lowlands of Heaven is an account of the love and dedication of the spirit world for us here on earth. It illustrates the enormous effort and organization which is responsible for our chaotic existence on our blue planet.

The Highlands of Heaven

A new narrator takes over, his name is Zabdiel and he resided in the tenth level of heaven. Zabdiel makes it clear that he is using just one method of classification of the many steps of heaven. He quite openly tells us that others have used different words for the hierarchy, but he uses the numbering system since it is simple and direct and easily understood.

Zabdiel takes us on a tour of many levels and the various functions of the higher spheres around our planet. He tells us one of the qualifications for entry:

"This is one of those things which make for difficulty in this life of the spheres. For not until a man has learned to love all without hating any is he able to progress in this land where love means light, and those who do not love move in dim places where they lost their way, and often become so dull in mind and heart that their perception of the truth is as vague as that of outward things."[10]

As with other spirits mentioned in Spiritist literature, Zabdiel is involved in helping others ascend. In one of the communications he is sent to help a brother and sister, who live on level ten, but aren't making progress. Zabdiel asks the spirit, Bepel, who knows the background story concerning the couple, why is this so:

> "Bepel smiled and replied, 'You know the man who lives here, he and his sister. They came over from Spheres Eight and Nine some good while ago together. Here they progressed and, from time to time, have returned to the Fourth Sphere, where they have loved ones and, in especial, their parents. This they have done in order to help them onward. Lately they have come to be some little less at their case in these surrounding for the love they bear to those behind. It would seem that these are making their progress very slowly, and it will be long before they reach this estate. These two, therefore, await the coming of someone who has the authority to permit them depart to take up their abode with those they wish to help, in order that their more continual presence should be at the disposal of them to enable them onward."[11]

This should serve to give you a flavor of the challenges of higher spirits. Dealing with the complexities of people's desires, even when they are already in a relatively high position, takes wisdom and care for those who may be able to help.

The book also has passages which demonstrate the power of a spirit. How they use their mind to create, instead of manual labor.

The spirit realm, arranged G. Vale Owen to psychograph these important revelations to us, so we can see what is ahead of us and to truly comprehend that any sacrifice we make on earth to be a better person is well rewarded in the spirit world.

The Ministry of Heaven

A new group of spirits present themselves to G.V.O. at the beginning of *The Ministry of Heaven*. The manager of the group is known by the moniker, Leader. Stories similar to what Zabdiel told are presented. The group employs a spirit, Kathleen, who is closer

20

to G.V.O. in her time spent on earth, so she may organized their thoughts and words in a manner to comport with the use of English at the time.

There is also a long account of a group that is sent on a mission down to the Lower Zone, where they assist those who are undergoing intense suffering. This account is reminiscent of the book, *Liberation*, by the spirit Andre Luiz, psychographed by Francisco (Chico) C. Xavier.

The descriptions of the types of spirits, their physical forms and their attitudes align with what has been reported in Chico's books and Allan Kardec's interviews with poor spirits in their own purgatories in his book *Heaven and Hell*.

The Battalions of Heaven

In the fourth book, Arnel, the spirit who speaks to G. Vale Owen, tells more about life in the tenth level and fully describes a city that encompasses a university. The majesty of Jesus Christ and the angels which surround him is documented in a moving narrative of His manifestation in the main center of the university.

One of the most compelling aspects of this book is the analysis of the power of Jesus and where it comes from. I haven't detected this depth of explanation into the role and the extent of His reach in our part of the galaxy from other Spiritist literature I have read to date.

The Children of Heaven

The Children of Heaven explores the process of training children in the spirit world. The book delves into great detail the methods and techniques for raising children to become full citizens of the spirit realm. The spirits Castrel and Arnel work with G. V. O. in the production of the messages in this book.

The Outlands of Heaven

The Outlands of Heaven has varied stories, one of which reviews life in the third level of heaven. Another long group of passages analyzes the progress of a colony and some of the improvements and education which transpires in that growing community. There is also a scene about an elevation from the third level of heaven up to the fourth level.

Paul and Albert

The book Paul and Albert, is the story of a once selfish surgeon, who, having abused his position for the satisfaction of his own lesser self and often cruel nature, finds himself in an unfamiliar place.[12]

Paul wanders through what he considers Hell and struggles to exist in a dog-eat-dog world where others like him are sent so they may learn what it is like to be treated as they have treated others.

The book is described on the Christian Spiritualism website as:

"The narrative shows by graphically explained example that every action which has been committed must have its consequences, and that such consequences must be faced by the doer of the action. Thus, for example, we see that those who willfully inflicted pain on others are in some cases subjected to having vicious and sickening 'operations' carried out on them by other equally cruel inhabitants who have learned how to control such situations; the pain is really felt, but the spiritual-body merely continues to live on. It is explained that some of the events in those dark conditions are beyond the power of description, and even if it was possible for them to be described, the content would be not be considered suitable by any reputable publisher."[13]

What we have learned from the book *Liberation*, by Andre Luiz and other accounts of the innate cruelty and depravity of the Lower Zone and the Abyss are all on display in this account.

The Kingdom of God

This book contains many of the Rev. G. Vale Owen's analysis of what he has learned from his communications with various spirits. He explains the concept of God and the science of God. He delves into the verses of the New Testament and how they are explained and expanded by what was brought to him.

Rev. G. Vale Owen – Life After

The first four volumes were a great success and garnered admiration from many who were looking for spiritual guidance. In 1920, the English newspaper, *The Weekly Dispatch*, ran a serialized form of the communications that Mr. Vale Owen received. His books were quite popular.

G. Vale Owen managed to go on a lecture tour in America and the United Kingdom. He gave more than 150 lectures in Great Britain alone. The British newspaper, *The Daily Mail*, described the scene at one of his lectures:

"There were all sorts and conditions of people – clergy-men, Army officers, city men, girl typists, Covent Garden porters, women in working garb, women of leisure, widows in their weeds, laborers in corduroys. These and other types of humanity were all there. When he left the church Mr. Vale Owen was surrounded by men and women who grasped him by both hands. Men bared their heads and a number of women wept. When Mr. Vale Owen freed himself he stood on the steps and the hushed assemblage addressed a few simple words. As he descended the steps hundreds of people again rushed to greet him. It was with the greatest difficultly that his friends, clerical and lay, were able to escort him to the rectory across the road. Thousands of people have written to Mr. Vale Owen congratulating him on his writings. Many people in yesterday's congregation traveled specially from the north of England, Manchester and Leeds in particular, to hear his address."[14]

The messages of love and the revelation of the extent of the spirits who surround and guide us, was too much for the officials of the Church of England, they removed G. Vale Owen from his parish in 1922. Thereby cutting off all income for G.V.O. and his family.

Only the kindness of Sir Arthur Conan Doyle, who organized a contribution from all of his fans was G. Vale Owen able to live the rest of his live from the proceeds of a trust fund. He died in 1931 at the age of 61.

The Rev. G. Vale Owen provided a great service for humanity. His dedication in working tirelessly every night, while still working as a Vicar for his church in Orford, is a testament to his love for us all. He began a spark of recognition of the spiritual universe in England. While it may seem to have died out in the heat and passion of World War II, it started a trend line.

The spirit world tells us that progress isn't a straight line but an upward spiral. It must began somewhere. Allan Kardec started Spiritism in France in the 1850's, G.V.O. supplied another curve up in the 1920's. Chico Xavier dramatically boosted the recognition and information about Spiritism starting in the 1930's to the present day.

Hopefully, the writings given to us by Chico Xavier and G.V.O., and other wonderful Spiritist mediums, will spur on another generation to explore Spiritism – to allow us, here on earth, to realize why exactly we are here, going through our lives, full of conflict, pain, and pleasure.

Introduction – How we are Guided by Spirits – Book 3 of Spiritism as Revealed to an Anglican Vicar

This book covers communications that pertain to three main themes:

1. Guiding humans on earth.

2. Spirit assistance.

3. The future of earth.

Book 3 illustrates the ground game of the spirit world. Via the messages of multiple spirits to the Rev. G. Vale Owen we are presented examples of how the spirit realm above us peers down upon their unruly students. The process of tracking and modifying behavior on an individual and a collective basis is revealed. Even the broader direction of human society in the future is posted for all to see.

To understand our place and the primary function of our spirit mentors one must look upon the earth as a campus. First, a wide range of students are admitted – beginning with souls who have recently graduated from a primitive planet, where the rule of law is kill or be killed. They come to earth and act in a most uncivil manner. Spreading waste and destruction in their path and creating chaos for polite society. What we don't understand is that it is our job to set strict parameters and to teach them the path to civilization – this is the task of the older and wiser members of the student body.

Others have been here from the beginning and are climbing up the steps to graduation. They are well acquainted with the earth and how it works. They know what to expect and have decided to either slowly improve themselves, or fight tooth and nail the impetus to become valued members of earth and of the spirit world around us. The year, or their last life on earth, of their graduation is up to them. They determine the trials and the parameters for promotion to a new, more exalted campus.

Next, we have a group of newly arrived students, who have transferred from a more distinguished campus. They land, look around, and are disgusted at the conditions they detect. They shouldn't be, for they were forewarned that continual misbehavior at their old school would get them expelled to a lesser world. Hence, while they are here, a portion of them tend to be the smartest but the most dissatisfied and prone to impulsively join or form a revolutionary cadre (or to corrupt an existing organization) – whose only aim is to overthrow what has been built and put themselves into power. So they can, with ruthless efficiency, make changes to fit their ideal. These same students forget, this type of behavior – walking over others, treating anyone who disagrees with them as criminal or to be reviled – is exactly what caused them to be expelled in the first place.

Lastly, there are a small minority of incarnates on earth who have come from advanced planets or higher levels of the spirit realm who are here to become beacons of light for the rest of us. They are the unselfish doctors who toil in service of their patients, not the paycheck; the honest politicians who strive to improve and guide their countries to a higher moral level, not the vote buyers who seek to lock their constituents into a cycle of dependence on government largess. They are the ones who rise to the top through their intellect, wisdom, and caring – not by stepping over others.

These four categories are the general representation of the incarnate students. But, there are additional slices of students who are in the spirit world (discarnates or errant spirits) all living in the spirit spheres around the earth at different levels of spiritual maturity. While, the spirits who reside in one of the levels of heaven, can be considered graduate students, who continue to learn, but also help other students – there are categories of spirits below them.

There is a detailed explanation of the levels of spirits in *The Spirits Book*, but for this short introduction, I will use their location to broadly describe their character. Errant spirits in the Lower Zone, that area below the boundary of heaven and starting on the surface of the earth are spirits who have not divested themselves of either their baser characteristics – such as hate, envy, revenge, selfishness, and general rebelliousness – or, they are still materially attached to the earth, whereby they have love for the money or property they have been forced to leave behind. And other reasons in-between the two aforementioned.

Then there is the Dark Abyss, the area which lies below the surface of the earth. Where light is dim and the air is putrid. This is the land of hardened criminals; unrepentant souls whose career, while physically alive, was to take advantage of others and to live a selfish existence. Now they dwell amongst others just like them.

To put these two classes of souls in perspective, the Brazilian medium, Francisco (Chico) C. Xavier told us that only about thirty percent of people that die travel up to the heavens. The rest find they wake up in a dismal landscape, where waiting gangs take advantage of the new comers.

Now imagine that these invisible students are allowed to walk the campus, unrestricted, whispering into the incarnated students' ear every conceivable bad piece of advice possible. Just like a Middle or High School near you! Think back to those years when you were in a closed campus, with a wide range of friends, acquaintances, bullies, druggies, and imbeciles. All with ready recommendations for every occasion. The vast majority of thought and speech generated being completely worthless, if not downright dangerous.

This mishmash of schoolchildren; incarnates and discarnates - combine to make up the total student body. Which brings us to the second point: The spirit realm, in the spheres of heaven surrounding our beautiful planet, is tasked to individually and collectively, enable us to grow and develop into civilized spirits.

27

Whereupon, one day we shall be a productive member of the spirit realm, instead of a burden.

And this is the most fantastic news – we are loved, all of us, incarnate and discarnate alike. Behind the great force of constant love is a vast organization with one primary objective – to help us, to promote our well-being, to enable us to learn and prosper.

The staff, toiling on our behalf, is composed of sweet, loving, caring, and compassionate workers. On the other hand, they expect a lot from us and aren't always sympathetic to our excuses. For instance, when Chico Xavier told his spirit mentor he couldn't psychograph one day because of pain in one of his eyes, his spirit mentor, Emmanuel, told him, that he still had one good eye and it was not an excuse to miss work.

In Rio de Janeiro I listened to a speech given by a Spiritist medium, he told us that after work he was relaxing with a glass of wine and thought it was good to be resting and doing nothing for a while. Then a spirit put into his mind - don't think like that, you are always working! It might have been a joke, but it does illustrate that we have a part to play in our own education and we are expected to perform at the highest level possible.

The spirits told the two men in the examples above, the same thing that a teacher who drives their students to success would also say. High expectations usually translate into higher performance. Spirits love us, but they also know us and they well understand our predilection to seek the easy answer – to rest when a little tired – to delay whenever possible – to choose immediate gratification over working toward a larger reward.

Living life after life could at times seem like Sisyphus, who had to roll a stone up a hill, only to have it roll back down and hit him, for all eternity. Unlike Sisyphus, we can determine to have a limited number of lives on earth and the level of struggle through each one … the exact amount is up to us.

During our travails, take comfort that we always have help at hand, assistance is only a soft thought spoken in our minds away.

Our caretakers are ready to guide us twenty-fours a day. But, don't rely excessively on guidance from our mentors. Demonstrate the ability to analyze past mistakes; ask yourself what you can learn from any situation that has been thrown in your path; focus on how well you can do in the future; strive to remove selfishness – and you will be surprised at how smooth the road ahead will appear.

Section 1 – Guiding Humans on Earth

When I think of the love that is showered down on us by spirits from heaven, I am astounded. I believe we are all well acquainted with love from our family, and even within our extended family. But beyond that, the concept weakens and often turns into contempt and an excuse to take advantage of anyone outside your circle of love and caring.

It is this tribal human instinct that we must learn to discard on our upward path. Spirits have told us, many times, in many manners, that we should extend brotherly love to all humans. This is a difficult concept, made harder by our culture of competition for a limited amount of material goods or financial rewards. To be truly selfless and fraternal is an arduous trek.

We are guided to remove not only selfishness, but other base character flaws. While Spiritism prefers to use the word "wrongs" for past harmful behavior, it may be safe to list the seven deadly sins, as blemishes that we should strive to remove from our being: pride, greed, lust, envy, gluttony, wrath, and sloth.

The holes that would appear in our personality from removing these unwanted characteristics should be filled with the seven heavenly virtues: prudence, justice, temperance, courage, faith, hope, and charity.

Our spirit benefactors certainly don't expect angelic behavior. In fact, making mistakes and learning from them is very important. I had the opportunity to learn from a man named Sergio who had a near death experience, in which he reviewed his life with a small team of his spirit mentors. As the life review unfolded, he found disturbing aspects to his behavior; he continually attempted to say stop, I want to analyze this episode; his spirit guides would invariably reply that it was unimportant. Finally he realized that his life was as important as it was unimportant – which at first sounds flippant, but when one looks at an eternal existence with multiple lives, one sees that in whatever we lived through, it was all part of a learning experience. That even if we failed during one episode, what we learned stayed with us, to enable us to be successful in the next trial, in the next life.

Therefore, be prepared, for we may be guided into situations where we fail; but, we fail for a reason. We may gain valuable insights into what we did wrong and learn to better analyze our intended actions. After all, when you are planning for the education of your child, you fully realize the benefit of failure, for only failure teaches one to understand that careful planning, dedication, and resilience is required for success – and even then victory can be close run. If all we did was travel from success to success we would be derailed by the first defeat.

Hence, life isn't meant to be easy, safe, or overwhelmingly pleasant. Life is supposed to be a challenge, in which either victory or defeat is useful. For whatever occurs, all that is important is that we learn from it. And we should take away the primary lesson, that if we would follow our conscience – that compass that always points to the higher path – that whatever the outcome, we emerge a better person. We may emerge poorer, less respected by many, considered a fool by society, and insults hurled at us … but all that doesn't matter, for we followed the road to the light.

Your conscience is always the answer sheet to any scenario. Resist the urge to rationalize away the right thing to do and follow your superior instinct and you shall be guaranteed success. It may not be apparent in your current life, but it will propel you upwards in your real life; your life as an immortal spirit.

Accepting our lessons and letting our conscience guide us, makes the job of our guardian angel and spirit mentors easier and a joy. Who doesn't love having a pupil try their best, through thick and thin, always trying to maintain a good attitude? In fact, as recorded by many messages from spirits to Spiritist mediums, the more willing and dedicated the student, the more assistance will be given.

Planned trials in your present life will be modified to make them less drastic and your future lives will concentrate on learning experiences instead of payment for wrongs, in which you have not yet learned the desired lesson. Angels guide us out of love, and giving them any excuse to increase that love, without denying you a valuable lesson, is a joy to them. Hence, an episode that may have been planned as extremely dramatic may be scaled back, because your attitude has changed and you are modifying your character along the right lines.

Our guardian spirits are always there for us; we may not notice their presence, but they are next to us – whether physically beside us or billions of miles away; they are constantly connected. They are the source of the whispers in our heads to do the right thing, or to think once more before making a certain decision.

Learn to discern the subtle messages coming from your guardian or your conscience. Ponder carefully the long term ramifications of each action. Look for signs that the spirit world is guiding you in a specific direction. When you embark upon a task and seemingly everything falls into place … this usually means that your path was the correct one. Or when you are searching for an answer, and out of the blue, your uncle calls you with a suggestion or a contact of a person who could help – most likely this isn't random, but synchronicity; a planned series of events orchestrated by the spirit world to assist in your endeavor.

The more you look, the more evidence you will find that you and all others around you are guided by bright and loving spirits.

Chapter 1 – The Value of Sorrow – Changing our Path

Many of us consider sorrow to be the opposite of joy. The spirit world knows better, they believe sorrow gives us the space and the time to analyze ourselves and others. We think again about our attitudes and beliefs and discover better paths in our lives.

Christ's Use of Sorrow

In the Reverend G. Vale Owen's book, *The Life Beyond the Veil*, there is a revealing passage about sorrow; what it is and what it is used for. In Book One – The Lowlands of Heaven, Owen's mother writes to him from the other side about the passage in the Bible when Jesus tells Peter that he is an adversary to him.

This event is in the context of Jesus preparing the Apostles for his death in Jerusalem. According to Owen's mother, Jesus wished to deliver the message to his disciples that his imminent death would not be a failure, but the start of a grand design. From his death a sequence of events would unfold which would change the world forever.

Vale Owen's mother explained further:

"Peter, by his attitude, showed that he did not understand this. Which is all plain and easy enough, so far, to understand. But what is usually lost sight of is the fact that the Christ was pursing one straight line of progress and that His death was but an incident in the way of His onward path, and that sorrow, as the world understands it, is not the antithesis of joy, but may be a part of it, because, if rightly used, it becomes the fulcrum on

33

which the lever may rest which may lift a weight off the heart of the one who understands that all is part of God's plan for our good. It is only by knowing the real 'value' of sorrow that we understand how limited it is in effect, so far as making us unhappy goes."[15]

Sorrow isn't a state of complete despondence, but a gateway to open our hearts and minds to the true state of our life. The feeling of sadness enables the lifting of the veil of self-deception in which we had been living and forces our vision to gaze on the light of the truth. Truths that we may have been consciously avoiding by letting our emotions and prejudices rule our conscience.

During our trials here on earth, we have all experienced sorrow. The events which brought us down to misery are often meant as a signal to change direction. A sign that our accumulated decisions made so far are not entirely correct and should be modified.

An example would be when family members are estranged from each other. When one of the group suddenly dies, the survivors realize, through their abject grief, the pettiness of past arguments and reconcile. Thusly, sorrow serves to awaken our priorities and place in perspective the trivial grudges and plans for revenge we all, at one time or another, hold against those who dared to slight us.

Owen's mother, who is now part of the loving legion of spirits who help guide our small destinies, discusses how sorrow could be used by the spirit realm to subtlety maneuver us onto the right path.

"For the problem which is the chief study of the new House in which I spend so much of my time is this same subject, namely, turning, or converting, of the vibrations of sorrow into the vibrations which produce joy in the human heart. It is a very beautiful study, but many perplexities enter into it because of the restrictions imposed on us by the sacredness of free will. We may not override the will of any, but have so to work through their wills as to produce the desired effect and yet leave then free all the time, and so, deserving, in a way and in a measure at least, of the blessing received."[16]

The paragraph above says so many things about the spirit world on so many levels. First, the amount of study and effort that is spent on our part. We, who are sent here to learn, completely unaware of the army of good spirits who care for us and attempt to illuminate the right path, are the objects of love so complete as to warrant such exertion and determination on our behalf.

Secondly, the set of rules in which our life is a predetermine set of events, but in which our choices are completely our own. Like children, whose every decision is usually the wrong one, our spirit benefactors must observe us stumble upon the earth in a seemly chaotic dance of wrong-headedness. Only pure love could possibly explain the dedication to our cause.

At the end of the day, when sorrow crashes upon us like a giant wave, remember to use it as a tool. A device to rethink and analyze, to put inside the deepest regions of your heart what is important and what is not. Let your conscience, that gift from God, which is the set of Divine Rules which is implanted into each of us, fashion your thoughts and your plan to move forward.

Chapter 2 – Life on Earth is an Extension of Life in the Spirit World

"How would you explain to one who had little idea of a spirit world about him the truth of survival beyond the grave and the reality of this life and all its love and beauty? First you would endeavor to bring home to him the fact of his present existence as an immortal being. And then, when he had really grasped the significance of that, as it affects his future, he would perhaps be open to a few words of description as to that life which he will find himself possessed of, and in touch with, when he puts aside the Veil and emerges into the greater light of the Beyond."[17]

So writes the mother of the Reverend G. Vale Owen, in *The Lowlands of Heaven* section, which is in a compilation of four of his books, *Life Beyond the Veil*. In the Lowlands section he communicates with his mother, who resides in the spirit world. His mother is attempting to explain the continuity of life from the other side to physical life, and back to the other side again.

We aren't here for one grand life, full of mixtures of misery, contentment, grand passion, mistakes, honorable and dishonorable deeds, then off to a life of leisure as a spirit, listening to harp music.

The life you are living now is an extension of your life in the spirit world. You came here for a purpose, to rectify what you had lacked before, to repair defects and build for the future. G. Vale Owen's mother warns us we should take our time here industriously:

"Now, it is no small matter that men should so live their lives on earth that when they step over the threshold into the larger, freer sphere they should take up and continue their service in the Kingdom without a more or less protracted hiatus in their progress. We have seen the effect of so many, as it is viewed in extension into this land, that we feel we cannot too much emphasize the importance of preparation and self-training while opportunity offers. For so many do put off the serious consideration of this, with the idea of starting afresh here, and when they come over they find that they had very little realized what that starting afresh really implied."[18]

In other words, upon death we don't start afresh, we merely complete one stage, as if finishing a degree at a college, and return to start exercising what we have learned. Imagine the embarrassment when you return and find out you have accumulated very little knowledge and didn't follow the course you laid out before you started the journey.

First, half the battle is to recognize that we are on earth to learn and to improve. Not to gather as much material goods as possible, but to raise our character, our spirituality, our love for our fellow humans up a notch. Knowing this puts the rest of life into perspective.

Secondly, as when you send children off to school, the spirit world doesn't lose interest into what happens to us. The Spirituality knows our plan, measures our progress, and alerts our guardian angels when we veer off in the wrong direction.

Chapter 3 – How to Facilitate Communication with Spirits

I have noticed that whenever I saw pictures of Chico Xavier psychographing I saw him with his hand against his head. I thought that may have just been how he felt best when he communicated with spirits.

I read a passage in the book, *Life Beyond the Veil*, in *The Lowlands of Heaven* section. It was a communication to the Rev G. Vale Owen from his mother in the spirit world. His mother tells him the best method to hear her clearly in his mind. The bold words are from G. Vale Owen:

"Place your hand against your head and you will notice that we are then able the more readily to speak to you so that you will be able to understand.

Like this?

Yes, it helps you and us, both

How?

Because there is a stream of magnetism proceeding from us to you, and by doing as we have suggested it is not so quickly dissipated

I don't understand a word of this.

Maybe not. There are many things you have yet to learn, dear, and what we are saying now is one of those things, little in itself but still of account. It is often these small things which help to success.

Now, while we are not over anxious to explain the methods we employ in the transmission of these messages, because we can only make you understand imperfectly, still we may say this: the power we use is best described as magnetism, and by means of this vibrations of our minds are directed on your own. Your hand being so placed serves as a kind of magnet and reservoir in one, and helps us."[19]

I hope this assists mediums understand some of the mechanism involved in communication between our physical world and the spirit realm.

Chapter 4 – Prayer – Is Not Merely Asking for Something – The Spirit Realm Analyzes our Requests

Our prayers receive more attention than many of us believe. One of the recurring themes in Spiritist literature is the care and consideration of our prayers. We are listened to in the spirit world. No matter how small or inconsiderable we think ourselves to be, our requests are analyzed.

The importance of prayer for ourselves and how the spirit world reacts to our devotions is discussed in the book, *Life Beyond the Veil*, in *The Lowlands of Heaven* section. It was a communication to the Rev G. Vale Owen from Astriel in the spirit world that touches upon the power of prayer and meditation:

"Prayer is not merely the asking for something you wish to attain. It is much more than that, and, because it is so, it should receive more careful consideration than it has yet received. What you have to do in order to make a prayer a power is to cast aside the temporal and fix you mind and spirit on the eternal. When you do that you find that many items you would have included in your prayer drop out from the very incongruity of their presence, and the greater and wider issues become to you the focus of your creative powers. For prayer is really creative, as the exercise of the will, as seen in our Lord's miracles, such as the feeding of the five thousand. And when prayer is offered with this conviction, then the object is created, and the prayer is answer – that is, the objective answers to the subjective in such a way that an actual creation has taken place."[20]

There are several concepts presented in the above that are not normally associated with prayer. First, is the aspect of thinking about the eternal, since we are here on earth to learn to be more loving and spiritual, praying for superfluous material possessions will get all of the attention it deserves! Which is to say, very little. On the other hand, desiring to be given strength to successfully end a trial with newfound knowledge, is an imperishable attribute we would take with us for life after life.

Praying for enlightenment, such as a solution to a problem, or for the benefit of others will always receive due consideration. This type of request which illustrates a desire for spiritual or intellectual self-advancement is a sign to the spirit world that one is serious about their assignment on earth.

The second concept is that our thoughts are translated into action. What we pray for, if it is worthy of an answer, is transformed into physical reality. Praying for help in finding shelter for your family, so they may strive through their own trials without the worry of homelessness, could, for instance, cause a person to decide to rent out their house to the requesting family at a lower rate or with a smaller deposit or no last month's rent. All actions brought about by the manipulations of the spirit world on behalf of the person requesting Divine assistance.

My example isn't merely an intellectual exercise. I have known people in dire straits, people who have selflessly helped others, receive free housing, which comes out of the blue. A woman, who was recovering from the aftermath of a near death experience, wasn't able to work, yet she still insisted in providing care for others, was given the opportunity to stay rent-free in a house. All she had to do was to take care of a small park. These are not coincidences, but planned assistance from the Spirit Realm.

While on earth, we consider our thoughts to be perishable. As quick as we think, they are gone. They are meaningless. This is not true. Our thoughts radiate outward from us. Each thought is tagged with our personal identification and most probably, a time stamp and a location.

41

We know this by two sources; first, by what is told to us in Spiritist literature and secondly, accounts from near death experiences. When people who have reported a life review during a NDE, they invariably describe the ability of the spirit world to recount their thoughts, second by second, and the feelings of others interacting with them. Nothing is lost or forgotten.

What Happens to a Misguided Prayer

Now that we have learned what a prayer should be, we would like to know what happened to all of those selfish prayers. Like the ones I used to make as a kid, wishing for a new bike, or the most regular prayer I had; asking that school be closed tomorrow, or the whole week if possible. We are told:

> "Then the project of the will glances off tangent, and the effect is only proportionate to the scattered rays by which the objective is touched. Also, when the prayer is mixed with motives unworthy it is proportionately weakened, and also meets with opposing or regulating wills on this side, as the case may require; and so the effect is not attained as desired."[21]

In essence, if we pray for something selfishly, it is duly noted, but mostly ignored. When we pray for what we should not have, the answer may come back to us in another lesson. Be careful where you turn your attention, for your thoughts and desires may have unintended consequences.

A woman recounted a near death experience, where she started it off by asking God to make her happy. She had a good job and a wonderful husband, but this wasn't enough for her. Her prayer was answered. She was in a terrible automobile accident where she was in intense pain. So bad, she could no longer work. It was the lowest moment of her life.

Then she yelled at God, telling the Supreme Intelligence that her life was even worse. Again, her prayer was answered. After taking her pain medicine and going out to dinner, she became so drunk, that on her way home she vomited in the car, and then insisting she could walk to the front door, without the help of her husband, she fell and hit her head. Her husband drove her to the hospital.

Only when she was recovering, did she feel a transformation. For the first time, she felt what others felt. Instead of being a stand-offish person, patients and even the staff gravitated to her to tell her their innermost thoughts. Her husband was astounded. She was a changed person. Her original prayer was truly answered. She became content with her life. She didn't miss the old job and the bountiful salary, she dedicated herself to helping others. But to come to this point, involved pain and anguish. It wasn't an easy road for her.

How Does the Spirit World Analyze Our Prayers

In the communication from the spirit Astriel to the Rev. G. Vale Owen, we are allowed to peek behind the curtains to discern the process by which are prayers are analyzed.

"For you must know that there are appointed guardians of prayer here whose duty it is to analyze and sift prayers offered by those on earth, and separate them into divisions and departments, and pass them on to be examined by others, and dealt with according to their merit and power."[22]

The process seems too earth-like, too much like how it would be done in a large corporation. This is because, as much as we would wish it to be otherwise, earth is a poor reflection of heaven. How people organize themselves, how work is done and other mundane tasks we bring our inclinations from our sojourn during our spirit life to our incarnated lifespan. Hence, in heaven, as on earth, there are vast organizations and levels of management and separation of duties. Fear not, spirit bureaucracy is not like ours; uncaring, stiff, arrogant, and full of pompous managers.

The vital point to be taken is the amount of care parceled out to every one of us. The Spirituality is listening and responding. We just lack the sensitivity to recognize the effect it has on our life. It can be done, by evaluating your life, the signals and synchronicities that have shaped your present, you can begin to reveal the marvelous ways in which you have been guided.

There are some prayers which must be referred to even higher authorities. Prayers which are beyond the capability of certain levels of heaven to determine the best course of action. Astriel tells us what is done with desires which are undecipherable.

> "These we pass on to those of higher grade, to be dealt with in their greater wisdom. And do not think that these latter are always found among the prayers of the wise. They are frequently found in the prayers of children, whose petitions and sighs are as carefully considered here as those of nations."[23]

Hence, the requests of children struggling in dysfunctional families or other dire circumstances are carefully reviewed. The love of children is equal or even more profound in the spirit realm than it is on earth. In heaven, without deep love, a soul can't enter, while earth is home to many levels of incarnated spirits, some who have no love for anything or anyone but themselves.

Finally, to dispel any doubt as to how prayers are analyzed and then acted upon, we are given this example:

> "'Thy prayers and thine alms are come up for a memorial before God.' You will remember these words spoken by the Angel to Cornelius. They are often passed over without being understood as the literal description of those prayers and alms as they appeared to that Angel, and were passed on, probably by himself and his fellow workers, into the higher realms. It is as if he had said, 'Your prayers and alms came before my own committee, and were duly considered on their merits. We passed them as worthy, and have received notification from those Officers above us that they are exceptional merit, and require a special treatment. Therefore I have been commissioned to come to you.' We are trying to put the case as emphatically as we can in your language of official business in order to help you to understand as much as you may be able of the conditions here obtaining."[24]

How often do we hear that communication from the spirit

world is wrapped in a parable, or the meaning is difficult to comprehend? Here is an example of a straightforward message, plain as day, as to how prayers operate.

In essence, when you pray, be worthy of what you ask for. Demonstrate previous spiritual growth or the desire for it. Ask only for what helps you or others to improve while on trial on earth or at least to successfully complete a trial.

Astriel tells us that prayers prove that Angels shed tears. They see and hear what is requested and their hearts cry out in pity and love. He asks us to remember that love and compassion are real objects in the spirit world. Just as is hate and greed are in the Lower Zone. We are told they take on a type of solid form, a recognizable pattern which are physical measurements of our progress and status on earth.

Chapter 5 – How to Interpret Dreams – The Spirit World Guides Us in our Sleep

The spirit Astriel, in a conversation with the Reverend G. Vale Owen discussed how the spirit world helps people when they ask for guidance for a pressing problem. We have all had days where there is something we just can't figure out. A homework assignment from school, a complex algorithm to be designed and coded for work, or a presentation to kick off a new project are just a few samples of what could occupy our minds just before retiring for the night.

Many ask for guidance from above in solving their problems, others focus on the conundrum at hand so diligently that the energy of their thoughts reach the spirit plane in a form of requesting assistance. Astriel reminds the good reverend that God gave people minds to use, not just to receive instructions. That part of our trials on earth is to learn to solve difficulties on our own. After all, if the teacher gave everyone the answers to the test, why have the test?

But, like a good teacher, inquiring minds aren't entirely left to their own devices. After a student has demonstrated their diligence the teacher will offer advice on how to solve the problem, hints to the path to pursue are supplied to the eager pupil. Astriel recounts how he helped a person to further their knowledge.

"I remember that once I was impressing a man who was investigating the laws of psychology in the matter of visions and dreams. He wanted to find out what was the cause of certain dreams being prophetic – the connection between the dream itself and the incident which it foreshadowed. He applied to me, and I told him that he must continue his investigations and use his own mind, and, if it were well, he would be given to understand."[25]

Therefore, if one demonstrates dedication and hard work toward a goal, you will be assisted. First the spirit realm must be convinced that a person deserves help. Once that has been established a whole world of information is opened up.

Astriel, in his communications to G. Vale Owen, documented in the book *Life Beyond the Veil*, published in the 1920's reveals to us one small facet on how the spirit realm guides and cares for us during our trials here on earth. One aspect of the invisible care we receive is what happens when we dream and how they are structured to help us.

Dreams are an Escape from Our Physical Body into the Spirit Realm

In the book *Spiritist Review - Journal of Psychological Studies of 1858*, published in 2015, by the United States Spiritist Council, there is a dissertation from an unknown spirit about sleep. It supplies a complete survey of what sleep means to souls at different levels and why our dormant state is vital for us:

"Poor human beings! How little you know about the most ordinary phenomena that exist in your life! You think highly of yourselves; you think that you have a vast knowledge and remain speechless before these simple questions framed by all children: "What do we do when we are asleep? What is the meaning of dreams?" I don't have the pretension of making you understand what I want to explain, since there are things that your spirit cannot submit to, because one can only admit what one can comprehend.

Sleep entirely frees the soul from the body. When we are asleep we are momentarily in the same state that we shall definitely be after death. The spirits that have quickly detached from matter, on the occasion of their death, had intelligent dreams; those, when sleeping, meet again with the society of other beings that are superior to them; that travel, talk to them and are enlightened by them. They even work on tasks that they find finalized when they die. This, once more, must teach us that we should not fear death, as we die every day as once stated by a Saint.

All this was said with respect to the superior spirits. The large majority of people, however, who may remain in that perturbation for long hours, in that uncertainty that you were told about, those individuals go to worlds that are inferior to Earth, attracted by old affections, or to look for pleasures that are even of a lower level than those found here. They will then learn doctrines that are even more vile, ignoble and harmful than those that they profess among you. What establishes the sympathy on Earth is nothing else but the fact that we feel attracted by the heart, as we wake up, to those with whom we have spent eight or nine hours of pleasure or happiness. What also establishes the irresistible antipathy is that, deep there in the heart, we know that those creatures have a different conscience, with respect to us; hence we know them not having ever setting our eyes on them. It is this that also explains the indifference, since we don't seek to make friends when we know that we have others that love us and wish us well. In one word, the sleep influences your lives more than you think.

Through sleep, the incarnated spirits are always in contact with the spiritual world, allowing then that the superior spirits, without much repulse, do agree to come to incarnate in your environment. God wanted that during the contact with vices they could reinforce their virtues in the source of goodness, so as not to fail, as they come to instruct others. Sleep is the door that God opened to them to meet their friends from heaven; it is the break after the work, waiting for the great liberation, the final liberation that should reintegrate them back to their real world.

A dream is the memory of what your spirit saw during the sleep. Notice, however, that you do not always dream since you do not always remember some of what you have seen or everything that you have seen. It is not your soul in its full detachment; often it is nothing more than the memory of the perturbation that follows our departure or arrival, added to the memory of what you have done or what worries you during the waking state. Without that, how can we explain those absurd dreams, of the scholars as well as of the simplest person? The evil spirits also use the dream to torment the weak and pusillanimous souls.

As a matter of fact you will soon see the development of a new kind of dream. It is as old as the one you know but ignored by you. It is the dream of Joan of Arc, of Jacob, of the Jewish prophets and of some Indian fore-tellers. Such a dream represents the memory of the soul, entirely separated from the body; the memory of that second life that I was telling you about some time ago.

For the dreams that you retain the memory try to distinguish well between those two kinds, as without it you shall fall into contradictions and cause dismal mistakes to your faith."[26]

At the end of the spirit's communication we are being told that some dreams can hold valuable information for us. It is our responsibility to separate the important and relevant dream from the vast majority of nonsense dreams we all have.

Astriel in his conversations with G. Vale Owen helps guide us to discern between the important and the fluff we encounter during our dream state.

How a Dream Helped

Astriel tells G. Vale Owen exactly how he guided the supplicant who wanted to know more about prophetic dreams:

"That night I met him when he fell asleep and conducted him to one of our observatories where we experiment with the object of portraying, in visible form, the events hovering about the present moment; that is, events which have happened shortly before, and those which will happen shortly in the future. We were not able to go far back or far ahead at that

49

particular establishment. That is done by those in the higher spheres."[27]

For those who absolutely reject determinism, like I did, the realization that our future is known rips out the foundation of your beliefs. This means that your life on earth is set, not in stone, only in the trials you shall encounter. You have free-will to choose your options and attitude during those lessons presented to you.

Spiritism also answers the question of the ability to see forward. Allan Kardec, who wrote *The Spirits Book*, in the 1850s provides the analogy of a high spirit standing on top of a mountain. There is a trail in the canyons below. The spirit can see a person walking along the path. The advanced spirit is able to detect where the person was and where they are going. Whereas, the person below, he or she only sees the immediate road ahead and can look to the rear to see what has already happened.

We are that person on the rough trail and the spirit world, made up on many levels of ascension, can, determined by the stage of purity, accurately foretell the road ahead. The person who is dreaming will get to see a bit of the road ahead, which was covered in mystery before:

"We set the instruments in order and cast upon a screen a picture of the neighborhood in which he lived, and told him to watch intently. One particular item was the entry into the town of some great personage with a large retinue. When the display was over he thanked us and we conducted him back to his earth body again."[28]

Hence, Astriel arranged for the inquiring gentleman a demonstration of a prophetic dream. Astriel gave him the gift of seeing ahead so he could determine for himself what the dream meant.

The Interpretation of the Dream

"He awoke in the morning with a feeling that he had been in the company of certain men who had been experimenting in some branch of science, but could not recall what it had been about. But as he was going about his work that morning the face of the man he had seen in the procession came to his mind vividly, and he then remembered several scraps of his dream experience.

On opening a newspaper a few days afterwards he saw an intimation that a visit was projected to the town and district of this same personage. The he began to reason things out for himself.

He did not remember the observatory, nor the screen pictures we had shown him, as such. But he did remember the face and the retinue. So he reasoned in this way: when our bodies sleep we ourselves, at least sometimes, go into the sphere of four dimensions. That fourth dimension is such as enables those who dwell there to see into the future. But coming back to this realm of three dimensions, we are not able to carry over with us all we have experienced when we ourselves have been in the realm of four. Yet we do manage to hold such items as are natural to this lower realm, such as the face of an earth dweller and a retinue in procession."[29]

Astriel explains the relationship between the dream and the reality of the experience:

"The connection, then, between such a dream as foreseen and the events themselves is the relation of a state of four dimensions to a state of three. And the former, being of greater capacity than the latter, covers at any moment a wider range of view, as to time and sequence of events, than the latter can do."[30]

We who live in a three-dimensional world, where we can place and view objects given width, height, and depth. Time is held constant. Our eyes can only view in two dimensions, but our brain enables us to infer the third coordinate.

Now suppose you are a creature of four dimensions, you detect width, height, depth, and time. You see the object not in a snapshot but in all phases of its existence.

51

Breaking this down further, I found another analogy from Wikipedia that postulates what a two dimensional being would think about a three-dimensional being:

> "Dimensional analogy was used by Edwin Abbott in the book Flatland, which narrates a story about a square that lives in a two-dimensional world, like the surface of a piece of paper. From the perspective of this square, a three-dimensional being has seemingly god-like powers, such as ability to remove objects from a safe without breaking it open (by moving them across the third dimension), to see everything that from the two-dimensional perspective is enclosed behind walls, and to remain completely invisible by standing a few inches away in the third dimension."[31]

Now take the analogy one more step, and think of us living our lives in a 3D movie. The movie has a beginning and an end, the plot spans hours. Although we, as actors in the film, notice only the part we are currently playing. Each scene is real life to us. But a high spirit standing outside our range of sight, sees the build up to the current scene and result of the actions we take in our present time. We, as the actors caught in the digital representation of the film, have no concept of the audience who hovers around us, watching our lives unfold.

What would happen if you took the actor out of the movie and placed her or him in the audience? They would have a difficult time trying to understand what precisely they are seeing and could only interpret it through their own point of view.

Hence, our dreams are invariably muddled. Our brains are able to cipher the simpler concepts and we, for the most part, misinterpret the fourth dimensional aspects of our dreaming experience.

Lesson Learned

Given the limitations of our physical bodies, the man who wished to understand prophetic dreams was able to unlock a key concept about dreams and the spirit realm. Astriel summarizes his achievement thusly:

> "Now, by such use of his own mental faculties he had arrived at as great an advance in knowledge as I could have given him direct; and by so doing he had also advanced in mental training and power. For although his conclusion was not such as would pass muster here without rectification in several points, yet is was roundly and broadly correct, and serviceable for all practical purposes intellectually. I could not have infused into him more than he had found out for himself."[32]

We are part of the spirit realm, our immortal souls live the vast majority of the time in a world with at least four dimensions, maybe more the higher one travels. Each time we incarnate, we temporarily lose our past and must live in the present. But we aren't left without any tools, we have our conscience and instincts, and we can journey back to the other side to receive assistance.

We have been granted the gift of leaving our bodies during sleep. It is up to each individual to determine for his or herself what their dreams mean to them and how closely should they follow the perceived lessons resulting from a vivid dream experience.

Chapter 6 – Goodness is to Evil – What Sight is to Blindness

The spirit Zabdiel, whom the Rev. G. Vale Owen, in the second book in the *Life Beyond the Veil,* a collection of four books, communicated with in the 1910's, explains the concept of goodness and evil. Zabdiel tells us that good and evil are "conditions of attitude"[33] toward God. Your perspective regarding the love of God determines the amount of benefit or harm any action we take, which, sooner or later, reflects back on us.

Zabdiel presents a universe full of the Supreme Spirituality's love and this constant permeates all. When we attempt to block out the radiated love from God, this is when evil persists. Zabdiel illuminates the concept:

> "The very intensity of the Love of God becomes terrible when it meets with an opposing obstacle. The swifter the torrent the greater the surf about the opposing rocks. The greater the heat of the fire the more complete the dissolution of the fuel which is cast into it, and on which it feeds. And although to some such words may seem horrible in the saying of them, yet it is the very intensity of the Love which energizes and flows through the creation of the Father which, meeting opposing and disharmonious obstruction, causes the greater pain.
>
> Even in the earth life you may test and prove this true. For the most bitter of all remorse and repentance is that which follows on the realization of the love borne to us by the one we have wronged."[34]

Holding back love and God's will is like attempt to dam an

ocean. It may work for a short period, but in time the barrier will fail. Therefore, evil is the absence of love. Where love is allowed there is good, where love is resisted there is evil. Zabdiel analyzes evil:

"Blindness is inability to see. But not only is there such a condition as blindness; there are also people who are blind. Blindness is a negative condition, or less. It is the condition of one who has four senses instead of five. But real it is, nevertheless. Yet it is only when one who is born blind is told of the sense of sight that he begins to feel his lack of it, and the more he understands the lack of it the more his lack is felt. So it is with sin. It is usual here to call those who are in darkness the "undeveloped." This is not a negative term, which would be 'retrogressed.' So of both I say not 'loss' but 'lack.' The one born blind has not lost a faculty but lacks it."[35]

Hence, when a person commits an evil act, it is because of his or her incapability to discern the good, the correct action to take. It is the absence of understanding the presence of love and how that should influence every decision we make.

Most spirits and all people are a balance of good and bad characteristics. There is not a living soul that is composed entirely of evil. We are all a mixture, we travel through life committing acts that we regret. Zabdiel explains why:

"Yet you may say that people do go back and fall from grace. Those who do so are such as those who are partly blind or of imperfect sight – color-blind as to one or more colors. These have never seen perfectly, and their lack is only unknown to them until opportunity offers, and then their imperfection is manifest. For a color-blind person is one whose sight is, in little or more measure, undeveloped. It is only by using his vision that he maintains what vision he has, and if he neglects to do this then he retrogresses. So with the sinner."[36]

Filling in What is Lacking

We, on earth at this moment in time, are in the process of

developing our good sides and removing our base emotions. We are all partially color-blind when it comes to perceiving the Light. We are on earth because we need to train ourselves to fully comprehend the love which envelops us and how to channel that love for our benefit and the benefit of others.

The process whereby we grasp what we have heretofore missed is our trials on earth. Our choices during those trials sets us up for where we will land in the spirit world and our course we must follow in our next life. Zabdiel tells us, "It is only by freewill that that person is held responsible for both good and evil in his heart."[37]

Through our trials we build up a range of experiences. Like a law library that contains case histories, which are used to guide the verdicts in future cases, we too, deposit what we have learned into our conscience. Hence, our need for multiple lives in multiple cultures. Zabdiel reinforces this point:

> "Also let it be remembered that what seems to be good or evil to one man does not of necessity so appear in the eyes of another. Especially is this true of those of different creed and habit of thought and manner of life in community. What, therefore, is possible in the matter of distinction between these two is that the broad and fundamental principles which underlie each should be grasped clearly, and the minor shades of these qualities be entrusted to the future when they will be gradually made more plain."[38]

The accumulation of knowledge to navigate through the shady maze of moral behavior is not lost upon entry into the physical life. We are given the infinite database of our conscience. Whereas, we may not be aware of searching for the correct answer, the feeling of anxiety in the pit of our stomach or that notion that we just did something wrong is the result of our brain retrieving thousands of years of results and notifying us of the findings.

This is why we have stress. Our conscience sends it signals out to all corners of the body alerting us that we are on the wrong track. The accumulation of these messages weakens our system and throws our internal harmony into disarray. This is why studies have shown that people who are more spiritual and are aware of their moral boundaries are healthier.

Multiple Lives are Required

"For a longer or shorter period sometimes, and often indeed for some thousands of years, as you reckon time on earth, a man may maintain his obduracy. But no man is created who is able to continue so everlastingly. And that is merciful limit which our Father Creator has placed around and in us lest He lose us, or any one of His children, away from Him, and without return for ever."[39]

Some of us simply do not learn the easy way. One life is not sufficient to fully embed living by the Golden Rule into the foundation of our character. I have been told, by spirits writing through mediums, that I have failed again and again. I was placed in a position of authority and instead of tending to my flock, I used them for my personal gain. I am certain I have maintained my stubbornness for thousands of years, much to my regret.

I am grateful for the overwhelming force of love that is slowly breaking down my walls of selfishness. Only by living through harsh realities was I able to understand that the absence of love, of caring, of compassion sets the stage for great wrongs.

My lack of virtue, caused by my ignorance is gradually being righted. I am a long way off, but now I welcome the journey. I look forward to learning to live amongst my fellow beings with a sense of love and purpose.

The first step is to listen closely to that governor in your head, your conscience. Attempt to follow what feels right. It's not easy since there are many cases that are still uncertain to most incarnated souls. But, as Zabdiel says, as we experience more lives, our moral compass will expand. Zabdiel leaves us with this message:

"Let us therefore, having looked on this phase of aberration from man's natural walking with God, now look the other way in the direction in which all things are tending. For truly, evil is but a transitory phase and, whether it pass away from His economy in whole or no, from every individual most surely it will pass away when its opposing force is spent, and he be left free to follow on in the glorious train of those who brighten as they go from glory to further and greater glory."[40]

As we shed our blemishes and ascend in the spirit hierarchy, we are given more responsibilities. In the spirit realm where faith and thought create reality, power is parceled out to those who have completed the requisite training. This is why we are on this planet, so we may one day complete our training and contribute to earth and other worlds, in helping other souls rise.

Chapter 7 – The Arc of Our Lives is Driven by Two Forces

Zabdiel, a spirit leader of a group of spirits, sent to communicate with Rev. G. Vale Owen, talked about how complex objects and processes are derived from basic principles. Zabdiel first begins with how our solar system operates:

"Out of the simplest wisdom are made the greatest things; and out of the most elementary of geometrical figures arise the most wonderful combinations of perpetual movement. For it is only the purest and simplest things that are competent to be used most freely and without entanglement. And this state of affairs alone gives warrant of perpetuity, whether on earth or in the vast reaches of space through which go these worlds and systems, eternally because perfectly ordered in their course.

Now, it is not too much to say that the appointed paths of all these bodies of the heavenly systems are shaped of two principles: that of the right line, and that of the curve. It is even more true and exact to say that their orbits may be said to be shaped out of one form only, and that the right line itself. All go onward impelled in a right and straight course and yet not one that is known to us but travels in a curve. Astronomers will explain why this is, but I will note one instance by way of example here.

The earth, we will suppose, is set forth on its journey. It travels in a straight line from one point. That is its potential movement. But directly it leaves that point it begins to fall towards the sun, and we find after a while that it is moving in an ellipse. There is no straight line here, but a series of curves worked together in one figure, which is the orbit of the earth.

And yet the pull of the sun was not in the fashion of a curve, but in a right line direct. It was the combination of these two straight lines of energy – the impetus of the earth and the gravitation of the sun – which, being perpetually exerted, bent the orbit of the earth from a straight into an elliptical shape, and one in which many elements of curve entered to build it up complete. I leave out other influences which modify this one again in order to concentrate your mind on this one great principle. I put it in formula, thus: Two straight lines of energy operating on one another produce a closed curve."[41]

Hence, the trajectory of an object is determined by the energy within it and the force influencing it. Without influencing force, the object would travel on a straight line forever. It takes a combination of energy to produce the orbit. Zabdiel explains the results:

"Yet each modifying the other, and the greater dominating the lesser without depriving it of its essential power and freedom of movement, these by their joint action – exerted and directed apparently in opposition – produce a figure of greater beauty than the two straight lines, which are as the parents to the child."[42]

From this Zabdiel is preparing us to think of our lives. We are an object that carries within itself its own force. We travel on a straight line until another force interrupts our course and causes us to be deflected. Think about what would happen to us if our life was frozen. No change in job, family, friends, and children stayed the same age forever. We would replay a similar day over and over again. No outside stimuli would alter our thinking or character.

Imagine being in a heaven as described by many religions. Where life is bliss, an Elysian fields, where there is no want of anything, no stress, and absolute zero conflict. Nothing to ever bother you again. You would continue on a straight line forever in time, never altering course, never growing as a person. It would be eternal monotony.

Instead of smooth seas our life is buffeted by high winds and waves. Zabdiel tells us why:

"You see a like opposition of forces in human life, and you say His plan is here imperfect. You think He might have made a better way; and many doubt His wisdom and His love because, seeing but a minute section of the curve of the great orbit of existence, they cannot but conclude that all is falling, falling to destruction; or at least that a straight and a right line would be the better course. And not these combinations which curve the impetus of human life from its direct onward way of evolution – without disaster and without pain."[43]

Hence, whereas we see nothing good in many adverse situations of our life, is actually a force pulling us off our easy path and onto a rougher, but more edifying road. Where we see a life cut down prematurely, is actually but a course correction at the proper time. All planned out in advance to make ready the soul for their next earthly episode.

Over the long run of our multiple incarnations, which is in fact a small portion of our eternity, the arc of our lives serve a purpose. Each existence is one more mile marker, signaling a chance for us to grasp the opportunity to advance. Zabdiel informs us how the spirit world, from on high, sees the struggle:

"We here do see not all nor much of the road ahead; yet more than you we see, and so much as enables us to content ourselves and press onward, helping others on the road, content and trusting that all will be well ahead however far we go. For now we do not seek with much labor to reckon on the course we are traveling wrapped round with earth mist which hinders us to see, but we view the way from the clear sunlight atmosphere of these heavenly realms; and I will tell you the orbit of human life, as it works out towards completion, is beautiful too – so beautiful and so lovely withal that we are full often brought to arrest in wondering awe at His Majesty of Love and blended Wisdom, to Whom we bow in lowly adoration not to be expressed in any words of mine, but only in the yearning of my heart."[44]

Each hurdle placed in front of us is there for a reason. It may not be apparent to us, in the midst of our daily dramas, but suffice to say, that it is one small force that diverts us from a straight path and onto the highway of learning and eventual perfection.

Chapter 8 – Courageous Thinking

The world is full of religious and political intellectuals who work full time convincing us to stay within certain ideological boundaries. For example, we are told the Bible must be interpreted literately, therefore the world must have been created in six days. Even though, all evidence points to the contrary.

Messages and books from spirits, brought to us by Spiritist mediums, tell us that the messages of the Bible were fashioned for the level of comprehension and society for the time in which the communications were delivered. Hence, the idea of a time span of billions of years and our planetary evolution would not have been remotely understandable to even the most sophisticated individual in ancient times.

Jesus, during his time on earth, preached love and respect for all, but many today still cling to the passages citing reasons to make certain groups outcasts. Again, Spiritism tells us that the messages of universal love and fraternity are eternal, while other passages were meant for the time in which they were delivered.

The spirit Zabdiel, in his communications with the Rev. G Vale Owen, talks about the narrow parameters that Christian orthodoxy imposes. Rev. G. Vale Owen was a Church of England minister who was later thrown out of the church for publishing his messages from high spirits. Zabdiel opens with telling G. Vale Owen that even after all things visible were created, what was left incomplete was mankind.

Humans are meant to evolve mentally, to find their spiritual path toward God. To accomplish this takes courageous thinking.

Zabdiel expands:

> "Nor doing this am I able to constrain myself within the limits
> of doctrinal theology as understood by you. For it is indeed
> constrained and straitened so greatly that one who has lived so
> long in wider room would fear to stretch himself lest he foul
> his elbows against the confining walls of that narrow channel;
> and hesitates to go at any pace ahead, fain as he is to travel, lest
> worse than this be his lot.
>
> No, my friend, shocking and startling as it be to those whose
> orthodoxy is as the breath of their body to them, more
> saddening is it to us to see them so much afraid to use what
> freedom of will and reason they have lest they go astray,
> mistaking rigid obedience to code and table for loyalty to Him
> Whose Truth is free."[45]

We are being told not to let the artificial boundaries of our
society constrain us. Granted this is difficult, where any perceived
transgression unleashes a barrage of criticism from the left and the
right if any deviation of political orthodoxy is detected. In some
countries, even the attempt to question religious dogma can lead to
torture and death.

Against this background, breaking free of past constraints is
truly courageous thinking. Zabdiel isn't asking us to be martyrs.
He is requesting that we internally free ourselves and determine
what the message of living by the Golden Rule, love, fraternity,
and charity really mean. We should ask ourselves what is the
logical conclusion to loving everyone like a brother or sister.

Zabdiel exhorts us:

> "Think you for a moment. What manner of Master-Friend is
> He to them who tremble so at His displeasure? Is it that He is,
> waiting and watching, with sinister smile, to catch them in His
> net who dare to think and think in error sincerely? Or is this He
> Who said, "Because you are lukewarm, and neither cold nor
> hot, I will reject you"? Move and live and use what powers are
> given prayerfully and reverently and then, if you do chance to

err, it will not be of obduracy and willfulness but of good intent. Shoot with strong arm and feet well and firmly set, and if you miss the mark by once or twice, your feet shall still be firm and the word "Well done!" for you shot amiss, yet in His good service, and as you were able to do so, so you did. Be not afraid. It is not those who strike and shoot and sometimes miss the mark whom He rejects, but the craven who fear to fight for Him at all. This I say boldly for I know it is true, having seen the outcome of both manner of lives when those who have lived them issue forth among us here, and seek their proper place and the gate by which they may pass onward this way."[46]

Study Spiritism and you shall soon see the path to the light. The road is not easy. To take the path one must shed old preconceptions, rid themselves of hate and envy, and begin to learn to not only control their actions and speech, but thought as well.

No one is asking anyone to join a monastery or divest oneself of all worldly goods. No, a tougher task is requested, to change your character and attitude. To actually live by the Golden Rule and to stay honorable in all circumstances. To accomplish this takes effort and study. Start today.

Chapter 9 – Love and its Opposite

Zabdiel starts out his communication with the Rev. G Vale Owen, on November 19, 1913, talking about how people from all around the world will come to know Jesus Christ. Whereas they may not know him as to his "Natural Divinity" , which I take to mean his composition and power as a spiritual entity, but will come to him because of His acts of kindness and love while in human form on earth.

Hence, it is through love that we must take the first step toward knowing Jesus and what he taught, for without the foundation of the feeling of love, nothing else can be built upon it. Zabdiel explains:

> "Foremost they must love. That is the first commandment of all, and the greatest. And hard have men found it to keep. They all agree that to love one another is good; and when they come to translate the sentiment into action, how sadly do they fail. And yet, without love no thing in the universe would stand, but fall into decay and dissolution. It is the love of God which energizes through all that is; and we can see that love, if we look for it, everywhere. The best way to understand many things is to contrast them with their opposites. The opposite of love is dissolution; because that comes from refraining from the exertion to love. Hatred is also of the opposite, and yet not the essence of it; because hatred of one person is often a mistaken method of expressing love to another."[47]

Dissolution or apathy is a major problem in our world today. People have a hard time feeling. We are buffeted with shocking or pornographic images on a constant basis, we lose the ability to

66

muster the energy to love. Hence, some take to drugs or alcohol to supply the stimulate to begin to feel, others become fanatical about a cause and lose all reason and empathy for different points of view.

Hatred is the welling-up of a primitive emotion. It is unfocused mental energy which leads to the radiation of confusion and bad feelings to all around the person dwelling on hate. There is power in hate, but it is destructive and causes more problems than one supposes it solves.

Zabdiel also tells us that hatred also affects doctrines. Where if one becomes a member of one organization, such as a religion or a gang, then you must hate all other rivals. He, quite rightly, warns us that constant hate makes it more difficult to love, to love anything else, when hate consumes all.

Lastly, Zabdiel notifies us that we must start with love, for without love we are unable to climb the ladder to perfection:

"This is one of those things which make it difficult in this life of the spheres. For not until a man has learned to love all without hating any is he able to progress in this land where love means light, and those who do not love move in dim places where they lose their way, and often become so dull in mind and heart that their perception of the truth is a vague as that of outward things."[48]

Your capacity to love greatly determines where you shall go after physical death. Zabdiel doesn't desire any spirit to have to live in the Lower Zones or the Abyss. In these undesirable places the common denominator is the absence of love for others.

The Spirituality loves us all and has illuminated a path for us to climb toward goodness. It's not a steep path, but it is also not the easiest. It simply takes effort to rid ourselves of our primitive urges and to open our hearts to love and kindness. To wait one moment before letting emotions run over us and consider the feelings of the other person and what they went through.

Chapter 10 – Music from the Heavenly Spheres

Music permeates the spheres of heaven. It winds its way down until a crude approximation hits the earth. Whereby, it becomes inspiration for music, tones, cadences, rhythms, notes, melodies, vibrations on strings, and harmonies.

The spirit Kathleen communicated to the Rev. G. Vale Owen, about music. She revealed the origin and the beauty of music to G. Vale Owen on November 12, 1917:

> "This, and almost this only, do we know, or think we know – it passes for knowledge with us in any wise – the Heart of God is the Source of harmony in music – not so much the mind of God as God's great Heart. From Him flow forth the love-strains of His melody, and those spheres which are most near to His attunement receive those Divine harmonies, and by them, with other influences combined, become more and more attuned to Him Who is the Source of all that is Lovely and Loveable. Thus, as the eternities glide on, they who inhabit those far high Spheres blend within themselves more and more of attributes awful and sublime, and compass, each within himself, more and more of Divinity."[49]

As the white light of Love originates from God, so does the Divine Harmonies flow from the vibrations carried by the Universal Fluid created by God, down from the highest to the furthest reaches of the universe. Why is music important? It releases emotions and feelings deep inside. It frees our imagination to soar above mediocrity and materialism.

The spirit Kathleen, answering a question from G. Vale Owen about music in the celestial spheres tells him:

"Yes, we have music of a like nature with yours of earth.

But – and there is a large But here – your music is but the overflow from the reservoir of Heaven's music. You do get the gleams of the glorious harmony we have here, as it comes through. But it is muffled by reason of the thick veil through which it all has to pass, even the finest of earth's masterpieces."[50]

Kathleen notifies us that we, on earth, are unable to conceive of the music in the heavens. Our physical and mental limitations imposed by our bodies preclude us from hearing the harmony from on high. But, we do receive a shadow, a poor representation of what is heard and felt in the heavens.

"Music elevates the soul" is a saying we have all heard. Music serves to channel our intellect and emotions to a different plane. Music reaches places deep within our spirit, it helps binds our force centers together and brings them into harmony.

Without the power of our emotions we stall on our ascendency toward the light. This is why women who have had to experience life after life of hardship under unfair treatment, who were still able to retain their ability to love and nurture - rise to one level after another – while men who block out and sublimate their emotions encounter roadblocks to fully unleash the power of their mind and faith to ascend. Music assists us to combine the naked power of emotion with rational thought.

Frederic Chopin

In the book *Nosso Lar*, by the spirit Andre Luiz, psychographed by Francisco (Chico) C. Xavier, he tells us of concerts in heaven, where contented spirits sat on a verdant lawn enjoying nature and inspiring music. In the book *Memoirs of a Suicide*, by Yvonne A. Pereira, in a city-sized complex to help and educate suicides, we are told that the spirit Frederic Chopin entertained the students, described by the narrator, Camilo Branco:

"Thus, we were able to listen to the great composer who had incarnated more than once, always dedicating his best mental energies to Art or the Belles Lettres as he translated his music via images and narrations in a stunning myriad of themes."[51]

Interestingly, the spirit Camilo describes Chopin as:

"An unhappy soul who now realizes that it is only in the humble carpenter of Nazareth that he will find the secret of the sublime ideals that will make him happy – he presented us with the dramatic poem of his earthly migrations in fabulous expressions of his enrapturing music, transported from the magic of sounds into the wonder of real expressions. One of his incarnations took place before the advent of the Great Emissary, when he was already serving the Arts, cultivating the Belles Lettres as an unforgettable poet that lived in the very midst of the empire of power, the Rome of the Caesars!"[52]

Souls who sense Divine Melodies and transform them to weave an edifying story occupy an important pedestal in the spirit world and in our physical world. Frederic Chopin is one of those. He shall return to earth once again to lift up our spirits and help us turn our eyes and minds to loftier goals.

Mozart

In the book *The Spiritist Review – Journal of Psychological Studies – 1859*, which is a compilation of articles in a monthly magazine edited by Allan Kardec, there is an interview with the spirit Mozart, who refers to ubiquitous nature of music in the spirit realm:

"5. Can the music in the world where you live compare to ours?

- You would have difficulty understanding it. We enjoy senses that you still don't have.

6. We were told that there is a natural, universal harmony in your world that we do not know here.

- It is true. You create music on Earth; here, the whole nature produces melodious sounds."[53]

Mozart echoes what the spirit Kathleen told the Rev. G. Vale Owen … that music is part of the environment, it is one more aspect of nature.

During the same session the mediums asked to speak to Chopin. Mozart replied that would be possible, but they were warned that Chopin was a sadder and more somber soul. After Chopin was evoked, here is the transcript:

"13. Do you miss your Earthly life?

- I am not unhappy

14. Are you happier than before?

- Yes, a little.

15. You say a little, meaning that there isn't much difference. What is it missing so that you can be even happier?

- I say a little for what I could have been, since with my intelligence I could have advanced more than I did.

16. Do you expect to achieve the happiness you miss now?

- It will certainly come but new trials will be needed.

17. Mozart said that you are more somber and sad. Why so?

- Mozart told the truth. I get sad because I did not accomplish a committed assignment and do not have the courage to restart."[54]

The mental state of Chopin was documented in a séance in 1859 and seconded by the writings of a spirit who had committed suicide in the late 1800's in a book published in Portuguese in 1955.

How Earth Receives Music

While advising us of the poor quality of the melodies we do perceive, Kathleen attempts to explain how humans catch a glimpse of what harmonies manage to reach our lowly plane:

> "Our business with you at this time is to tell as best we may, in what few words suffice, some of that we take note of as this same stream descends upon us and passes onward, broadening as each molecule of tone expands of itself and thrusts it fellows outward, until by the time that stream impinges on your boundary it has become much grosser and more coarsened in its texture, and so suited to those almost tangible vibrations available in your sphere.

> This stream from above us finds a receptacle here, and more than one receptacle. This used as a reservoir, and the music is molded into airs and melodies and started forth once again as a small but intense stream earthward. Immediately, it begins to expand, as I have already told you, and what you receive therefore is not sterling essence but the attenuated expansion of the original creation. It is like a small hole in a shutter of a darkened room. Through it streams a small jet of sunlight, but when it reaches the opposite wall it is much thinner in quality and the stream is filled with dancing motes which only tend to obscure the brightness with which it enters through the small aperture."[55]

According to Kathleen, we are like a traveler, lost in a large city, off in the distance we hear, what may be music, but it is difficult to decipher amidst the noise of cars honking, engines roaring, and tires squealing. But still – a discernible melody pulls us in the direction of the harmony which gives us comfort. Some of us, in a meditative or relaxed state can hear the notes and use them to create an earthly representative of the sound dancing in our head.

Kathleen parts with the subject by saying:

> "Well, but even so, your music is both lovable and uplifting.

Oh, bethink you, then, my friend, what must the music of these Spheres be. It ravishes us with ennobling pain and pleasure, and each becomes in himself an accumulator of energy to give forth again what he has received, interpreted and molded, by his own personality for the benefit of those who are not so progressed as he. So is the exquisiteness and potency tempered by those among us whose special aptitude is of such a kind, in order that it be not too fine in nature for the comprehension of those higher souls of earth who catch, and in some degree retain, what thus reaches them from the Master of Music here aloft."[56]

Hence, the receptive souls, such as Mozart, Frederic Chopin, and others hear harmonies that rain down upon us in their minds and fashion, as well as they are able to, utilizing their native genius, compose music to approximate the sounds emanating from heaven.

Chapter 11 – Sex – Marriage – It's All Part of the Spirit World's Plan

A group of spirits, with the spirit Kathleen, who is the main connection between a group of spirits and the Rev. G. Vale Owen, discussed the role of sex and marriage. They presented that we all must combine four aspects of sex roles and characteristics:

"Now we turn to detail more especially and speak of that outcome of marriage, the human unit, male or female as the case may be.

He is born, you will note, of fourfold element. There is the male and female element of the sire, and also the female and male element of the dame. In the father the dominant expression is that of masculinity, in the mother that of femininity. By the incorporation of these four elements, or rather four aspects of one element, or more nearly still these two aspects and two other sub-aspects of one thing, in the one person of the offspring, there is first multiplied and then unified once again some of these variations which are the outer expression of the inner principle of sex.

So he begins to live his own life, this child of the eternities past, and to look forward to the eternities of the future."[57]

You could read this to state we must all have a balance between feminine and masculine qualities. And that a woman possessing masculine characteristics expresses them differently than a man does ... and vice versa. Hence, we must learn all four aspects of a two-sided equation.

As we travel forward in our quest to ascend the ladder of spirituality and goodness, we need to combine the outstanding qualities of each aspect. There are other Spiritist writings which back this up, as well as reports from near death experiences.

Yvonne had a near death experience in which she felt she personally encountered Jesus. I wrote about her experience in my book *The Spirit World Talks to Us - 12 Accounts of Near Death and Other Experiences*. If the spirit wasn't Jesus, then at the least it was a high spirit that has been ascending for eons. She was transported to a heavenly location. Yvonne, in the middle of a luminous fog, looked around. "Suddenly from a distance I saw something."[58] Yvonne reported in her YouTube interview. She described what she saw; "Imagine a flame of fire, instead of fire it was energy. Imagine a face".[59]

She knew it was Jesus, she said, "He engulfed me with his body that was made of energy".[60] Yvonne felt what she had never felt before – pure love. She tells us what she thought as she first embraced the high spirit she recognized as Jesus:

"I knew it was Jesus"

"He engulfed me with his body that was made of energy"

"At that moment I felt the love of a father and a mother blend in one"

"It was not a he and not a she"

"It was one"

"I think on earth love has been divided into a male type of love and a female type of love"

"Jesus has blended in both"[61]

What Yvonne identified in Jesus is what is in store for us. As we ascend in the hierarchy of spirits, becoming more loving, caring, fraternal, and wise, we begin to combine the masculine and feminine sides more completely. This is part of our reason for incarnating on earth. We must be trained in active and passive behavior, in bold action and in quiet sympathy.

The spirit realm, under the direction of Christ, has fashioned our planet to train us in both aspects of male and female behavior and characteristics. And they used the differentiation of the sexes to not only serve as training for us in countless lives, but also to push civilization to a higher plane.

The Reason for Sex

"The control center of sex is not located in the dense body, but in the sublime organization of the soul"[62]

I read this in the book *In the Greater World*. It is a book written by the spirit Andre Luiz, who died and found himself in the Lower Zone. Eventually he was rescued by spirit workers in the celestial city of Nosso Lar. He became a member of various groups to assist humans and spirits still tied to earth. He wrote a series of books about his life in the spirit world through the great medium Francisco (Chico) C. Xavier.

I was intrigued by the passage about sex. If there was anything about us that seemed to be rooted in our dense primitive and often brutish bodies it is sex!

But Andre Luiz's mentor tell us what sex means in the higher spiritual regions and how it molds us here on earth.

"Down on earth, men and women are distinguished according to specific organic features. As for us, in transit to higher spiritual regions, the remembrance of our earthly existence is still preponderant. We know, however, that in such higher regions femininity and masculinity are characteristics of souls that are highly passive or openly active."[63]

Hence sex is an attitude, or more succinctly an attribute. Attributes that we acquire throughout our many lives. He describes this process further:

"Consequently, we know that, in the variations of our experiences, we gradually acquire divine qualities such as

76

determination and tenderness, strength and humility, power and gentleness, intelligence and sentiment, initiative and intuition, wisdom and love, until we attain our supreme balance in God."[64]

As we progress we learn to balance the active and passive sides of our nature. Every spirit is unique and all will have different degrees, but all who ascend into purity will achieve a balance.

The mentor tells us that the human race started out like animals, where the male possessed the female, but given millennia of slow evolution the combinations of woman-mother and man-father migrated to the concept of the tribe, the primitive shelter changed into the home and the quest for wild game transformed into the farm. From this, the spark of sex, civilization arose, the wooden club of the caveman became the gift of flowers to his love.

We all must travel this road to prefect balance. The mentor describes our journey:

"Sometimes, humans take years, centuries and many lifetimes to go from one level to the next. Few individuals are able to keep themselves above the fray with the equilibrium that is required. Very few have crossed the territory of ownership without battling cruelly with the monsters of selfishness and jealousy, to which they have completely surrendered. A small number travel the road of tenderness without shackling themselves for a long stretch to the many chains of exclusiveness. And sometimes, only after millennia of excruciating, purifying trials, can the soul reach the luminous zenith of sacrifice for its final deliverance in route to new cycles of unification with the Divinity."[65]

Therefore, we own no one, we direct no one, we merely love, cherish and help one another. Always providing feedback for the spiritual benefit of our partner. Each one of us learning to weigh our active and passive sides. Learning to know when one is better than the other in different circumstances.

Even Further Back

Given how we all accept the need for two sexes to carry on the human race, our belief in the inevitability of a male and female form and function is absolute. But it is not – it was a conscious decision – one made for a purpose.

G. Vale Owen was told:

"We speak first to you of Marriage as of the union of two personalities in creative faculty. The people take it as quite in the ordinary course of things that sex should be, and also that sex should be complete in blend of male and female. But it was not of essential necessity that this should be, humanity might have been hermaphrodite. But far away beyond the beginnings of this present eternity of matter, when the Sons of God were evolving form, in its ideal conception, they took counsel together and afterwards decreed that one of the laws which should guide their further work should be, not so much a division of the race into two sexes, as you and earth philosophy have it, but rather that sex should be one of the new elements which should enter into the further evolution of being when being should shortly enter into matter, and so take form. But form endowed personality with individuality, and so the element personality, by evolution of concrete form, issued in its complement of persons. But as from one element persons came, so sex is unity composed of two species. Man and woman form one sex, as flesh and blood form one body."[66]

Therefore, while the physical aspect of sex is part of our experience, the more subtle personality traits, and graduations of aggressive and passive behaviors is all part of our training.

Hence, as we are told in *The Spirits Book*, by Allan Kardec, in our many lives, we may come back as a male or female:

202. Does a spirit, when existing in the spirit-world prefer to be incarnated as a man or a woman?

"That point in regard to which a spirit is indifferent, and which is always decided in view of the trials which he has to undergo in his new corporeal life."

Further in *The Spirits Book*, we are told that marriage is a union of two spirits – there is no mention of male and female. Therefore, marriage is two spirits assisting each other to understand the different aspects and to be sympathetic to those differences. To help the other, to learn from the other, so as one unit they may both improve.

This point is enforced by what the spirit Kathleen passed on to the Rev. G. Vale Owen:

"Two great principles which are included in the Unity of Godhead were made to appear as two separate things in order that those two principles might be studied in detail by those who were not competent to study them as One. But when the male considers the female he is but getting a more clear understanding of a part of himself, and so when the female reasons on the male. For as they were not separate in the eternities of development which went before this present eternity of matter and form, so the two elements shall become one again in those eternities which shall come after."[67]

The spirit world, the High Lords of our system, who are the messengers and implementers of the Word of God, knew that for us to understand the duality of natures, we needed the problem broken down. It is simple heuristics, a plan to present the need to explore all aspects of our behavior in such a way that we live the solution ... throughout many lives. It is like tricking your children to play a game in which they are accumulating new knowledge; enjoying themselves and learning at the same time, otherwise they would have resisted.

While we may have started out as asexual personalities, with no need to reproduce from the mixture of two parents; in our present intellectual and social level of maturity, we require a course in comprehending the many facets of our behavior. Our sojourn will result in newfound awareness:

"By this experience of the two in unity, the perfected human being, ages hence, in other higher worlds of onward press towards the state of Being consummate, man shall have come to the knowledge how it is possible in loving other and giving to other by denying of self he is loving himself the more and but the bountifully giving to himself by that same denying of self."[68]

We shall eventually become what Yvonne saw during her near death experience. A glorious mixture of love and kindness. In fact, the spirits who spoke with the Rev. G. Vale Owen, in 1917, revealed the same aspect about Jesus:

"So of the blend of the two elements, spiritually as bodily, there is born a Third Who within Himself unites these two elements in His one Person. The Lord Jesus was the perfect Son of Humankind and His nature, spiritually considered, is a blend of the male and female virtues in duly equal parts."[69]

There you have it, our daily dramas trying to understand our partners is all part of a grand plan. A plan so perfect, we don't even realize that we are in deep study while we try to figure out how to live with each other. Therefore, go forth, unafraid, learn the hard or the easy way what your spouse desires, why they desire it, and what motivates their desires – because the insights you gather will be used for your ascension up the spiritual ladder.

Chapter 12 – Fear of Being Different – Don't Let Society Silence You

A minister, of an unspecified religion, passed away. He was assigned a house on the second sphere of heaven. The spirit realm sent a woman to him to discuss why he was unable to speak, what he knew was the truth, to people who needed help with communicating with loved ones who have passed. Instead of assisting those in need he guided them elsewhere, for he was afraid to be exposed to scorn and ridicule from his colleagues.

It is easy to tell everyone to stand-up for what you believe in; to not be afraid to speak the truth. But, we all know it's not easy. When others are all professing a certain belief, we become tentative in any differences in our own thoughts.

I remember, when I was in college, I was invited to a study. I was told to listen to a series of beeps and to tell the leader at the head of the table the number of beeps I heard. There were about four or five other participants. Using headphones I heard the beeps and kept track of the correct number. After the first round each of us were asked what was the number of beeps we heard. My answer was different from all the others.

This caused instant confusion on my part. I tried to go through the instructions I was given, what was the definition of a beep, etc. On the second round, again I had a different answer. I was now worried about my hearing; was the static sound supposed to be a beep too? On the third round I conformed to what the others said. I had given up. Obviously, there was something wrong with my thinking or my hearing.

After a few more rounds, we finished. Then I was told, that all the other participants were told what to say, I was the only variable. The experiment was to determine the effect of group pressure. What I had heard was true, but I lacked the confidence and conviction to report the truth. I had failed.

But, I am eternally grateful for being allowed to learn a very valuable lesson. In fact, as I look back, I am certain the spirit realm guided me to that room and experiment so I could learn to have faith in what I knew and to not let others influence me. The embarrassment I felt caving in to group pressure so easily was intense. I have never forgotten how disappointed I was in myself. What a complete fool I was!

This moment made a lasting impression on me. No longer would I suffer changing my belief, if I had the facts to support it, in the face of social pressure from others. While I can certainly say, often, instead of speaking out, I remained silent, in order to keep my job, each time feeling small for doing so. On the other hand, in other circumstances I have spoken out or refused to go along. Which could explain my lack of advancement in my career!

Hence, I am sympathetic to the poor soul who was confronted in heaven for what he did, or more rightly, what he did not do, on earth. His case was discussed with the Rev. G. Vale Owen. They began with a description of a house in the second sphere of heaven where those who have recently passed over stay for a time to recuperate and to determine their eventual place in the heavenly spheres:

> "One of our band not long ago went to this Home and sought out a man who had come to such a forward state as this. On earth he had been a minister of religion who had read somewhat of what you call psychic matters, and the possibility of speaking one to other between us and you, as we do at this present. But he could not come at the thing in thorough, and was afraid to say out even so much as he in his own heart knew to be true and good. So he did what many of his fellows are doing. He put the matter aside from him. He could find other ways in which to help his fellow-men, and this other matter

might await the time when it was more and more widely understood and accepted of men, and then he would be one of the foremost to proclaim what he knew, and would not shirk his duty in that time."[70]

In other words, when the coast is clear, he would pop his head out and become part of the group. I once heard a wonderful explanation of how senior and executive management operates in large companies. Each manager wishes to lead, to make him or herself noticed as a performer, but on the other hand, they don't wish to stick out too far. Because to be too different is to not be part of the group. Hence, their behavior was described as constantly swimming in a bait ball. You don't want to be too distant out of the bait ball, otherwise a predator will pick you out. Therefore, you want to change direction with the rest of the fish. Huddling together in relative safety, hoping some other fish, close to the outer ring, or completely outside, will fall prey.

This is why one sees some of the dumbest ideas gain traction and even thrive in corporations and governments. The fish aren't thinking of the actual direction, they are merely trying hard to keep up with others, so as to not expose themselves.

This man didn't want to reveal that we, the incarnates, are able to speak to the other side. For doing so would expose him to derision and malicious gossip from his peers. Therefore, when members of his flock came to him enquiring about communicating with deceased loved ones, this is what would occur:

"But when others came to him and asked him first whether it was possible to speak with their dear ones who had come over here; and second, whether it were God's will so to do; he put them in mind of their Christian belief in the Saintly Communion, but urged them that they be patient until the Church should have tested and sifted and should have issued guidance for those who were of the fold. And while he waited, lo, his time on earth was fulfilled and he was carried over into this Home, where he might rest awhile and come to some decision on what attitude he had assumed on diverse matters of his calling, and of the use he made of his opportunities."[71]

People came to this man of the Church because they had seen evidence and clues about the other side. Before the internet made possible the gathering of near death experiences from around the world; before the power of the Catholic Church had diminished to the point where people could freely talk about psychic phenomena – still there was an acknowledgement amongst the masses that a life beyond death existed and that loved ones still lived in another dimension.

People talked, they either knew or had witness themselves … a feeling, a sense, an intuition of a future event, or an actual near death or other experience with the spirit realm. The Catholic Church's position, and others as well, that one can't communicate with the other side didn't match their own understanding.

The Conversation

Hence, the spirit world sent an emissary to speak to the newly departed man of the Church. She, the spirits called her Naine, sought him out in his resting place in sphere two. She found him in a peaceful garden. Surrounded by plants and flowers of indescribable lights and colors:

"She went to him and stood before him, and he bowed and would have passed on, but she spoke to him and said, 'My friend, it was to you I was sent, to speak to you.'

And he replied, 'Who sent you to me?'

'The Angel who has to answer to our Master for your life-work while in the earth sphere,' she said.

'Why should he have to answer for me?" he asked her. 'Surely every one must answer for his own life and work – isn't that so?'

And she said, 'That is surely so. Yet, to our sorrow, we here know that it is not the whole of the matter. For naught you do or leave undone ends with yourself alone. He who had you in charge made effort, time and again, for your welfare and, in part, succeeded, but not in whole. And now the earth period has been closed for you, he has to sum up your life, and answer for his charge of you, to his joy and also to his sorrow.'

'This seems hardly fair, to my mind,' he answered her. 'It is not my idea of justice that another should suffer for one's failures,' Naine said, 'And yet, that is what you taught the people yonder – it was your understanding of the doings at Calvary, and you handed it on to them. Not all you said of it was true, and yet it was true in part. For do we not share joy on behalf of another's joy, and shall we not also share in his sorrowing? This your Angel does for you even now. He both joys and sorrows over you.'

'Please explain.'

'He joys in that you did good work in charity, for your heart was much bathed in love for God and man. He sorrowed for you in that you were not content to do what you taught was done for you on Calvary. For you were not willing to become scorn for men, and to be withered with their disapproval, for you valued the praise of men more than God's praise, and hoped to be able one day to buy more cheaply your reward for having spread light upon the darkness when that darkness should begin to pass from night into the twilight of the dawning day. But you did not see, in your weakness and lack of valiant purpose and of strength to suffer shame and coldness, that the time for which you waited was the time when your help would be needful, and the fight all but won by others of more stalwart mettle, while you stood with the onlookers and viewed the fight from a fair vantage ground, while those others fought and gave and took blows good and strong and fell forward in the battle when they would not surrender their cause to those who opposed them.'"[72]

Oh how I feel for that poor man, doing what he thought he could while weighing the pros and cons of his actions. Afraid of the consequences of fighting a large and brutal organization. I have faced the same dilemmas and have been gutless time and time again. I remember, back in high school, walking home with some friends, passing two other young high school boys, when they attacked us. I ran leaving my friends behind. What a spineless coward! I vowed to never do that again.

But of course I did! In management, I allowed people to be fired or given bad reviews just because a certain percentage of employees had to be found wanting. I performed such despicable acts because I selfishly desired to keep my position and – much worse – I wanted to demonstrate my usefulness in carrying out orders. Unlike the man of the cloth, he at least engaged in charity and good works, while I, only wished to make money.

Upon hearing what he did from the emissary, he asked:

"'But why all this?' he inquired, 'What is your reason for coming to see me at all?'

'Because he sent me,' she said, 'and because he would that he also might come to you, but is not able until you are of a mind more clear of purpose, and until you have mastered and acknowledged the various elements which made up your earth life in their true values and appraisement.'

'I see, partly at least. Thank you. I have been in a cloud all this time. I came here, away from the others, to try to understand it all better. You have said some pretty straight things to me. Perhaps you will add to this service by telling me how I am to begin.'

'That is my mission here and now. It is the one thing with which I was charged. I was to probe your mind, to make you look inward upon yourself and, if you showed any will to progress, I was to give you a message. This will you have now shown – not very heartily, however. And this is my message from your Angel guide who awaits you to lead you on when you have trained yourself some little more. You are requested to take up your quarters in a home, which I will show you, in the First Sphere. From there you will, from time to time, visit the earth plane and help those there in their communion with their friends here in these spheres of light, and also aid them in speaking comfort and encouragement to those who are in the darker spheres, that they may progress into the light and peace of His Presence. There are even among those to whom you ministered, several who are trying to do this good work for those in anguish, and also to give and to get gladness by their speaking with their loved ones here. They sought your guidance in this matter and you had no courage to give it to them. Go and help them now and, when you are able to make known to them your personality, unsay what you then said, or say what you lacked courage then to tell them. In this you shall have some shame, but they will have much joy and will deal very kindly with you, for they have scented already the fragrance of love from Realms higher and brighter than this in which you have been resting. But the choice is still for you. Go or go not, as your heart inclines you.'"[73]

Naine left him pondering upon his decision, whether to travel to a lower sphere and facilitate communication between the earthly and heavenly planes or to remain in his home in the second sphere. Whatever his decision, it will be his alone. Free-will is one of the Divine Laws, we are not forced to become better. We are presented opportunities in which we may learn.

In the spirit world, for those in one of the heavenly spheres, we are given options and choices. We move up or down at our determination. On earth, we encounter episodes that have been predetermined to allow us to learn what we had lacked in the previous life. Again, we have the choice to either absorb the lesson or completely ignore it.

While in the Lower Zones and the Dark Abyss (also called purgatory) those spirits are placed in a location where they are daily reminded of who they are and what they believe and are given the exact environment they so desired while on earth. Although now that they are in the middle of it, they shall have second thoughts and one day emerge.

In our physical life, we are given challenges. Just like the man who was given a chance to spread his knowledge, but declined the sublime summons because it was too risky - we too face difficult choices. Our decisions will not only affect our life here on earth, but our future path in the spirit world. Remember, for any sacrifice we make on earth, in the pursuit of dong good, we shall be rewarded a hundred fold when we return back home, after shedding our physical bodies.

Chapter 13 - Stillborn Children – Raised in the Spirit Realm

All life is sacred and precious to the spirit world. Spiritism tells us that upon conception, the merger of spirit to flesh occurs. A distinct spirit gestates in the mother's womb. While some pregnancies are terminated naturally or unnaturally the question answered by the spirit Arnel to the Rev. G. Vale Owen, is what happens to babies who have never taken a breath of fresh air?

Arnel tells us about the children who are raised in the spirit world. In addition, Spiritist literature relates there are different paths that could be taken when a pregnancy is aborted.

Some spirits are taken from the fetus and put back into their original spirit body. They may have been originally assigned to a particular mother, and if an abortion occurs, they may wait until the next opportunity. This may be the case where the spirit waiting to be born has a connection with the mother that needs to be played out in a mother to child relationship.

Damaged Perispirit

Nevertheless, the majority of babies that die either soon after birth or are stillborn do so for a reason. The purpose lies in the relationship of the spirit and the perispirit and the perispirit to the body. The perispirit connects the body to the spirit. The perispirit can influence the body as it is forming and even during life. When a person harms their own body through a drastic event, such as a suicide, they not only harm the physical vessel but the perispirit too.

If a person threw themselves in front of a train, or causes a similar devastation of a corporeal body, the injuries to the perispirit – which is influenced by the form of the body, is immense. Only a reset of the perispirit to a normal human form can ensure a safe birth.

In the book, *Memoirs of a Suicide*, an instructor tells a group of spirits how a person who had severe injuries must go through certain steps in order to attain a successful birth and incarnation:

> "Unfortunately, they will reincarnate just as they are! Nothing can be done for them except return them to the flesh. That is the therapy imposed on them to correct the overall imbalance of their vibrations, thus creating a sort of 'trial run' for new attempts at growth in the future. This therapy, made easier to bear by the prayers that are ministered to them daily in sympathetic, gentle and beneficial currents emitted from here on their behalf, is all that these poor brothers and sisters can receive for the time being, despite our great desire to see them serene and happy!"[74]

"Trial run" means a union of the spirit to the body via the perispirit. This may mean a still birth or just a brief time alive outside the mother's womb. This short episode is enough to reform the perispirit to the intended structure of a human body.

It is as if a cast was made for a statute that was imperfect. The metal was poured into a broken mold, then when the mold was removed the statue was flawed. The mold would be replaced by the corrected version and the metal would be re-melted and re-poured into the mold thereby creating a perfect statue. The perispirit must be perfect to create a healthy human. Hence some type of birth event must be used to repair the extensive damage.

The Problems of a Stillborn

> "We speak of childbirth into these realms of those who come forth from the earth sphere but have not been endowed with a separate individuality therein. These children come here asleep, and you will realize that their first awakening is that process

90

here which answers to birth on earth. They have never breathed the atmosphere, nor seen the light, nor heard any of the sounds of earth. In brief, none of their bodily senses have been exercised in the way for which they were prepared by their natural formation. The organs of these senses are, therefore, nearly, but not quite, perfect in their structure. Moreover, the brain has never been called upon to interpret their messages. And so the child of earth lacks earthly qualities empirically, while have them potentially. These conditions do not apply to a child who has been actually born into earth life, even though he have but a few moments, or even less, of life before he pass on hitherward."[75]

Arnel tells us why the spirit world must take special care of a stillborn, but he leaves unanswered as to why does the spirit realm spend so much time and effort in raising a spirit, from before their natural term in the womb all the way to spirit adulthood. Wouldn't it be better just to let the spirit return to their damaged form and wait for the next opportunity?

I have not yet seen the answer to this question in any Spiritist literature I have read to date … but I have a theory. I believe, that in the infinite wisdom and love that the spirit realm has for us, that for spirits who have suffered so much in life and came to an ignoble end, most probably after repeated lifetimes of failures, that these spirits are given a radical reset. A chance to completely retool their character. They are re-raised in the spirit realm, surrounded by love to give them a chance to return to a normal path of ascendancy in their spirit quest to become a pure spirit.

Without, this boost, this major operation on their character and personality, out right failure could persist for eons, which would be a tragedy for the aspiring spirit and for the many loving spirits who have tried to assist.

The Nurturing Process

The spirit Arnel then explains what must be done to prepare the stillborn for life in the spirit realm:

91

"The problem, therefore, which they have to solve who take these children in hand is not a small one; for it is necessary both that the organs be dealt with so that a natural progress may attend the child, and also that the brain receives its lesson. In the case of an infant a few minutes old this connection between the brain and the organs of sense has been established and can be used in the maturing of those faculties dependent for their exercise on those organs. But a stillborn child brings not that connection, and it has to be made on this side. Once that is done, the progress is merely a matter of orderly development, on the same lines as that of ordinary children."[76]

Arnel explains the preferred method to complete the connection from the baby's spirit to his perispirit to the spirit remnants of his physical body. The first method is to expose the child, in spirit, to the spirit of his mother. This is accomplished while the mother is asleep and free to wander the spirit world. When the baby and mother are brought together, a type of birth is experienced by the baby. Only after that, does the child feel to be a separate entity.

The bond between a mother and her child is stronger than you may believe. The process of a normal birth and childhood is revealed in the book, *Missionaries of the Light*, inspired by Dr. Andre Luiz, psychographed by Chico Xavier. The process of building a body up for full independence in a new reincarnation takes seven years. From the time of birth to the seventh birthday, a child will have a guardian spirit constantly looking out for them.

Andre Luiz's mentor explains thusly:

"You are aware that the human body has its vegetative activities per se, but you may not yet know that the perispiritual body, which gives form to the cellular elements, is strongly rooted in the blood. In the fetal organization, the blood elements are a gift from the mother's body. Soon after rebirth, a period of a different assimilation of organic energies takes place, where the reincarnated 'self' rehearses the consolidation of its new experiences. In this new cycle of physical life, it is only at age seven that it can begin to preside on its own over the blood formation process, which is the basic element for the equilibrium of the perispiritual body or pre-existent form. Blood, therefore, can be regarded as the divine fluid that underpins our activities on the physical plane, and through its continual flow within the physiological organism, it furnishes us with a symbol of the eternal movement of the sublime energies of the Infinite Creation."[77]

Hence, a child's body is still forming to its spiritual outline until around seven years of age. Mother's out there reading this, the cutting of the umbilical cord is just a symbol … your vital energies (love, of course is always there!) still assists your child years after their birth.

Imagine, the care for a child jettisoned from their mother prematurely. The mother's spirit is still tied to that child, visiting their loved one at night and giving love and comfort so the child may restart building their personality in the spirit world. Throughout the childhood of the stillborn, they are, if possible, kept in contact with their physical mother. Thus supplying them an anchor of love from the earthly sphere.

Arnel tells us there are differences between children who never reached the earth alive:

"There is always some little difference between such children and those others who have been born on earth. They are lacking in some of the sterner virtues; and, on the other hand, they are more spiritual in their personality and outlook. But as earthborn children progress in spiritual development, and the stillborn children develop their knowledge of earth by contact with their mothers, and later with their other relatives, so the differences is minimized until they are able to associate on quasi-equal terms of loving friendship, and to help in the mutual giving of what each lacks.

So the earthborn are mellowed in sweetness, and the others are strengthened in character, and, both being included in a community, infuse an element of variety which is pleasurable as it is of profit."[78]

Arnel states that the association with the parents of the spirit child is vital for the child's development. All of this goes on in the mist of dreams for the parents. Unknowingly, the mother and father are responsible for raising a young spirit – and all they have are fleeting remnants of dreams.

Tragically, if the parents are of a wicked disposition, the child must be separated from the mother and father, until the child is mature enough to understand the circumstances. Often, the child will assist the parents from the spirit world to follow the path of the light.

Motherhood and fatherhood starts before the birth of a child, it begins at the conception of the child. Life is precious and it serves a purpose. We, our children, seen and unseen, are on this planet and in the surrounding spheres so we may learn to become mature and civilized spirits. So we may become a productive member of the spirit realm and contribute the force of our will to the creation of worlds and life to promote even more spirits.

Chapter 14 - Your Spirit Brain Dwarfs Your Human Brain

The Doctrine of Spiritism, and many religions, tell us that we are immortal souls. Spiritism reveals that we live forever and we incarnate on earth, and other planets, as part of a learning process to improve … to become pure spirits. But if that is so, how and where do we retain all of our past memories and knowledge about life in a physical body and life during the times we were errant spirits?

The answer is we have all memories stored in our spirit brain, which is vastly superior to our limited physical mind. It is like comparing one of the first personal computers which had a storage capacity of 512,000 bytes of data to a storage device today of one terabyte – one trillion bytes of data. – 1,000,000,000,000.

How do we know this? The spirit Arnel discussed with the Rev. G. Vale Owen, about a tour of a temple G. Vale Owen took when he was asleep and free of his physical body. G. Vale Owen could only remember parts of what he saw, and some he misunderstood.

Arnel told G. Vale Owen why he was unable to correctly recall the event when he returned to his physical consciousness:

"In the brain of your spirit-body which gives out of its storehouse from time to time, so much as the lesser capacity of your physical brain can hold and use. Most of the scenes you have described in your previous Script have thus been stored in your spirit brain and reproduced in this way."[79]

Hence, when we recall our dreams – our time in the spirit world – we are unable to precisely remember the details of our experience. It is as if, one took a picture, of immense detail and beauty, then drew back until the picture appeared hazy and non-distinct.

This is how we evoke our dreams. Our interpretation is only on a gross level. The details we think we know fade into symbols, as our weak physical brain attempts to categorize that which we had never encountered on earth into something we can process.

Most times, the only true recollection is the mood of the dream. Even looking at a fuzzy picture we can still see the happiness or sadness of the subject. Our physical brain can process emotion. Hence, if the dream is pleasant, then something good happened or you were told of a positive event which may occur. If the dream felt foreboding, then a future path may be a mistake or information was revealed about a person or place that could mean harm.

Chapter 15 – To Be Human is only a Temporary Condition

We, as humans, believe ourselves to be on top of the food chain. Masters of the planet. It only appears to be this way. In reality, we are immature souls who are in a tightly controlled classroom, with twenty-four hours per day monitoring. We should all thank God for this.

The human form as it is expressed on the planet Earth, was specifically tailored to the conditions which exist on this little orb, the third from the sun.

We have been presented with an encasement which was designed to further our education. It allows our spirit intelligence to be filtered and gated, to only transmit a limited amount of data, back and forth, via the perispirit, to our organic brain. The human body acts as a governor on our spirit personality to set us up to gain the maximum knowledge from our experiences assigned to us on earth.

Living for a small amount of time in a human body is a privilege. One that shouldn't be taken lightly. The gift of reincarnation provides us with a vehicle to remove what is wrong and to add what is good to our spirit personalities. Our whole existence is that task.

We are on earth to learn, to improve, to be educated ... to love. This is the reason you are on earth.

Yes, our human instincts have been modified over the millennia. Yes, we are born with certain urges. Yes, the DNA from our parents and their parents affect our bodies and minds. But all of this is known, and planned by the spirit world.

Our primitive impulses, which helped us survive during the dawn of mankind, are now those very desires we are challenged to learn to either modify or ignore. One may regret those yearnings which boil up and invade our thoughts, but its all part of the process of training ourselves to reject that which runs counter to our conscience – the set of universal laws embedded in our brain by the Divine Presence.

As we mature we shall learn to follow the signs and signals given to us by our conscience and from spirits who are here for our benefit. We shall place deep into our heart the need to do what is right and honest, given what options we may be able to choose in any type of circumstances.

The spirit world doesn't expect us to give away all of our possessions and live life as a wandering monk. Only that we constantly attempt to be on the side of good, to try and maneuver around the obstacles that face us. To select the path that harms the least people, does the most good, and follows our inner voice of purity.

Section 2 - Spirit Assistance

We look upon guardian angels as kindly manifestations of spirits who shine, have wings, and smile lovingly down upon us at all times, with unbounded unconditional love. That we are forgiven all wrongs, all malicious deeds, everything, no matter what. All we need to do is drop to our knees and ask for a pardon – then heaven's gate will open to us. The truth is more complex.

Yes, all is forgiven – but not all penalties are withdrawn. Yes, we are loved unconditionally – but its tough love, love fashioned to shape us, to make us more responsible. Yes, heaven's gate is always open – but we must earn entrance.

Spirits, who have been in our shoes, who know the little lies we tell ourselves, who recognize our desires and weaknesses; work on our behalf to lift us up out of the mire of our normal human behavior. They attempt to enable us to not look at any sideways glance as an insult. To not envy what others possess. To not obsessively make plans for revenge of perceived wrongs. To not grab at any opportunity to enrich ourselves. To not lose our temper at the slightest provocation.

We are watched and guided to stay true to our original plan for our life. A blueprint created by higher and concerned spirits, with our input, to experience the pain and disappointments we have caused others. As well as supplying opportunities to hone our skills, broaden our outlook, and accumulate more wisdom.

Hence, our guardian spirits, and other spirits as they are called in to give assistance, may exert negative influence to stop us from committing wrongful deeds, while at different times may apply positive pressure to urge us to perform an action, create something new to move the world, or simply fill in a missing component to a problem that has been vexing us.

The tools guardian and high spirits possess and the techniques which are employed to measure, evaluate, and inspire us are partially uncovered in the section which follows. Resources, time, and effort are deployed on our behalf on a planetary scale which would dwarf any human endeavor. The combined might of Axis and Allied armies during World War II are nothing compared to the row after row of angelic battalions dedicated to our welfare.

Literally, billions of high spirits from all levels of heaven, circling the earth, plus untold number of spirits residing in advanced spheres and other planets are toiling on our behalf. Every minute there are thousands of daily dramas, whereupon spirits are trying to guide individuals to make the right choice, as low spirits fight to retain their comrades to remain tied to materialism and selfishness.

In our trek for purity of spirit and heart, we are meant to walk through fire. Each misstep causes a tear to drop from the eyes of our guardians. They live with disappointment and hope. Every day is a battle. While victories may seem few and far between; they are intensely celebrated. For each success means there is one more soldier to add to the army of Christ.

Above all else, as you read the revelations brought from the spirits who spoke, via mind to mind, with the Rev. G. Vale Owen, remember that we are cherished, loved, and guided with the utmost kindness. Every action taken on, for, and to us are always meant for our own edification. From the petty thief, the crooked politician, the narcissistic self-promoter, the shy person who plods through daily life, the doctor, the parent who toils and sacrifices for their children … are all loved with equal passion.

While each incarnate on earth may be at different levels of spiritual maturity, with the help of our guardian angels, we shall all end up pure of heart. And ready to lend our assistance to a struggling soul on a planet who is looking to improve.

100

Chapter 16 - Helping Souls Who Just Passed Over

I have previously written about the help given to the dying and the souls who have passed over from the physical world to the other side. In the series of books by the spirit Andre Luiz, psychographed by Francisco (Chico) C. Xavier, this subject is discussed from many angles. The caring and effort to help people make the transition is considerable.

This subject is also reviewed in the Reverend Owen's book, which is a collection of four of his books, *Life Beyond the Veil*, in *The Lowlands of Heaven* section, his mother talks about the assistance given to the newly dead:

> "Now let us see if we can impress you to write a few words of the conditions which we found when we arrived here – the conditions, that is, of those who pass over here when they first arrive. They are not all of an equal degree of spiritual development, of course, and therefore require different treatment. Many, as you know, do not realize for some time the fact that they are what they would call dead, because they find themselves alive and with a body, and their previous vague notions of the after-death state are not, by any means, lightly thrown away."[80]

As we have seen in Spiritist literature, among those who have slight spiritual inclination or knowledge are quite rightly confused. Even those who are spiritual and practice one of the religions are often taken aback. Most are taught we become another being or we are sent to heaven right away in the form of an angel. We cast off not only our bodies, but our baser characteristics and are transformed into graceful and noble entities. Imagine the surprise when they find out we are who we are.

Process of Awakening

Vale Owen's mother takes us through the regular process to wake up a confused soul who has come over to the spirit realm.

"The first thing to do, then, with such as those is to help them to realize the fact that they are no more in the earth life, and, to do this, we employ methods.

One is to ask them whether they remember some friend or relative, and, when they reply that they do so but that he is dead, we try and enable them to see this particular spirit, who, appearing alive, should convince the doubter that he is really passed over. This is not always the case, for the ingrained fallacies are obstinate, and so we try another method.

We take him to some scene on earth with which he is familiar and show him those whom he has left behind, and the difference in his state and theirs.

If this should fail, then we bring to his recollection the last experiences he underwent before passing, and gradually lead up to them when he fell asleep, and then we try to connect up that moment with his awakening here.

All these endeavors often fail – more often than you would imagine – for character is built up year by year, and the ideas which go to help in this building become very firmly imbedded in his character. Also we have to be very careful not to overtax him, or it would delay his enlightenment. Sometimes, however, in the case of those who are more enlightened, they realize immediately that they are passed into the spirit land, and then our work is easy."[81]

The last thing that most of us expect to be when we die is the continuation of what we were before death. Andre Luiz wished to explore exactly how a spiritually aware person felt after their death. In the book, *Workers of the Life Eternal*, psychographed by

103

Chico Xavier, Andre Luiz is given permission to ask questions to Dimas, who had just passed away.

What a Spirit Feels Right After Death

Dimas was an untiring medium, who worked for the good of incarnates and discarnates. Hence, Andre was part of a spirit team who was sent to help Dimas disconnect from his physical life. It is worth noting, that one of the main obstacles, was the desire of his family for him to recover and once more be part of their life. The thoughts emanating from Dimas' wife and children kept him tied to earth. The spirit team had to resort to the camouflage of making Dimas appear to recover, so his family would leave the spirit team a few hours of peace to begin the process to bring Dimas over to the spirit realm.

Upon his death, Dimas was placed in a coffin. Next, the coffin was taken to the cemetery, where the funeral procession included at least twenty discarnates, including the newly departed. At the cemetery, where the coffin containing the remains of Dimas is being buried. Andre asks his director if he can pose some questions to Dimas. The Director gives his permission to explore more what it feels like to be newly dead.

Andre turns to Dimas, now a spirit and asks:

"'Are you still experiencing any physical pain?' I began.

'I still have a clear impression of the body I have just left behind,' he responded politely. 'But I have noticed that, in wishing to remain close to my own loved ones and to continue on where I had been for so many years, I relive all the suffering that I endured. However, when I resign myself to accepting the higher designs, I immediately feel lighter and comforted. Despite the short amount of time that I have been awake, I have already been able to make such an observation.'

'And what about the five senses?' I continued.

'They are in perfect working order.'

'Do you feel hunger?'

'I actually can tell that my stomach is empty and I would be glad if I had something to eat, but this physical desire is neither uncomfortable nor torturing.'

'And thirst?'

'Yes, although I do not suffer because of it.'"[82]

As usual Andre poses the questions we would all like to know. There are an enormous number of gems of information in each one of Andre's books. I encourage our readers to discover more about the spirit world by reading the books of Andre Luiz, starting with Nosso Lar, his story of his death and eventual rescue from the Lower Zone (or Umbral) to his time at the celestial city of Nosso Lar.

An Example of a Soul Who Just Passed

Vale Owen's mother tells us of an actual case she was on. She and group were sent to assist a woman who was on the cusp of passing over. They arrived to see the dying lady surrounded by sad friends. All were extremely sorry to see her leave the earth. The narrative starts:

"She fell asleep, and the cord of life was severed by our watching friends, and then, softly, they awoke her, and she looked up and smiled very sweetly at the kind face of one who leaned over her. She lay there perfectly happy and content until she began to wonder why these strange faces were around her in place of the nurses and friends she had last seen. She inquired where she was, and, when she was told, a look of wonder and of yearning came over her face, and she asked to be allowed to see the friend she had left.

This was granted her, and she looked on them through the Veil and shook her head sadly. 'If only they could know,' she said, 'how free from pain I am now, and comfortable. Can you not tell them?' We tried to do so, but only one of them heard, I think, and he only imperfectly, and soon put it away as a fancy.

We took her from that scene, and, after she had somewhat gained strength, to a children's school, where her little boy was, and, when she saw him, her joy was too great for words. He had passed over some few years before, and had been placed in this school where he had lived ever since. Then the child became instructor to his mother, and this sight was a pretty one to see. He led her about the school and the grounds and showed her the different places, and his schoolmates, and all the while, his face beamed with delight; and so did the mother's.

We left her awhile, and then, when we returned, we found those two sitting in an arbor, and she was telling him about those she had left behind, and he was telling her of those who had come before, and whom he had met, and of his life in the school, and it was as much as we could do to tear her away, with a promise that she should return soon and often to her boy."[83]

To those who have read that the mother was taken from her child, do not worry, she was taken to a place where she could recuperate after her release from physical life. This process is intended to calm the stresses of coming back into spirit form and to make her ready to restart her true life, as a spirit.

A Recollection of Helping the Newly Dead from a Medium

There are many examples, which are quite like the one above in the books by Chico Xavier. From the 1850s, when Allan Kardec codified Spiritism, to the present, we have been given a clear and consistent picture of what death really is.

Independently of any communications from spirits about helping the dead, I had a series of e-mails with a medium who had retained memories of her life in the spirit realm. She read my blog and was fascinated how close Spiritism was to her own experiences. Then she read the book *Nosso Lar*, which talked about spirit guides who assisted the recently passed.

A team of spirit helpers were responsible for rescuing Andre

Luiz, the spirit who dictated the book to Chico Xavier, about his death, time in the Lower Zone and subsequent life in the celestial city Nosso Lar.

She wrote me:

"My most recent adventure involved Chico Xavier's Nosso Lar. As someone who remembers being a helper, it was exciting to see Home identified. I thought I was the only one who knew about/remembered Home. :) I must have worked there for hundreds of years, helping spirits. Then I came back here to learn some new things (for a couple of short lifetimes plus this one). Anyway, I want to vouch for Home as a reality. The details about its structure might vary but it is an amazing place of love.

 And from Home, you can access any place on earth. It's not uncommon for people who have reached the helper level to enter the dreams of the embodied, which can be done directly from Home, to offer help and advice."

Once again, a person who hadn't been aware of Chico's books or Spiritism, finds verification of their own ideas and memories. She did write to say that unlike Andre's experience where he spent time in the Lower Zone, not all people experience this frightening episode after death.

"One item that I feel needs a minor correction regards the purgatory-like experience of Andre Luis, prior to his going Home. He experienced a dark, scary landscape, but I want people to know that the arrival zone is different for everyone. It will basically be your own mind-created object. With sudden or unexpected deaths, people often don't know they have crossed over; they look for familiarity and their own mind creates that for them. The good news is that someone like me (what I used to do, anyway) will meet you where you are, and help you through the process."

Of course, she is completely correct. In Andre Luiz's book there are many instances of spirit helpers assisting people right from their deathbeds and other locations. Andre Luiz was in the Lower Zone, or the Umbral, as it is referred to in Portuguese, because he was an unconscious suicide.

In the case of suicides, the spirit who takes her or his own life is generally obligated to remain in the Umbral until such time as their normal death would have occurred. Hence, the spirit world frowns on people leaving the earthly campus before they are dismissed.

In Andre's case, he didn't deliberately kill himself, but he allowed his behavior, drinking and syphilis, to cut short his life. Hence, he unconsciously committed suicide. The second lesson is, not only must we finished the classes assigned to us, but we have to take care of the materials we are given (our bodies).

She then conveys more of her recollections:

"I remember many instances of having to adjust my vibration to see what the new arrival was seeing. People often see their place of work, or their home, or the beach ... or hell, if they think that is where they were going. I had to help them through that.

So, for instance, one man wanted to find his office. So I helped him. And while we located his office we talked. At some point, when the time is right, I would always ask, "Do you remember what you were doing just before you met me here?" This conversation would eventually lead them to the realization that they had passed-on to the next life. Then and only then could I lead them to Home, for what amounted to sessions with a social worker examining their lives. It wasn't judgmental, it was more like, "what went well?" "What could have been better?" etc. And sometimes I felt bad when people were sent back - which would only happen after the counselor and person both agreed that this was for the best.

Another I remember was a very take-charge, upper class kind of man who mostly sneered and barked orders at me, as he tried to find his way to familiar surroundings. I just smiled and helped. And eventually the question... the realization... and then we would go Home.

It's always Home."

Again, what she has written is not only verified by other accounts in Spiritist literature, but these types of friendly encounters after the fact life reviews are a theme in many people's NDEs (Near Death Experiences).

I wrote her back that the last person she mentions could have been me. Before my rough edges were softened by my discovery of Spiritism (although my wife may have a different view), I could see myself trying to order spirits around to do my bidding, thinking that I had to take charge of every situation.

She replied about her experience in assisting this bombastic gentleman:

"Time doesn't mean much when you're Home, but the incident I referred to was probably in the 1800's maybe? The gentleman was a victim of an accident on a sailing ship, and found himself on shore looking out at the water. He saw me and demanded I summon a carriage to take him into town. He wanted to get in touch with his family and tell them what happened. He was kind of surly in that way that people who expect others to jump when they speak tend to be. So I explained in a loving and compassionate way that his transportation would be along soon, and why don't we talk while we wait?

So he complained about the lack of service and general incompetence of others, along with my perceived lack of helpfulness. We sat on the hillside and waited. And he talked a bit of his life. I don't remember the details, though. Eventually as he calmed down (though still frustrated), I asked the question, 'Do you remember what you were doing just before you met me here?'

And he told me about being on the ship and how it heeled over and he got knocked into the water, he thought.

109

'So do you remember how you got here?'

'No, I don't remember. I swam to shore, would be my guess.'

'That's interesting, why aren't you wet?'

'I don't know, I dried off.'

'Really? When did that happen?'

And so on.... and eventually a light clicked on.... 'Did I die?'

'Your feelings are true. Listen to them... You can see this place is not where you were, and you don't know how you got here, and this will tell you what you want to know.'

'So what happens now?'

'Come.... I will show you.'

I stood up and reached out to him. He stood up and took my hand. As we turned away from the sea, a city he had not seen before seemed to rise up before us.

'We're going home,' I said. 'Come!'

And we walked to Home together, where he was met by a counselor, who took over from there.... Home was simply 'there' when he was ready to see it."

The talented medium's account of her work in the spirit world is inspiring and comforting. Knowing that we are surrounded by such benevolence and love should give us all the courage to continue our struggles in our daily lives.

Spiritism is arranging these messages, recollections, and books to notify us of what lies beyond our mere physical existence. The Rev. G. Vale Owen, was selected to send volumes of great detail concerning life in the spirit world to England in the 1920's, right after the horrible tragedy of World War I, which people thought of as The Great War, "The War to End all Wars", since no one could conceive of losing so many young men again.

The medium that I conversed with told me her story in 2015, ninety-five years after the publication of *Beyond the Veil*. Spiritism told us the great secret that when we pass we are still ourselves in the 1850s. In a span of one hundred and sixty-five years, the message has stayed the same.

At the end of the day, we should realize that we are on earth for a purpose. As we go about our pre-planned life, with trials custom-made for our benefit, we are being watched.

Chapter 17 - Spirits - Helping a Child Pass Over – And her Parents Cope

The spirit Arnel tells of a time when he and a young spirit, Habdi, was called to assist the transitioning of a child from the earth to the spirit life:

> "So we went without delay and came upon them where they were gathered about the bed of a little girl-child. She was of some six summers. I could see that she was about to come hitherwards. The home was that of a man of moderate wealth. He was not rich but worked to earn his bread. The room when I arrived there was full of lights of many colors."[84]

Colors, lights; the emanations which come from spirits. The level of brightness denotes their spiritual purity. During medium meetings I have attended, I have heard some mediums talk about how bright was a particular spirit; they knew then they were in the presence of a high spirit. They could see and feel the calming vibrations surrounding them, just by being in the same area as one who lives at the most harmonious level.

Arnel shared this story with the Rev. G Vale Owen, who wrote of this account in *Book Five – The Outlands of Heaven*. He received the message in 1920.

Arnel tells us more about the parents of the little girl:

> "There were but few strains of dullness in their auras. The woman was not quite so spiritual as the man. But both were very good people. Only, as the child grew weaker and they began to understand that she was slipping beyond their grasp,

there gathered about them colors more somber and the radiance became more dim. Their faith began to fail somewhat, their faith in the goodness of God.

They were earnest souls, however, and that is why these high beings had come down to help them in this dark hour.

There were one man and two women spirits tending the child. These were there to see that all went well with her in her passing. To them I led Habdi. The company who had called me meanwhile stood in a group aside and concentrated upon the man and his wife to help them."[85]

The spirit realm takes special care of children when they pass over the veil. Their love for the more innocent creatures among us is boundless.

Love for Children

Benevolent spirits help children from all environments, even those raised in a household devoid of spirituality. Their attention is not limited to children who are leaving the physical life, but even to children who had a near death experience. And just like the spirits who requested Habdi to come and help them with another child, the spirit realm knows that children seeing other children feel more comforted at certain times.

A woman named Sandy, had a near death experience when she was five-years-old, years later, she wrote an account of her NDE (near death experience):

"In August of 1985 when I was only 5 years old, I was on a boat trip on a local lake. I was bitten by a mosquito and developed encephalitis. 'I died' and drifted into a safe black void of comfort and ease, no pain and no fear. This was a place where I felt right at home. Off in the distance I saw a very small light. It was drawing me to it. I felt myself rushing towards this light with a great amount of speed. I was not frightened. When I came into the light, it represented peace and joy, but most of all a deep unconditional love. The light was a sparkling, glowing cloud. From inside I heard a voice in my head and I knew it was God. Since my parents never discussed God or took me to church, I really don't know how I knew, but I did. Furthermore, I felt like this was my real home, this place where I was with this beautiful light which was God. I felt surrounded by the light and was one with it. The feeling was like being scooped up and held by my daddy when a barking dog was biting me just a few months earlier, only more so."[86]

As with so many other accounts by children, upon separation from their body, their soul is bathed in a sea of warmth. And like others, Sandy felt love, a love which saturated every pore.

At the time Sandy was a five-year old with no concept of the afterlife or a Supreme Being. Her parents never felt the urge to expose her to any type of prayer or devotion, yet immediately, as her soul rose, she knew she was in the presence of Divinity.

To comfort the innocent child another child appeared, a girl who seemed to be about ten years old:

"Another beautiful light, only smaller, joined us. It was a girl about 10 years old. She looked somewhat like me. I could tell she recognized me. We hugged and she said, 'I am your sister, I was named after our grandmother, Willamette, who died one month before I was born. Our parents called me Willie for short. They were waiting to tell you about me later when you were ready.' I was talking to her and she to me without words. It was too strange looking back on it, but it seemed natural at the time. She kissed me on the head and I felt her warmth and her love."[87]

The spirit realm takes care of us when we emerge from our restrictive bodies. Guides are on hand to help children and assist those who have demonstrated their adherence to the Golden Rule. People who have lived an honest and compassionate life toward others are not left alone in the great transition back to the real world, the spirit world, where we shall spend the vast majority of our immortality.

When Jesus declared, in Luke 9:60, "Let the dead bury the

dead, but you go and proclaim the Kingdom of God", he wasn't, as many believe, only telling us to ignore all else and perform our duty to God. He also gave us a glimpse as to how the spirit realm operates. He knew the extent of the care the newly deceased were given. He wasn't telling us to neglect our obligations, He was telling us there is a support group around us the moment our soul begins to detach from our corpse.

Sandy's sister met her in the light to make her feel comfortable and to send her a message. Her message was that she must return. Like so many other NDEs, the aura of the spirit world was enticing, as if you had dived into a sea of warm love and felt the glow of complete tranquility. A feeling one only has for fleeting moments during our sojourn on earth. Moments like lying on a beach, the hot rays of the sun penetrating your skin, the sound of the waves and birds mixing to create a harmony of bliss.

Habdi Helps a Child

As Sandy was met by her sister, the little six-year-old girl was given the same loving treatment. There are no coincidences in the spirit realm, each death, each NDE is planned and orchestrated by the powers that watch over us.

Arnel recounts the last moments of the small sweet child:

"At length the little one breathed deeply, and did not breathe again. By this time her spirit body had risen from out of the body of the flesh, and was almost free. So the two women attendants took her in their arms and laid her to rest for a few minutes. Then they roused her and Habdi came to her and took her by the hand and smiled upon her and kissed her upon her brow and called to her merrily. Soon she smiled in answer and so, hand in hand, the two children went away, the man and the two women following in their wake."[88]

The child, as all children do, followed the pleasant and intriguing path. She saw another playful friend and immediately gave over her will to his; to be led into another world, where love was the oxygen they would breathe and nothing bad would ever happen to her.

Even older children are carefully guided to the other side.

A Teen Passing to the Spirit World

In the book *Message from a Teen in the Spirit World*, by the spirit Neio Lucio, psychographed by Francisco (Chico) C. Xavier, we are presented with how a young boy, Carlos, fourteen years old, felt as he was passing away from a severe disease. He couldn't speak because his lungs were no longer supplying the amount of oxygen required to maintain his life.

Carlos' mother and father were next to him by his bed. Other family members and the doctor were in the room, waiting for his last breath. He could only think, how sad everyone looked and he wanted to help them. He begun to be afraid of dying, when an event occurred:

"When everything seemed beyond hope, something happened that grabbed my attention. A faint noise aroused my curiosity.

I looked toward the doorway and saw that, in some unexplainable way, delicate flakes of a phosphorescent substance had begun appearing there.

Those points of light seemed to be forming a fine cloak of airy gauze and it looked like someone was moving beneath it …

I was watching this oddity in amazement, when the light curtain split apart and a pretty young lady appeared. I recognized her right away.

She was the same lady that was in the big painting that Mom kept in the house. It was Aunt Eunice, Mom's little sister, who had died when you and I were still small.

She was wearing a light green dress decorated with shining lace. A beautiful, radiant, bluish light surrounded her, especially her head and upper body, as if she were holding a hidden lamp. Her dark eyes radiated unlimited sympathy and kindness.

I was greatly surprised as Aunt Eunice entered the room, gave Mom a hug (without Mom seeing her), and then sat down beside me and said, 'Well, little Carlos, you are so brave. Are you afraid now?'

If it had been any other occasion, I think I wouldn't have behaved so well, because I had always heard that the dead are ghosts and our aunt was already dead. But I was so distressed that I felt greatly comforted by her words of encouragement. I needed someone to cheer me up.

I noticed Dad's nervousness, Mom's tears, and Dr. Martinho's discouragement and sadness as he sat beside me, and I concluded that Aunt Eunice's good mood was just what I needed.

Actually, in the good old days when I had been well, I had heard strange stories about 'hauntings from the other world.' Which had left such an impression on me that I couldn't sleep, but Aunt Eunice couldn't inspire fear in anyone. She was beautiful and smiling, filling me with trust and optimism.

So I felt alive again, although I noticed an unpleasant stiffness in my body, which I couldn't move, not even a bit."[89]

Carlos couldn't move his physical body, which would no longer be possible, he was freed of his ties to earth and taken to a shelter to rest by his loving Aunt. As Carlos was sent a caring family member to help his transition, the little six-year-old girl was taken care of by another child who could help her accept her new world.

The Grieving Parents Comforted

The spirits who focused their minds on the parents did so for a purpose. As their precious daughter, the love of their life, slowly faded away from their embrace, both parents were permitted to glimpse an aspect of the spirit realm.

The mother, sensing her child had breathed her last, was about to give way to deep emotional pain. Arnel tells us what happened

117

next:

> "But instead the woman put her left hand on her bosom and, starting back, placed her right upon the shoulder of her husband, and looked steadfastly at that place which was above the head of the bed, and a little to the left of the center as she viewed it. There she saw her little one looking eagerly into the laughing eyes of a boy who seemed to be talking to her of something very pleasant to think on. He was clad in a cream-colored tunic belted with gold; and the little girl was much like him in her tiring. The boy had given her a beautiful spray of flowers of white and blue which she held in one hand, the other clasped in the hand of her young companion to give her strength. Slowly they went away, he talking, and she smiling her prettiest. Then there arose from the bedside a man and two woman in radiant dress who followed after the children."[90]

In essence, the mother was given the gift of peering into the spirit realm. She accurately saw what occurred in the other dimension. After the vision ended she asked her husband if he saw the same thing. He didn't, he felt a different kind of other-worldliness; he told his wife:

> "'I felt a strong breeze about me. It was not quite like wind, but rather was a kind of influence – a stream of influence, I might call it. It seemed to go through my very being and carry away all bitterness and sense of loss. And I heard, or seemed to hear, some voices talking together. One said somewhat after this fashion, 'The boy knows the way right well and will not err away from it. We will let him guide her and ourselves will follow after and aid them with our strength for the journey.' It was in no language I know, dear, and yet I understood quite clearly. But I saw nothing but a faint cloud of light exactly in the spot where you were looking. It seemed first to gather about our little one, then to rise above the bed and float to the left as I looked at it. That is the spot where you saw your vision, was it not?'

'Yes, dear,' she replied, 'and I thank God for that, for had I not been given that vision I do not like to think what wicked thoughts I would be thinking at this moment.'

Then she went to him and, kneeling by his chair, laid her face against his breast and burst into tears. They were a simple-minded pair, those two, and moreover, their mode of life had been such to enable these high angels to come and do service to them. Nor did they deem it of so small importance as that it should not have enlisted their concern. Nay, my son, we do not reckon matters greater or lesser by the gauge which men have made. We have our own measures, and they are more true than those of earth."[91]

A simple couple, not simple in native intelligence, not simple in faith and caring, but simple as in honest and straightforward folk, whose word is their bond and always helpful to their neighbors. They came to earth, they respected their fellow beings, they didn't fall for the lure of rampant materialism; in other words, they were working hard in learning the lessons they were assigned.

And such devotion and demanding toil is rewarded. Certainly, not on earth, where the good and decent are often overlooked, or worse, denigrated. Where steadfast couples, individuals, and families go about their daily jobs, doing the best they can and caring for others. This is victory on earth. This is success.

There was a reason for the couple to lose their child. There was a reason for the child to come and stay for a short time on earth. Nothing was done to punish, only to benefit and instruct. No life was taken away forever, no future struck down, since mother, father, and child are all immortal souls … who are still alive at this moment and for all the millennia to come.

They like you, experienced a chance to grow, to mold their character to be loving, charitable, fraternal, and honest. And in their deepest trial, the spirit world was right there, beside them, working to smooth out the pain and to let in the knowledge that God is good and all flows from that.

Chapter 18 – Angelic Ministry – Helping Discarnates into Heaven

We, in physical form, on earth, forget the multitude of souls who are trapped in a narrow band on or near the surface. These are spirits who wander the Lower Zone. They haven't the spiritual fortitude to understand how to ascend to the first level of heaven, where they will be safe and supported. Instead, they are subjected to cruelties and injustices that stretch our imagination.

Christ doesn't forget these souls, all are his children. He sends spiritual workers out to recover as many as possible. Those who are ready to follow the light will receive assistance.

The Reverend Owen's mother, who communicated to him in his book, which is a collection of four of his books, *Life Beyond the Veil*, in *The Lowlands of Heaven* section, talks about one such rescue operation. She tells us:

> "We received a message a short time ago of the arrival of a sister at the Bridge, who had come over from the further side where lie the regions of gloom, and I and another were sent to conduct her to this Home. We went quickly and found our charge awaiting us. She was quite alone, for her attendants had left her thus in order that she might profit by a quiet period of meditation and reflection before beginning her further advance."[92]

One can detect the extent of the spirit organization. First there are guides who find a willing soul in the Lower Zone, then others are notified to pick up a spirit at a specified place to finish the trip from just inside the Bridge to a colony where she could receive treatment.

The Bridge is a gateway from the Lower Zones to heaven. There are many such portals. Each one is guarded, so as to not allow unrepentant spirits entry. Only those who have demonstrated a true desire to change are allowed entry.

Next, the group finds their woman:

"She was seated on a slope of grass under a tree whose branches spread like a canopy over her. Her eyes were closed, and we stood before her waiting. When she opened them she looked at us for some time in an inquiring manner. As she did not speak, I at last addressed her 'Sister'. At that word she looked at us hesitatingly, and then her eyes begin to fill with tears, and she put her face in her hands, bowed her head upon her knees, and wept bitterly.

So I went to her and laid my hand upon her head and said, 'You are our sister now, dear, and as we do not weep, so neither must you.'

'How do you know who or what I am?' she replied, as she raised her face and tried to force back her tears, while there was just a touch of defiance in her voice.

'We do not know who you are,' I answered.

'What you were we do know. We know that you were always a child of our Father, and so, always our sisters. Now you are our sister in a fuller sense. What else you are lies with you. You are either one whose face is set toward the Sunshine of His Presence, or one who, fearing the task before you in that direction, will turn back again across the Bridge.'

She was silent for a while, and then said, 'I dare not. It is all too horrible over there.'

'But,' I urged, 'you must choose; for you cannot remain where you are. And you will come the upward way, will you not? – and we will lend you a sister's hand and give you a sister's

121

love to help you on the way.'

'Oh, I wonder how much you know of what lies yonder,' she said, and there was agony in her voice. 'There they called me sister, too; they called me sister in mockery, while they heaped upon me infamy and torture and – oh, I must not think of it or it will drive me mad again. But I don't know how I shall proceed; I am so stained and vile and weak.'"[93]

The group helped the woman stand up and make her way toward their destination. A place where the poor soul could recover in peace. But as she made progress, the group could discern that something was holding her back.

They found out that when she was detected near the opening of the Bridge, a spirit worker went out to help her. Since the spirit worker was at a higher level, she couldn't see her appointed guardian, but felt a presence. Being afraid, she shouted out, "May you be cursed if you touch me!"[94]

After that she blacked out and awoke on the other side of the Bridge, awaiting the group that came to help her. She felt terrible about the curse she made, to one who had come to assist her.

For us, on earth, the mere speaking of words in fear or anger, would be quickly forgotten. But, in the spirit world, where thought is action, such negative announcements have real meaning.

Vale Owen's mother takes us through the reasoning:

"She had cursed one of God's ministers, and she was afraid of the light because the words were evil. Truly, she did not know whom she had cursed; but a curse is a curse against whomever directed, and it lay upon her heart."[95]

The group headed back to the gate, where the kind spirit, a high spirit, knew of her desire for forgiveness waited for them. With love in his heart, he smiled and blessed the unfortunate woman.

Then, once more, the group made their way to the house where she would be allowed to recuperate from her ordeal.

Chapter 19 – Just Passed Over – Coping in the Spirit World

Who are we, what do we feel when we just pass over from the physical to the spiritual realm? The transition is difficult for many. We are told about the complexities of adjusting by the Reverend Owen's mother, who communicated to him in his book, *The Lowlands of Heaven*. She tells us about one person who experienced the learning curve:

> "I have, only lately, seen a very learned writer, who had published several books, talking to a lad who, in the earth life, was a stoker in a gasworks, and being instructed by him. He was glad to learn, too, for he had partly learned humility; and the curious thing was that he did not so much mind sitting at the feet of this young spirit as going to his old friends here and owning up to past mistakes, and his vanity of intellect in his past life. This, however, he will have to do sooner or later, and the young lad is preparing him for the task. It is also whimsical to us to see him still clinging to his old pride, when we know all about him, and his past and present status, which latter is rather low, and all the time trying to think he is hiding his thoughts from us."[96]

Social position on earth is no indication of one's place in the hierarchy of the spirit world. A person may be a senator or a chairman of the board of a prestigious company and find themselves at the lowest level after death.

What you are born as and what profession you have in life is not dependent on your spiritual level. Allan Kardec tells us:

"In the course of their different corporeal existences they may descend in rank as men, but not as spirits. Thus the soul of one who has been at the pinnacle of earthly power may, in a subsequent incarnation, animate the humblest day laborer, and vice versa; for the elevation of ranks among men is often in the inverse ratio of that of the moral sentiments. Herod was a king, and Jesus, a carpenter."[97]

Hence, we should all try to maintain our inner humbleness, to know we aren't better or superior to others. While we may be on a different spiritual level of understanding, it is our duty to assist all those we are able to help. Without condescension, with love and kindness from the bottom of our heart.

All the while, training our mind to focus on positive thoughts and to not look upon our fellow brothers and sisters as beneath us. Yes, this is difficult, for I fail constantly, for my pride often gets the better of me. But, I try to remind myself, as Chico Xavier once said, that I am as inconsequential as a grain of sand.

Judgement

Many come over from the earthly life with deep regrets and guilty consciences. They actively seek to be put on trial for wrongs they deem they have committed.

One of the companions of G. Vale Owen's mother, who has been working in the spirit world for some time after she returned to the spirit world, asked the group's Mother Angel when her judgement will occur? She received the following answer:

"My child, your judgement will take place whenever you desire; and from your own words I can tell you that it has already begun. For you own that your past life is worthy of punishment, and that is the first step in your judgement. As to the Judge, well, she is here; for you yourself are judge, and will mete out to yourself your punishment. You will do this of your own free will by reviewing all the life you have lived and, as you bravely own up one sin after another, so you will progress. Much of your punishment you have already inflicted upon yourself in those dark regions from which you have lately come. That punishment, indeed, was dreadful. But that is past and over, and what you have now to endure will be dreadful no longer. All dread should now be past. Painful, deeply painful, I fear it will be. But all through you will feel that He is leading you, and this more and more as you go on in the right way."[98]

Our desire to atone for our wrongs, mentioned from Jesus, to Emanuel Swedenborg, to Allan Kardec, to the volumes psychographed by Francisco (Chico) C. Xavier, all direct us to our most severe critic: Ourselves. Our purgatory, our future trials, will, for the most part, be demanded by our longing to remove our imperfections. To right what we have wrongly produced.

Once, we come back in contact with the spirit world, we realize how important it is to cleanse ourselves of our wicked inclinations. We know this because we see the high spirits who are on the road to success. We can determine, with our own eyes, their state of bliss and their beneficial impact on the lives of others. We wish to expend whatever effort is required to obtain a similar state.

Some may be seek redemption and others seek praise. Vale Owen's mother explains the conundrum that many experience upon their return to the spirit world:

> "That is what perplexes many who come over here. They expect to find all set ready for their dismissal from the Presence into torture, and cannot understand things as they are.

> Others who have cultivated a good opinion of their desserts are much disappointed when they are given a lowly place, sometimes a very lowly one, and not ushered immediately into the Presence of the Enthroned Christ to be hailed with His 'Well done.' Oh, believe me, dear son, there are many surprises awaiting those who come over here, some of a very joyful kind, and others the reverse."[99]

Therefore, we should keep our expectations low and accurately weigh our actions on earth, so we may enter the Kingdom of Heaven in the right frame of mind. Be prepared to listen and

126

follow the advice of those superior to us, for there will be many. Be thankful for their input, for it is meant for our benefit.

Chapter 20 – Helping a Family Stay Together – A Recently Departed Mother Helps her Husband and Children

As we live through challenging trials in life, we often feel abandoned. Life may seem completely hopeless at times. This is how a father with three small children must have felt after his young wife died. Unbeknownst to him, the spirit world knew of his plight. His recently departed wife knew that life without her would be hard. She asked to journey back to the surface of earth to determine how she could assist her beloved mate and children.

I read this story in the book, *Life Beyond the Veil*, in *The Lowlands of Heaven* section. It was a communication to the Rev G. Vale Owen from his mother in the spirit world. His mother tells him about how a loving spirit sought to keep her family together:

"She was so anxious that at last we took her, and arrived at evening time just as they were all sitting down to supper. The man had just come in from work and he was going to have his meal before putting them to bed. There were two girls, aged about seven and five, and a little boy of two. They all sat round the table in the kitchen, a fairly comfortable room, and the father told the eldest girl to say grace. This is what she said, 'God provide for us all, and mother, for Christ's sake. Amen.'"[100]

The spirit mother of the little seven year old stood next to her and put her hand on her head, to try to communicate with her. Unfortunately, the mother being a new spirit couldn't get her

128

thoughts across to her child. But after a few moments of silence, the oldest girl spoke to her father, "Dad, do you think mommy knows about us, and Auntie Lizzy?"[101]

Given the pressures of work and trying to raise young children, the father was planning to send the children to their aunt. The father thought for a bit:

"'I don't know,' he replied, 'but I think she does, because I have felt very miserable the last few days, as if she was worrying about something; and it might be Auntie Lizzie.'

'Well,' said the child, 'then don't let us go. Mrs. – will look after baby, and I can help when I come home from school, and we shan't have to go then.'

'Don't you want to go?' he said.

'I don't,' answered the child. 'Baby and Sissie would go, but I don't want to.'

'Well, I'll think about it,' he said. 'So don't worry. I dare say we shall manage all right.'

'And mother will help, and the angels,' persisted the little girl, 'because she can speak to them now, and they will help if she asks them.'

Now, the father said nothing more, but we could see his mind, and read it in the thought that if this little child had such faith, he ought to have as much at least, and by and by he made up his mind to try the thing and see how it would work out. For the parting with his children was not to his mind, and he knew he was very glad to find an excuse to keep them."[102]

The spirits went back to their home in heaven after their sojourn. The mother, new in the spirit world was disheartened. The group which accompanied her told her to have faith. If her daughter and her husband could have faith, then the both of them would combine to form a beacon of light which would attract help.

When the group returned, this is what happened:

129

"On our return we reported all to our Mother Angel, and immediately measures were taken to ensure that the family should not be broken up, and the mother was bidden to strive to progress in order that she should be able to help also. Then a change came over her. She set to work in real earnest, and will soon be allowed to join parties on their journey earthward now and then, and to add her little mite to their stronger service."[103]

Have faith and good intentions; you will be assisted. The Supreme Intelligence wants all of us to succeed. As we demonstrate our willingness to learn and to stay on the upright course, we shall have invisible hands ensuring our well-being.

We should also derive from this tale of the spirit realm, that when we return to where we our truly ourselves, our spirit selves, we haven't finished learning and growing. One life on earth is but a small detour within our immortal existence.

We inhabit a physical body to accumulate the lessons we require to improve. Upon shedding that dense encumbrance, we continue our studies. There are schools and colleges where you will learn the truth about the universe and the power of your own mind.

Chapter 21 – An Obstinate Man Learns to Open His Eyes in the Spirit World

Many of us are stubborn in our beliefs. I know I am, I have a tendency to hold on to a concept past the point where facts have refuted it. People like me have a predilection to have inordinate faith in their own decisions and may seem harsh, even when they try to approach situations with love.

I read a story in the book, *Life Beyond the Veil*, in *The Lowlands of Heaven* section. It was a communication to the Rev G. Vale Owen from his mother in the spirit world. His mother told him about a spirit, a man, who had recently passed over and was wandering in a lower level of heaven.

The lost soul thought he was alone, but in fact his guardian walked behind him. Following him on his journey, the guardian knew the man possessed good traits and strived toward the light, but he had a certain hardness of heart, which precluded him from fully seeing all of the aspects of heaven.

As the man approached a small celestial colony, one of the spirits came over to him to see if he could be of help to the soul with a perplexed look on his face. As the kind assistant walked toward the lost man, the man's guardian sent him the facts about who was the wanderer he was approaching.

In the message to G. Vale Owen, the spirit who started a conversation with the lost soul is "A" and the man wandering about is "B". "A" walked up to "B" with a kind expression and began the conversation:

"A. You seem to be not very familiar with this region. Can I help you in any way?

B. *I don't think so, although it is kind of you to offer to do so.*

A. Your difficulty is one which we might deal with here, but not so thoroughly as we would like to do.

B. *I am afraid you don't know what that difficulty is.*

A. Well, partly, I think. You are perplexed because you have not met any of your friends here, and wonder why.

B. *That is so, certainly.*

A. But they have met you.

B. *I have not seen them; and I have been wondering where I could find them. It seems so strange. I always thought that our friends were the first to meet us when we pass over, and I cannot understand it at all.*

A. But they did meet you.

B. *I didn't see any one I knew.*

A. That is quite correct. They met you and you did not know them – would not know them.

B. *I don't understand.*

A. What I mean is this. When you came over here you were immediately taken charge of by your friends. But your heart, good in some respects and even enlightened, was hard and blindly obstinate in others. And this is the reason you did not recognize their presence.

B. *What is wrong with me, then? Everybody I meet is kind and happy, and yet I don't seem to be able to join any party, or to find my own proper place. What is wrong with me?*

A. The first thing you must learn is that your opinions may not be correct. I'll tell you one which is at fault, to begin with. This world is not, as you are trying to imagine it, a place where people are all that is good or all that is evil. They are much as they are on earth. Another thing is this: your wife, who came over here some years ago, is in a higher sphere that the one in which you will be placed when you have at length got the correct perspective of things. She was not mentally your equal in the earth life, and is not so now. But you are on a lower plane than she is on general lines and all things considered. That is the second thing you have to accept, and accept ex animo. You do not accept it, as I can see by your face. You will have to do so before you can advance. When you have done so, then you will probably be enabled to communicate with her. At present that is not possible."[104]

When the kind spirit "A" told "B" that he must accept the fact that he is on a lower plane than his wife and he must take that deep into his heart (i.e. ex animo), he presented to all of us one of the eternal truths of ascending into heaven. It is not how smart, how clever, how quick you are that counts. It is your capacity for empathy, kindness, service toward others; in other words the amount of love you possess in your heart. True love, love which transcends family ties, race, class, or prejudices of any type.

"A" also does not hesitate to present the truth of the matter to "B". The spirit world loves us, but it doesn't mean that we are sheltered from harsh realities. The same tone of clearly delineating the facts, without placing blame can be seen in the individual accounts of near death experiences. People have reported their past transgressions are laid bare for them to analyze. Shielding us from the facts only stalls our progress.

"B" thought for a time, and then he said:

"B. *Is it vanity, then, that is my fault?*

Yes; but vanity of a rather difficult kind. In many things you are sweet and humble, and not without love, which is the greatest power of all. But there is a certain hardness in your mind rather than in your heart, which must be softened. You have got into a mental rut, and must get out of it and look

133

farther afield, or you will go about like a blind man who can see – a contradiction and a paradox. There are some things you see clearly enough, and to others you are totally oblivious. Learn that to change your opinions in the face of evidence is not weakness or backsliding, but is the sign of an honest mind. I will tell you this, further; had you heart been as hard as your mind you would not be wandering here in the fields of God's sunshine, but in darker regions yonder beyond those hills – far beyond them. Now I have explained, as well as I am able, your rather perplexing case, friend. The rest is for another to do."[105]

"A" then summoned "B"'s guardian. The guardian came to "B"'s side, but "B" didn't see of feel his presence. "A" took the hand of "B" and asked him if he could now detect anything. "B" wasn't sure.

"A" asked "B" to feel for the hand of his guardian, which also in his hand. When "B" felt the invisible hand, he immediately burst into tears. "B" had thought about what he was told and when he came into contact with a higher spirit, full of love, he felt the full force of what he knew he wanted to become too.

"A" left "B" alone with his guardian. G. Vale Owen's mother told us that soon "B" would be able to see and hear his mentor. He had realized his need to be open and flexible. To err on the side on compassion is always preferable to strict rejection imposed by rigid ideals.

Learning to identify the differences between moments where we must be strong and untiring and other periods where we should relax and allow a different path for others is one of the reasons why we are sent to this planet. Our quest isn't easy, it is full of events that take us unawares. Maintaining a calm head throughout permits us to fully interrogate our conscience for the correct approach to any problem.

Chapter 22 - The Spirit Realm Concerns Itself with Small Details

Before I discovered the Doctrine of Spiritism, I believed in God, but I thought of God and Jesus as remote entities. Peering down at us on a periodic basis to check-in on our paltry progress. I considered the situation of the human race to be similar to those first prison colonist sent to Australia, abandoned on a beach, with a few guards, and told to fend for themselves as best as they could.

Nothing could be further from the truth. We are watched, tracked, measured, analyzed, led, and herded into situations in which we thought were our decisions. The frequency in which our normal daily life is manipulated by the spirit world is much greater than one would suppose. No detail is too small to lay unnoticed.

The depth of the spirit realm's intrusion into our life is revealed in the book, *Life Beyond the Veil*, in *The Lowlands of Heaven* section. It was a communication to the Rev G. Vale Owen from Astriel in the spirit world that explains the care in which our lives are directed.

The machinations undertaken when the Rev. G. Vale Owen began to build his church begins innocently enough with a question from Astriel. The bold text is the answer from Vale Owen:

"On the top of your church tower there is a weather-vane in the form of a cock. You will call to mind that you yourself decided the form that this should take. Is that not so?

I had entirely forgotten it until you called it to mind. You are quite correct, however. The architect asked me about it,

and I hesitated between a fish and a cock, and eventually decided on the latter. I am wondering, however, whatever you have to say of it.[106]

Astriel is reminding Vale Owen of a decision that he automatically assumed he made. In fact, he believed he deliberated between putting a rooster or a fish as the weather vane on top of his church. Now he learns what really occurred:

> "No doubt. You see, these things are trifles to you; but there are few things which are trifles to us. Now, the fact that the likeness of a cock stands above your tower is the direct consequence of certain activities which took place in your mind five years ago. That is a case of creation. Many would smile at this, but we do not mind that, for we, too, are able to smile, and some of our smiles would perplex you, I assure you.
>
> The meaning you had in your mind when your apparently not very important decision was made was that all might be reminded that St. Peter denied his Lord. I suppose you meant it as a caution against the repetition of such offense today. But you did not realize that that apparently trivial decision was registered here and dealt with quite seriously."[107]

"There are few things which are trifles to us." reflect on these words. What we consider to be inconsequential decisions in our lives may, in fact, be vital. They may be the fulcrum upon which our life turns. When it is said the butterfly flaps their wings, from there a hurricane is born, it is meant that through seemingly trivial events large alterations in our lives may occur.

When a child is told that God watches over you, little does the parents or the child realizes the true extent of the words. Not only are our actions, but our thoughts, our innermost desires are an open book to the spirits that guide us. Our life and by extension everyone's life around us are on tracks. While we have free-will to respond to the events and scenery on both side of the tracks, we are monitored to make sure we don't derail. That we keep moving forward, because only by traveling ahead can we experience the life courses that have been assigned to us.

Astriel explains that not only is Vale Owen directed in certain actions, but a wider net is cast:

"I must tell you that the building of a new church is an event which is the cause of much activity here. There are officers to be appointed to attend the services and guard the building, and a whole host of ministering spirits to be allotted to the different departments of duty in connection with a new place of worship. Your clairvoyant friends have seen some of these already, but only a very few comparatively. Every detail is considered, not only in respect of the character of the minister and congregation and choir and so on; and the best among us, that is, the most suitable, chosen to help you according to the traits we observe; not only these things but the structure and all structural details are considered minutely, especially where symbolism enters in, for that has an importance not realized among you as it is with us. So it came about the weather vane was also considered, and I have chosen that because of its seemingly triviality in order to show you that nothing is missed."[108]

The last words of the paragraph stand out, "nothing is missed", all minutiae painstakingly reviewed, re-reviewed, and passed on to higher-ups for modification and approval. Spirits who have attained a celestial level are part of the immense army that serves to regulate and direct all life on earth. They ascend to heaven because of their attributes, their capacity for love and their selflessness. Hence, the battalions which surround us are an army driven by love. Motivated by their desire to supply the lessons we all so sorely need.

Spirits not only direct but they add to our lives. Astriel tells the Rev. G. Vale Owen how the bell for the church was paid for:

"It was decided that, as the cock had been chosen in preference to other symbols, we would answer that choice, according to our custom, by giving to the church some appropriate offering in response. And that offering was the church bell, for which a choir-boy collected the money. You had no bell when first your church was consecrated. The bird stood aloft, but could not

137

utter his warning as his original had done to St. Peter. And so we gave him voice, and your bell today gives tongue – as it did tonight at evensong."[109]

Actions and events, great and small, are planned and directed by the spirit world. Individually and collectively we are being pushed to become better spirits. The history of the world is like an upward spiral, where conditions motivate us, either through times of prosperity or cataclysms brought to mold our character. All designed to elicit particular responses to promote our advancement.

Chapter 23 – We are Inspired by Spirits

The spirit Zabdiel in his messages to the Rev. G Vale Owen, reveals to us that we are inspired by spirits. And inspiration is given to our hearts, to fortify our strength, to increase our wisdom, and our will to carry out our trials on earth. Other Spiritist authors have documented the same, that we are assisted by the loving presence of good spirits.

Allan Kardec, the Codifier of Spiritism, presented to the world the communications from the Spirit of Truth and other high spirits that we are immortal souls who live life after life to better ourselves; and to one day become pure spirits. Our path to ascension is to fortify our hearts with love, charity, and fraternity for all humankind. And to rid ourselves of the baser emotions of hate, envy, pride, and selfishness.

According to Allan Kardec's book, *The Book on Mediums*, written in the 1850s, we are all "Inspirational Mediums".[110] All of us are influenced by the good and bad spirits around us. Allan Kardec explains:

"Inspiration comes to us all, from Spirits who influence, for good or evil, in every circumstance of our lives, and in every resolution we make, and it may therefore be truly said that, in this respect, every-one is a medium, for there is no one who has not about him his familiar spirits, who do their utmost to suggest salutary or pernicious counsels to those with whom they are connected; a truth which, were we duly penetrated with its reality and importance, would frequently lead us to oppose a more effectual resistance to the suggestions of evil, by seeking the inspiration of our guardian-angel in our moments of uncertainty as to what we should say or do. At such times, we should invoke that watchful guardian with fervor and confidence, as a Providentially-appointed friend; and, if we did so, we should often be astonished at the new ideas which would arise in our minds, as though by enchantment, whether for the taking of an important decision, or for the accomplishing of our special work."[111]

We all have had moments of inspiration, flashes of brilliance, which provides some key piece of knowledge that we have been searching for; these sparks are caused by spirits, who chose to influence us. Kardec recommends that we use the gems given to us, but first filter the idea through your conscience and instinct to determine the validity of the suggestion.

Allan Kardec goes on to say that people of genius are mediums without being aware of it. These people have the innate sense to call superior spirits to provide the assistance they seek. Allan Kardec completes the section on inspirational mediums with this communication from the spirit world:

"What is the primal cause of inspiration?

'The communication of his thoughts by a spirit'

Is inspiration confined to the revelation of great things?

'No; it often has reference to the most commonplace circumstances of your daily life, for instance, you may have thought of going somewhere, but a secret voice tells you not to go, because there is danger in the way; or it tells you to do something which you have not thought of doing; this is inspiration. There are very few people who are not more or less 'inspired' in this way, at certain moments.'"[112]

Through the time and effort Allan Kardec spent with many mediums throughout Europe to codify Spiritism, the act of inspiration by spirits was documented. Although many religions have known this to be a fact for thousands of years, Spiritism gave context and reason for spirits, good and ignorant, to send us thoughts and feelings.

In the 1920s, Zabdiel, a spirit who lives on the tenth level of heaven, added to the discourse of how spirits inspire men and women in Book Two of the book *The Life Beyond the Veil* called *The Highlands of Heaven*. He explained to Rev. G. Vale Owen what inspiration from spirit to incarnate really entails; first he spoke about the word inspiration:

"Now, this is a word very expressive if understood aright; and very misleading if not so understood. For, that we inbreathe into the hearts of men knowledge of the truth of God is true. But it is only a very little of the truth. For more than this we do give to them and, with other things, strength to progress and to work God's will, love to work that will from high motive, and wisdom (which is knowledge blended with love) to work God's will aright. And if a man be said to be inspired, this is not a singular case, nor one exceptional. For all who try to live well, and few do not in some degree, are by us inspired, and so helped."[113]

Zabdiel went on to explain that breathing in the suggestions from a spirit may not be adequate, it is more like a person absorbs a wave of vibrating energy. Which flows into the body and the mind of the recipient. It may be a feeling of peace or of renewed vitality. Zabdiel supplied us the types of inspirations we receive:

"But we would not limit the meaning of the word to those alone in elegant words tell out to the world some new truth of God, or some old truth refurbished and made as new. The mother tending her child in sickness, the driver of the engine along the railway, the navigator guiding the ship, all, and others, do their work of their peculiar powers self-contained, but, as occasion and circumstances require, modified and supplemented by our own. This is so even when the receiver of our help is unaware of our presence; and this more often than not. We give gladly while we are able; and we are able so long as no barrier is opposed to us by him we would help."[114]

We may never realize the exact time and circumstances when we are touched and aided by a divine spark. The important point to keep in mind is to open yourself up to let the light in; not to erect fences whereby good intentions are blocked. Zabdiel tells us factors that can cut-off help from on high:

> "This barrier may be raised in many ways. If he be of obstinate mind, then we may not impose on him our counsel; for he is free to will and to do. And sometimes when we see great need of our help being given, the barrier of sin is interposed and we cannot get through it. Then those who counsel wrongly do their work, and grievous is the plight of those to whom they minister."[115]

Zabdiel, as did Allan Kardec, warns of the advice given by ignorant or inferior spirits. Once we open our gates to hate, envy, selfishness, and pride … we shall be visited by spirits who wish to encourage us in our base behavior. Demonstrating our human weaknesses gives pleasure and entertainment to poor souls who haven't risen above enjoying other people's mistakes and pain.

Spirits who mean us harm, do so out of spite, they wish to see and feel the same acts they committed accomplished by others. Temporarily unable to allow love inside themselves, they cling to what they know best and wish the world to do likewise.

To combat unwarranted interference by low spirits cultivate love and caring in everyday life. Zabdiel said, "Kind words later beget kind deeds. And so is love multiplied, and with love, joy and peace. And they who love to give, and give for love's own sake are shooting golden darts which fall into the streets of the Heavenly City, and are gathered up and carefully stored away till they who sent them come and receive their treasures once again with increase."[116]

Hence, love and assistance is everywhere, we merely have to tap into it. We have to make it part of our being and a daily habit. We are told a simple process:

> "So do every one these two things – see that your light is kept burning as they who wait for their Lord, for it is His will we do in this matter, and it is His strength we bring. Prayers are allotted us to answer, and His answer is sent by us His servants.

So be watchful and wakeful for our coming, who are of those who came to Him in the wilderness, and in Gethsemane (albeit I think they would be of much higher degree than I).

And the other to bear in your mind is this: See you keep your motive high and noble, and seek not selfishly, but for others' welfare. We minister best to the progress of those who seek our help for the benefit of their brethren rather than their own. In giving we ourselves receive, and so do you. But the larger part of motive must be to give, as He said, and that way the greater blessing lies, and that for all."[117]

We are constantly guided on our path by the spirit world – we just need to keep our heart and mind open. The signs will come to light the way, to select the right option, to find the right person. The more you expend yourself on others, the greater will be your reward in the afterlife.

Chapter 24 – How Not to Prepare for Life After Death

According to Zabdiel, there are two types of spirits on earth, which includes incarnates and discarnates. One is the type which realizes the earth is a place of learning, a location to mold their character, and then return to the higher spiritual spheres. The other is bound to the earth. Attached to earthly pleasures and material goods.

Zabdiel, in his communications to the Reverend G. Vale Owen, talks about the surprise of those who arrive at the spirit world unprepared for their new reality. Zabdiel tells us, "Many are very much surprised to find themselves allotted to a place of which they had heard with their outer ears, but had not further inquired as to its reality."[118]

When men or women, who never gave the possibility of life continuing forever a second thought, leave their bodies, many do not even realize they have passed on. They believe themselves to be in some strange earthly location, and quite can't place where it is.

Zabdiel illustrates his point with how he helped a man who had just died:

"I was once sent to receive a man who required some careful dealing with, for he was one who had many rather decided opinions as to these realms, and whose mind had been filled with ideas of what was right and proper as to the life continued here. I met him as his spirit attendants brought him from the earth region, and led him to the grove of trees where I awaited him. He walked between them and seemed dazed somewhat, as if he sought what he could not find.

I motioned the two to set him to stand alone before me, and they retired some little distance behind him. He could not see me plainly at first; but I concentrated my will upon him, and at last he looked at me searchingly."[119]

Zabdiel had to make himself denser in order for him to be seen. The higher the spirit, the less material and more energy, whereas those in lower spheres are composed of a greater ratio of matter to energy. Hence, spirits from superior planes can't be detected, by residents in inferior levels. Therefore, using his mind to transform his spirit body into a more solid object, Zabdiel became apparent to the newly passed over man.

Next, Zabdiel was able to engage in conversation:

"Then I said to him, 'Sir, you seek what you cannot find, and I may help you. First tell me, how long have you been to this country of ours?'

'That,' he answered, 'I find difficult to say. I had certainly arranged to go abroad, and thought it was into Africa. I was going. But I do not find this place in any way what I expected.'

'No, for this is not Africa; and from that country you are a long distance away.'

'What is the name of this country then? And what tribe of people are these? They are white and very handsome, but I never came on any quite like them, even in my reading.'

'Well, there you are not quite exact for a scientist such as you are. You have read of these people without realizing that they were anything more than puppets without life and natural qualities. These are those you have read as saints and angels. And such am I.'

'But,' he began, and then paused. He did not believe me, and feared to offend, not knowing what consequences should

145

ensue; for he was in a strange country, among strange folk, and without escort.

'Now,' I told him, 'you have the biggest task before you you have ever encountered. In all your journeys you have come to no barrier so high and thick as this. For I will be quite plain to you and tell you the truth. You will not believe it. But, believe me, until you do believe it and understand you will not have peace of mind, nor will you be able to make any progress. What you have before you to do is to take the opinions of a lifetime, turn them upside down and inside out, and own yourself no longer a scholar and great scientist, but the veriest babe in knowledge; and that nearly all you thought worthy of any consideration at all as to this country was either unworthy a thinking being, or absolutely wrong. These are hard words; they are such of necessity. But look well on me, and tell me, if you can read me, whether I be honest and friendly or no.'

He looked on me long and very seriously, and said at last, 'Though I am altogether at sea as to what you mean, and your words seem to me like those of some misguided enthusiast, yet your face is honest enough, and I think you wish me well. Now, what is it you want me to believe?'

'You have heard of death?'

'Faced it many a time!'

'As you are now facing me. And yet you know neither one nor the other. What kind of knowledge call you that which looks on a thing without knowing what it is?'

'If you will be plain, and tell me something I can understand, I may be able to get the hang of things a little better.'

'So. Then first of all you are what you would call dead.' At this he laughed outright and said, 'Who are you, and what are you trying to do with me? If you are bent on trying to make a fool of me, say so and be done with it, and let me get on my way. Is there any village near at hand where I can get food and shelter while I think over my future course?'

146

'You do not require food, for you are not hungry. Nor do you require shelter, for you are not bodily tired. Nor do you observe any sign of night at all.'

At this he paused once again, and then replied, 'You are quite right; I am not hungry. It is strange, but it is quite true; I am not hungry. And this day, certainly, has been the longest on record. I don't understand it all.'

And he fell into a reverie again. Then I said, 'You are what you would call dead, and this is the spirit land. You have left the earth, and this is the life beyond, which you must now live, and come to understand. Until you grasp this initial truth, further help I cannot give you. I leave you to think it over; and when you wish for me, if you should so wish, I will come to you. These two gentlemen who led you here are spirits attendant. You may question them and they will answer. Only, this remember: You shall not be suffered to ridicule what they say, and laugh at them, as you did but now at my words, Only if you be humble and courteous will I allow you their company. You have in you much that is of worth; and you have also, as many more I have met, much vanity and foolishness of mind. This I will not suffer you to flaunt in the faces of my friends. So be wise in time and remember. For you are now on the borderland between the spheres of light and those of shade, and it lies in you to be led into the one, or to go, of your own free will, into the other. May God help you, and that He will if you will.' "[120]

The man was unready for the unexpected termination of his life. He compartmentalized all notions of life beyond what he could see and hear for himself as fairy tales or wishful thinking. He was a product of the current arc of earth's destiny. He grew up in a culture which categorized all religious sentiment as romantic notions.

Whereas, early in human history, we collectively lived close to the spirit world; for that was all we had, as human knowledge expanded, we grew away from it. The spirit world knows that this is an expected result of intellectual and technological advances.

Mankind would travel from one extreme of the pendulum; complete reliance upon spirituality to the other extreme; recognizing nothing except what can be materially proven.

Our obsession in ridiculing any spiritual phenomena will eventually cease, due to irrefutable facts. The spirit Emmanuel tells us that the very scientist who are ardent non-believers are working, unknowingly, towards proving the existence of a spiritual plane.

Zabdiel told G. Vale Owen that the man was helped by his two companions, but he couldn't adjust and wandered down into the lesser planes. Only after a considerable length of time, did he call Zabdiel to meet him once again in the grove:

> "There I went to meet him, in that same spot in the grove of trees. He was a much more thoughtful man, and gentler, and less ready to scoff. So I looked on him silently, and he looked on me and knew me, and then bent his head in shame and contrition. He was very sorry that he had laughed at my words.
>
> Then he came forward slowly and knelt before me, and I saw his shoulders shake with sobbing as he bid his face in his hands.
>
> So I blessed him, with my hand upon his head, and spoke words of comfort and left him."[121]

We, as the human race, will go through the same cycle as the man who didn't realize he was in heaven. That it was before him all of the time, but he never saw it. Only when he opened his eyes and heart did everything reveal itself.

Chapter 25 - Go Forth and Talk with Spirits

Zabdiel in his communication with the Rev. G Vale Owen, on December 1st, 1913, states the primary reason Jesus was sentenced to death by the ruling Jewish religious order was because He told the people that life wasn't just on earth; our dusty plane was only a lowly way station … and those in charge of humans on earth were poor reflections of the governance of high spirits.

Zabdiel explains further:

"Throughout His teaching this is the one great motive, and for this it was that His enemies put Him to death. Had His Kingdom been of this world alone He had not discounted their temporal aspirations, nor their manner of life as to its ease and grandeur. But He showed that the Kingdom was of those higher realms, and that the Church on Earth, was but the vestibule to the Presence Chamber. This being so, then the virtues by which nobility should be measured were those which governed rank in these brighter regions, and not the mixed conditions of the lower portion of that Kingdom, as interpreted by the world."[122]

Being compared to decent, loving, caring, and honest souls residing in the spiritual realm was unacceptable to the rulers on earth. They knew that in comparison they would constantly fail. And this is still true today. The vast majority of regimes are built on corrupt edifices, who are mainly concerned with command and control of the population; not their welfare.

Zabdiel exhorts us to seek out higher spirits and learn about their loving presence. He tells us:

> "Also, it is on our part a marvel that men should be found who hesitate on the way, and fear that to speak to us is a wrong, and displeasing to Him Who Himself came into the world for this same reason; that He might show how both spiritual and material were but two phases of one great Kingdom, and the unity of both together."[123]

Many religions today, the Catholic Church being one of them, attempt to dissuade their followers from direct contact with benevolent spirits. They seek to control knowledge and access. Religions which preach that talking to spirits are really talking to demons, have a point. There are many low and malevolent spirits wandering the earth which may fool the unwary.

The remedy is education on how to detect spirits with our best interests at heart to those that use us for amusement or worse. Spiritism was revealed to us to supplement our knowledge and take it out of the hands of secretive orders.

Allan Kardec wrote about how to discern the quality of spirits in one of the 1858 editions of his magazine, *Spiritist Review*. He wrote about a young medium who was fooled by a lesser spirit into performing nonsensical acts.

The United States Spiritist Council, published the entire editions of Kardec's magazine for the year 1858 and it makes fascinating reading. The title of the book is, *Spiritist Review – Journal of Psychological Studies – 1858*, published in 2015.

In the article about a young medium and how he was tricked, Allan Kardec lays out eight main points to remember when dealing with spirits. Each one is worth keeping in mind when dealing with the "Other World".

> "1. The spirits are not all equal nor in power, nor in knowledge or wisdom. As they are no more than human souls detached from their corporeal body, they present a variety even greater than that of people on Earth, because they come from all worlds and, among the globes. Earth is neither the most basic

150

nor the most advanced. Thus, there are very superior spirits as there are very inferior ones; very good and bad; very wise and very ignorant; there are those of levity, malevolence, liars, astute, hypocrites, polished, sharp, jokers, etc.

2. We are incessantly surrounded by a cloud of spirits that occupy the space around us, despite the fact that we cannot see them, watching our acts, reading our thoughts, some to do us good, others to do us harm, whether good or bad spirits, accordingly.

3. From the physical and moral inferiority of our globe in the hierarchy of the worlds, the inferior spirits are more numerous here than the superior ones.

4. Among those spirits that surround us there are those that attach to us; that act more particularly over our thoughts, giving us advice, and whose influence we follow unnoticeably. Good for us if we hear the voice of good spirits only.

5. The inferior spirits only bond to those that listen to them, that give them access and to whom they connect. If successful on dominating someone, they identify with their own spirit, fascinating them, obsessing them, subjugating them, and leading them as one does to a child.

6. Obsession can never happen but by inferior spirits. The good spirits don't produce any kind of coercion, combat the influence of the bad spirits and stay away when they are not listened to.

7. The degree of coercion and the nature of the effects it produces determine the difference between obsession, subjugation and fascination.

Obsession is the almost permanent action of a strange spirit that leads the person to be solicited by an incessant need to act by this way or the other and to do this or that.

Subjugation is a moral bond that paralyzes the free will of the one that suffers it, pushing the person to the most reckless attitudes, frequently most contrary to their own interest.

Fascination is a kind of illusion produced by the direct action of a strange spirit or by his cunning thoughts. Such as illusion produces an alteration in the comprehension of moral things, leading to misjudgment and to mistake evil for good.

8. Human beings can always disengage from the oppression of the imperfect spirits by their will power, by the choice between good and bad. If the coercion achieved the point of paralyzing the will and if the fascination is such that it obliterates reason, then the will of a third person may replace it."[124]

Therefore, for those in the process or just curious about communicating with the spirit world, one must be on guard and weary to whom you let into your house and mind. I recommend you find Spiritist centers where conditions are tightly controlled to communicate with spirits approved by higher spirits. There are never any charges for this service.

Zabdiel lets us know that until we gain a better communion with the spirit world, our progress remains difficult:

"For that they killed Him; and today there is remaining too much, as we see it, of their sentiment, both in the Church and in the world outside. And until men do realize us our presence, and our right of consideration as fellow-members of this same Kingdom of the Father, and not until this come to pass, shall men make much advance in the discerning between light and darkness."[125]

During the nineteenth, twentieth, and now the twenty-first centuries, there has been an increased activity in the spirit realm on our behalf. With the advent of Spiritism, in the 1850's the seeds for the complete transformation of the earth have been planted. Zabdiel defines it as, "light being directed into the darkness."[126]

A plethora of new knowledge about the realm that put us here and guides our daily life is at our doorstep. It is up to each individual to determine whether it will be picked up and acted upon or not. All according to our free will.

Chapter 26 – Guardian Angels – They Stay with Us in the Spirit World too

Guardian Angels, the mere word conveys a deep feeling to your body; as if your favorite cozy blanket was covering you on a cold day, bringing warmth and comfort. We do in fact have a guardian angel, a mentor who guides us in our path to improvement. Spiritism notifies us that we are always watched, viewed with love and kindness … sometimes from afar and other times very close and intimate.

The spirit Zabdiel, communicated with the Rev. G Vale Owen in 1913 about his spirit guide. At first the presence of a guardian angel for one who is in heaven seems out-of-place. But that type of thinking is self-centered for us here on earth. We are spirits, encased in a physical body. The majority of our immortal existence will be in the spirit world. Our goal is to ascend up the levels of heaven, to one day, become a pure spirit. Hence, we require mentors to assist our quest. Not only when we are on the physical plane but also in the spirit realm.

Zabdiel describes the time when he was standing on high mountains, at the upper limits of the tenth level of heaven. He was peering across a valley to the mountains that were the beginnings of the eleventh level of heaven.

He liked to go there to meditate and to feel the presence of his sphere and the sphere above him. From that vantage point he could feel the all-embracing love of the Divine's universe. Zabdiel tells G. Vale Owen what happened:

"Once I stood thus, with face turned towards my future home, and closed my eyes, for the intensity of light as it moved before me was more than I could bear continuously. It was there I first was permitted to see and speak to my guide and guardian.

He stood upon the summit over against me opposite; and the valley was between. When I opened my eyes I saw him there, as if he had suddenly taken on a visible form for me, that I might see him the more plainly. And so it was indeed, and he smiled on me, and stood there watching me in my perplexity.

He was clad of glittering silk-like tunic to the knees, and round his middle was a belt of silver. His arms and legs below were bare of covering, and seemed to glow and give forth light of his holiness and purity of heart; and his face was the brightest of all. He wore a cap of blue upon his hair which was like silver just turning into gold; and in the cap shone the jewel of his order. I had not seen one of this kind before. It was a brown stone and emitted a brown light, very beautiful and glowing with the life which was all about us.

At last, 'Come over to me,' he said; and I was thereupon afraid, but not with any terror, but rather abashed of awe. In that way I feared, not else."[127]

Zabdiel, who resided in the tenth level of heaven, had never, until now, come face to face with his guardian angel. Imagine traveling through life after life, sensing a benign presence, a compassionate friend but never quite grasping the image and form of that companion. Now, finally, Zabdiel was only a valley away from his mentor.

Zabdiel stood in awe, not because he felt small or inferior, but of meeting a spirit that has accomplished what Zabdiel has dreamt of attaining. Not acquiring by luck or by who he knows (for that is impossible in the spirit world), but a spirit that has risen through his own dedication and discipline. As in our fascination with athletes, whom we admire, not because they are famous, but we look up to because we understand the work they put into their profession, day in and day out, to achieve the status they have attained. We stand in awe because we too, would like to match their work ethic and self-control.

Next, Zabdiel, shaking off his astonishment said:

"So I said, 'I know you for my guide, sir, for my heart tells me this much. And I delight to look upon you thus; for it is very lovely and sweet to me. In presence you have been with me often on my heavenly road, but always just before, that I have not been able to overtake you. And now that I am given to see you thus in visible form I am glad to thank you for all your love and tending. But, my lord and guardian, I fear to come to you. For, while I descend into the valley, the brightness of your sphere will dazzle me and make my feet unsure. And when I should ascend to you I think I should faint by reason of the greater glory which is about you. Even here I, from this distance, feel it scare to be borne for long."[128]

As spirits move on higher in the stages of heaven, they and the surrounding environment, become brighter, more energy and less material, more of the all-encompassing love from God is reflected from their ethereal bodies. Hence, an inferior spirit, sees only white light and is unable to make out features and is uncomfortable in such surroundings.

Therefore, in order to physically meet his guardian angel, Zabdiel will require assistance. His mentor supplies the solution:

"'Yes, for this time,' he replied, 'I will be your strength, as many times before I have been, not always of your knowledge; and at times again when you have known me near but only in part. We have been so much together that I am able now to give you more than hitherto. Only be strong, and with all your courage to the fore; for no harm shall fall upon you. It is to this same end that I have impressed you to come to this place, as often I have come to you."[129]

Zabdiel, thought that he wanted to walk to his favorite place to meditate and ponder about his future, was actually motivated to be at the exact place and time determined by his guide. If Zabdiel was easily manipulated by a higher spirit, examine how easily we, on earth, must perform deeds or come up with ideas that we thought were our own, but actually were implanted in us by our guardian spirits.

Don't doubt, even for a moment, that many of our actions, we believe that come from ourselves alone, are covertly placed in our minds by higher powers. Yes, we still have free will to make important choices, but we are led to certain episodes in our life according to our life's plan.

Zabdiel's spirit guide then begins to construct how he and Zabdiel will meet in person for the first time:

"Then I saw him for awhile stand very still indeed, as he might have been a statue very well. But presently his form took on another aspect. He seem to be in tension as to the muscles of his arms and legs; and I could see, beneath the thin gossamer-like garment, that his body there was in like manner exerting its every power. His hands were hanging at his side, and turned outward a little, and his eyes were closed. Then a strange thing happened.

From beneath his feet there came a cloud of blue and pink mingled; and it moved across from him to me until it was a bridge between the two summits, and spanned the valley below. It was in height little more than that of a man, and in breadth a little broader. This gradually came upon me and enveloped me, and when I looked I could see him through the mist, and he seemed very near.

Then he said, 'Now come to me, my friend. Tread firmly forward to me, and you shall have not hurt.'

So I began to walk to him through the shaft of luminous cloud which was all about me, and, although as I went it was elastic beneath my feet, like very thick velvet, yet I did not sink through the floor of it into the valley, but continued my way uplifted with great joy. For he looked on me and smiled as I went to him.

But although he seemed so near, yet I did not reach him, and yet again, he stood still and did not retreat from me.

But at last he held out his hand to me and, in a few steps more. I had it in mine, and he drew me on to firmer footing.

Then the shaft of light faded and I found I stood on the further side of the valley, and looked across on my own sphere. For I had crossed over by that bridge of heavenly light and power."[130]

Zabdiel's guardian angel, through the force of his mind, created a bridge across a deep and wide valley. The higher the spirit the more they are able to conjure according to their will. This, in essence, it why spirits, and ourselves, strive to improve.

The more disciplined one becomes, by following the Doctrine of Spiritism, to be loving, kind, fraternal, charitable to all in all circumstances, yet exercising authority with gentle calmness, the capabilities a spirit possesses increase. Whereupon, billions of years from now, a spirit from earth starting out in an immature state, will someday lead the destiny of a planet in the same manner as Christ leads us. We too, just like Jesus, could become the governor of a planet or planets, to help millions of young spirits rise and become working members of the spirit community.

The entire organization of the spirit realm revolves around promoting spirits to their utmost capabilities. To enable them to weld great power for the benefit of others. To achieve that goal, spirits must be rigorously trained to never violate the Divine Laws while always allowing spirits their free-will.

We live in a just universe. It doesn't appear so to us on earth, trapped amongst corrupt officials and criminals, but this is for our own good. Only by living with the results of the lack of love and brotherhood can we see for ourselves the tragedies that occur. The philosophy is the same as allowing your children to occasionally make their own mistakes, so they will know … since you realize they believe they know better than you … the results of their ill-considered actions. We are no different.

Talking with His Guardian Angel

Zabdiel, having reached the side of his mentor, now, for the first time, had the opportunity to speak directly with the unseen hand that has for so long, steered him to the correct path. We are told:

"Then we sat down and communed together of many things. He called to my mind past endeavors, and showed me where I might have done my task in better ways; and sometimes he commended me, and sometimes did not commend, but never blamed, but only advised and instructed with love and kindliness. And when he told me something of the sphere on the borderland of which I then was; and of some of its glories; and how the better to sense his presence, as I went about my task to which I should presently return to finish it.

And so he talked, and I felt very good fettle of strength and delight, and of greater courage for the way. So did he give me of his larger strength, and of his higher holiness, and I understood a little more than hitherto of man's potential greatness, in humility, to server his Master the Christ, and God through Him."[131]

The past accomplishments of Zabdiel were discussed in a sympathetic and caring manner, with gentle suggestions of how to perform better next time. We have seen the same consideration and kindness from spirits in stories by people who have had near death experiences.

James' Life Review

A good example is the NDE of James. When James' heart stopped, a woman spirit approached him and led him out of our world to the spirit world. Where, as many others before him have noted, the flowers and trees shined as if lit from within.

James then describes where his life would be reviewed:

"I was led by the lady through the forest. I asked where we were, what had happened to me, where were we going. I was told everything was fine and my questions would be answered soon. I didn't feel concerned in fact I felt calm and Peaceful. I was led by the lady to a clearing in the forest in the middle of which was a large wooded oval table with 10 or 11 people seated around it and one chair empty which I was indicated to sit at. Then the lady left. The people at the table seemed very familiar, but in an 'other' worldly way and also had the same young but old looking qualities. I was warmly welcomed and told that I had left my physical body, and the purpose of the council was to decide if I should stay or return to it, and that a review would take place to determine this. The review consisted of a screen which appeared above the table in the center which began to play a 'film' of my life from the moment I was born. Members of the council paused the film at different parts and we looked at the circumstances surrounding specific events, sometimes from the different perspectives of the other people involved, but mostly they were interested in how the experiences had affected me, and my feelings about things." [132]

As on earth, in the spirit world we all have our group of friends. Friends who have been with us since we were in school and who have always been concerned with our welfare; constantly checking on our progress, with the noble aim of assisting us in our major life challenges. We have our friends in the spirit world, who are all the more special because sometimes they watch over us and other times they reincarnate to share our trials together.

Additionally, as in the case of Zabdiel, we have our guardians as well as mentors, more mature and wiser spirits who we look for advice and guidance. The group that worked with James is most probably made up of friends and mentors, souls that he has intimately known before, but due to his recent separation from his body, his memory before the commencement of his current physical life is hazy. Hence, he seems to know them and feels comfortable in their presence.

Next, James' life is reviewed. And not just his actions, but the emotional affect he had upon others and the motivations that caused his actions are analyzed. This is one of the central tenets of Spiritism, our thoughts are actions, for with thoughts all begins and

160

actions are merely the completion of a plan. It gets more complex, for our very thoughts influence events and others around us. We are all like radio towers, beaming our innermost musings and emotional highs and lows to all around us. The spirit world tells us we have a responsibility to control the waves emanating from our brains.

This all sounds extremely difficult to perform, but think about why this must be so for a moment. As we progress and become higher and pure spirits, the power of our minds also increase in force. Therefore, to ascend in the ranks of the spirits, we must learn to control that which shall, in the future, possess great power.

James then tells us about the analysis of his life to date:

"The experience was uncomfortable at times, I had to see myself warts and all, I saw the best and the worst in myself. But never at any time did I feel I was being judged by anyone present. We reached my present circumstances and I saw that my lung condition had been created by myself to give me an exit opportunity. We had a long debate after the film about my life blueprint and whether or not I had fulfilled my chosen experiences which were mostly linked to previous lifetimes and spiritual 'baggage' that needed to be cleared and healed. I felt that I needed more time on earth and this was agreed by the council, who also told me that I would need to go back more spiritually awake to accomplish this."[133]

James understood completely the reason for his life on earth when he writes the words, "life blueprint". All of us follow a trajectory planned by the spirit world for our educational benefit. Zabdiel, has been on both sides of the equation. When he was an incarnate, he too was on a pre-programmed path, so he could pay for his past wrongs and learn what he required. All the while, watched over by his guardian angel.

Parting with His Guardian

We are always in view of someone superior in the spirit realm, whether we are in physical form or in spirit; there are higher spirits

161

evaluating our performance, not with malice but with kindness and caring. For, as stated earlier, the goal of the spirit realm is the successful promotion of souls, so they too, can contribute to others.

Zabdiel tells us of his parting:

"He came back with me by way of the valley, with his arm about my shoulder to help me with his power; and we talked all the way down and across, and then, as the ascent of the hill on the other side began, we slowly fell to silence. Instead of words we communed in thought and, when a little way up returning I looked upon him, I noticed that I could not see him quite so plainly; and began to be sad at that. But he smiled and said, 'All is well my brother. Always it is well between you and me. Remember that.'

Still he grew more faint to my sight, and I was minded to turn back again for that reason. But he impelled me gently and, as we ascended, he surely faded away from my sight. I did not see him again. But I knew him now as I did not till that time. I felt him in touch with me all the time I lingered on that summit. I turned and looked into the brightness of his sphere across the valley, but I did not see him on the other side."[134]

Our lives are precious and our time here on earth shouldn't be squandered by stress over temporary material pleasures. Our current society lays a very alluring trap for us, advertising happiness is within our grasp, if we just earn a few dollars more. To the seller of the goods or services, it doesn't matter how the money is earned, via licit or illicit means; only that is ends up in someone's coffers.

None of the products, homes, and toys acquired will accompany you to the spirit world. Only the sum total of your deeds. Your guardian angel attempts to tell you that whenever you pause from the daily grind to listen.

Pause a little more in your life. Stop, pray, and meditate … allow those you really have your best interest at heart guide you. When you sit calmly, ask for guidance from heaven; it will be given.

Life in the spirit world is worth sacrificing that one more purchase you wished to make. Live your life, so you can be proud that you have never knowingly hurt another, of if you had, try to find the means to atone is the greatest victory you could possibly have in this life. Feel free to reward yourself on earth with whatever you have earned through honest dealings, for your life's plan may entail a comfortable living.

Live according to the Golden Rule and while your friends may believe you are a bit gullible and not very successful, you and your guardian angel will know that your life on earth has not been in vain. In fact, just the opposite, while others grasped for the golden ring, trampling over whoever stood in their way, you meekly (in the true sense of the word as meant by Jesus, acting honestly, with focus and determination) pursued a life with a minimum of regrets; will exit this incarnation richer than you believe possible, into a bright light of love and ready for an even higher ascent the next time.

———— •◆•◀• ———◆

Chapter 27 – The Highland Watchtower of Heaven – Processing Prayers

High on the upper boundary of the tenth level of heaven, there exists a colossal tower, with ten sides. Each side processes the prayers and requests of a specific stage; from the lowest level of heaven up to and including the tenth level. A grand central station of thoughts, quandaries, conundrums, and problems which all need a response. The spirit Zabdiel describes the location; the facility is on a plateau. The ground covered in stone, the color of fire; the reflection of the stone permeates the air above to a height of one hundred yards. Next he describes the building itself:

"On this level space was one building. It was of ten sides, and each side was diverse in color and in architecture from all its fellows. Many stories it had, and rose a glittering pillar whose top caught the light which came above the peaks of the mountains, some far, some near – so high was this tower, as it stood there, a sentinel among the mountains of heaven, a very beautiful thing to see. It covered some eight part of the square, and it had porches on each side. So there were ten ways to enter, and once facing each of the ten ways. A sentinel in truth it was; for this is the watchtower of the highest regions of that sphere. But it was more than this.

Each side was in touch with one of the first ten spheres; and those who watched there were in constant communication with the Chief Lords of those spheres. There is much business passing between these Heads of the different spheres continually. Here it was gathered up and coordinated. If I might

164

descend to earth for a name, I would call it the Central Exchange of that vast region comprised in all those spheres stretching from that which borders on the earth zone, over the continents and oceans and mountains and plains of the second, and then of the third, and so onward to the Tenth."[135]

Heaven isn't just an ethereal group of clouds in the sky. It is organized, it has controls in place, and it has a command and control center, just like any large city or country. This knowledge of heaven is what Spiritism brings to us.

Andre Luiz, the spirit who told of his ascent to one of the initial stages of heaven, to the celestial city of Nosso Lar, described the various ministries and organization which controlled the life of his beloved spirit home. While the names of the departments may differ from a city on earth – the purpose remains the same – running a complex organization, full of souls, all who have work to perform.

In the book, *Nosso Lar*, Andre was told that while work is expected from everyone in the spiritual planes, rest was also important. The one person who never seemed to rest was the Governor of the city. When Andre asks if he ever leaves his work, he was told, "Only on occasions when the public welfare demands it."[136]

One could imagine the head of Nosso Lar would be well plugged in to the watchtower. Where the daily business between various cities and colonies, from one sphere to the next, from heaven to the earth would command the full attention of those entrusted with running a fair size metropolis.

The spirit Zabdiel, communicated with the Rev. G Vale Owen during December, 1913 about his visit to the watchtower. He described the people working at the tower as a superior caliber, a higher spiritual level than most spirits residing on the tenth level. They never seemed excited, going about their business in a cool and level-headed manner. Always courteous and would go out of their way to make all feel comforted and special.

Zabdiel described them as stately and they, "received all reports, information, requests for solution of some perplexity, or for help in other ways, in perfect quietude of mind. When something more tremendous than usual burst upon them, they were unmoved and ready always, quietly confident in strength to cope with their task whatever it might be, and with wisdom to make no mistake."[137]

Zabdiel was invited into the tower and he reports what he found there:

"There was a large hall or triangular shape and, high up, the floor of the next apartment. We went to the wall, where it met in angle, and there my friend bade me stand awhile and listen. I soon heard voices, and could discern the words they brought. These were being dealt with in a room above us, five stories aloft, and were transmitted downwards, passing through the floor into the round below, where there were other chambers. I asked the reason of this and he informed me that all messages are received by those who had their station on the roof of the building. These extracted what words they needed for their part of the work, and allowed the residue to proceed downwards into the chamber below them. Here the message was treated in like manner, and again handed on downwards. This was repeated again and again until what was left passed down the walls of this ground floor room to be once again sifted and the residue passed on below. In each room there was a great multitude of workers, all busy, but without haste, going about their task.

Now, you will thing this a strange way to go to work. But the reality was stranger still. For when I say I heard the words, I tell you only half. They were audible visibly. Now, how shall I put that in your tongue? I can no better than this: As you gazed at the wall (which was treated in different metals and stones, each vitalized by what principle here answers to electricity with you) you saw the message in your brain rather than optically and, when you were sensible of its import, you heard the voice which uttered it in some region far away. In this manner you were aware, in your inner consciousness, of the

166

tome of the speaker's voice, of his aspect and stature and manner of countenance, of his degree and department of service, and other details of help to the exact understanding of the meaning of the message sent."[138]

An analogy on earth for the watchtower would be a government listening post. These are stationed throughout the world to intercept radio, cell, and satellite traffic; to pull from the airwaves any snippet of vital information that a government may wish to know about other governments or individuals.

When a cell phone transmits a voice, it doesn't just send over the digitized representation of a voice, but other information as well. It transmits the phone number that sent the message, the destination, the geographic location, and the time, plus other information.

Our Thoughts Are Tagged

In the book *In the Realms of Mediumship*, published in 1955, the spirit Emmanuel, told us of our unique identification in the introduction, titled, "Rays, Waves, Mediums, Minds..." He reveals that as our thoughts flow out, they are tagged with our ID.

Hence, we are a walking radio tower, transmitting our thoughts out to the universe on a second by second basis. Imagine seven billion radio towers all broadcasting at once, twenty-four hours a day ... the sky would be filled with trillions of pieces of information. Each packet labeled precisely, as to who sent it, the time, the feeling, the emotion, what was seen, and the thought that started it.

In computer science and the software industry in general, there is the concept of the data following you. Whereupon, whenever you require information, it would be there, ready to answer any question you may have. This concept is what has spurred the rise of the cloud. Information living outside, always available to be pulled and analyzed.

Why shouldn't the spirit world trump this concept a thousand fold? Data is everywhere, data is in everything, data is everything, data creates, data lives. Spirits manipulate data, and the higher the spirit, the greater the ability to sift, shape, and move it. All it takes is a listening post, a facility to filter the data flowing about the spirit universe, to only catch that which is pertinent; and then to process it and act upon it.

An Example

Zabdiel watched the entire process, but he couldn't translate the strings of messages completely enough so he could understand them. They were too complex, too dense and full of information. His guide offered to translate one of the string of messages, so Zabdiel could see what type of help is requested. The guide offered this example:

> "It was to the effect that a party had been sent from the Sixth Sphere into the Third to help in the construction of some works there proceeding. Those who had designed them had been of high development, and had included in the apparatus and structure to contain it, a somewhat more advanced scheme that it was possible to construct out of the substance of that sphere. I might put the problem to you thus: If you were to endeavor to build up a machine for the manufacture of ether, and the conversion of it into matter, you would find no substance to your hand on earth of sufficient sublimity to hold the ether, which is of a force greater and more terrific than any force which is imprisoned within what you understand as matter.
>
> It was a somewhat similar problem they had to encounter now, and wanted advice as to how best to proceed in order that the scheme might be carried out to as large an extent as possible. This is one of the simpler problems these higher ones are given to solve."[139]

Help is always at hand in the spirit world. Help is always available in our world too … we do not always request or perceive it. There are listening posts for our physical sphere. There is an army of spirits who gather, filter, and respond to our thoughts, meditations, and prayers.

168

The spirit realm built the earth, so spirits may reside there to undergo intensive training. So we humans may learn the difference between the dark road and the path of light. The goal is to enable all of us to become valuable members of spiritual society. Participants who contribute, as opposed to students requiring training. We are all still students, learning to calmly solve problems with love and kindness in our hearts, no matter how difficult or urgent the situation.

Chapter 28 – Angel Visitors to Earth

The spirit Kathleen told the Rev. G Vale Owen about the complications of high spirits, angels, coming to earth:

> "It is no light matter, I do assure you, to receive the command 'Go forth downward.' For as we proceed earthward, both the brightness of our environment and of our own persons also grow less and less, and by the time we reach the neighborhood of earth we can but with difficulty see about us."[140]

The higher the level of the spirit, the less dense – meaning more energy and less matter – is the spirit. Even for spirits traveling within different levels in the spirit realm the transition is not simple.

The Solar System – The Galaxy

In the book *Workers of the Life Eternal*, by the spirit Andre Luiz, psychographed by Francisco (Chico) C. Xavier, Andre Luiz, who resides in one of the lower levels of heaven, was part of a group who had to prepare a special chamber to receive a high spirit. Collectively they were requested to concentrate their will to create a pleasant atmosphere inside the chamber, so the spirit could materialize there and talk to the group.

The organizer of the group who invited the high spirit, Asclepios, told them more about who was coming:

> "Asclepios belongs to the redeemed communities of the Plane of the Immortals in the highest regions of earth's spiritual realm. He lives far above our notions of form, and in conditions that are inconceivable to our current concept of life.

He has already lost all direct contact with the earth per se, and could only make himself felt there through messengers and missionaries of great power. His sacrifice in coming to visit us is to be appreciated, despite our improved position in relation to incarnate humans. He rarely comes here."[141]

Andre then finds out that a spirit like Asclepios will only reincarnate on earth every five to eight centuries. Then Andre asks if Asclepios is the highest spiritual form to be found in the universe; he receives the following answer:

"Not at all. Asclepios is associated with other self-denying mentors of terrestrial humankind; he is part of the highest echelon of the community to which he belongs, but in reality he is still a spirit of our planet, although working in the highest realms of life. We must travel for a long time in the evolutionary arena before we can follow in his footsteps. However, we believe that our sublime visitor longs to be part of the board of representatives of our orb in the glorious communities that inhabit Jupiter and Saturn, for example. In turn, the members of those orbs anxiously await the moment in which they will be summoned to the divine assemblies that govern our entire solar system. Among these latter are those who carefully and watchfully await the minute in which they will be called to work with those who maintain the constellation Hercules, to whose family we belong. Those who guide our group of stars naturally aspire one day to make up the crown of celestial spirits who support life and guide it in the galactic system through which we move. And did you know, my friend, that our Milky Way, a breeding ground and fount of millions of worlds, is just one single detail of the Divine Creation, a mere corner of the universe?!..."[142]

Hence, there are an unknown number of levels to climb before one sits at the table with the Supreme Intelligence. And at each step one is transformed into an ever higher ratio of energy to matter. Until one day, billions of years from now, a spirit living around the earth will become pure energy.

171

An Angel on Earth

Kathleen tells G. Vale Owen how she must become accustomed to the conditions of our planet when she descends from her heavenly sphere:

"This at first; but by and by our eyes become attuned to the coarser vibration impinging on them, and then we are able to see. This also comes more readily by practice. But it is a blessing only in that it enables us to do our work among you, and not by any means to be desired of itself alone. For the sights we see are mostly such as do not give us cheer, but much heart-rendering to take back with us into our brighter homes."[143]

Kathleen reveals that high spirits are not devoid of emotion. On the contrary, they are love personified and as such are deeply troubled by the acts we commit on each other here on earth. When we see selfless individuals who travel to war zones as part as organizations like Doctors Without Borders, we get an idea of the dedication and love that motivates high spirits that come to us … into this chaotic and violent planet.

Kathleen dives deeper into the process of adapting to our primitive environment:

"As we approach the earth, the effect of it is not so apparent to our senses. But it is about us, nevertheless, laves us, penetrates through us and permeates all our being, and by it we are sustained, as the air tube sustains the diver in the ocean floor, where the light from the wider freer atmosphere above is dim and he goes heavily by reason of the denser element in which he moves. So it is with us, and when we find difficulty in speaking so that we be heard of you, or make mistakes in our wording or even in the manner of the message, then be patient, and do not ever be thinking that some deceiver is at hand. For, bethink you, friend, how difficult it would be for one diver to speak audibly to another, both helmeted and with water between them, and then you realize how much of patience and steadfast endeavor on our part is needed, and will perchance, more readily, give us a more patient hearing on your own."[144]

Kathleen lays out the hurdles that stand in the way of open communications between two dimensions. Yet the obstacles, while formidable, are not insurmountable; love and dedication will win through. After each attempt, high spirits return and are refreshed:

"But when we, our labor done here below, face us about toward the upper reaches of the heavens of God, then we the more readily feel the stream of life flowing from the distant Home of Rest and Refreshment."[145]

There is an immense effort to facilitate information about the spirit world and why we must strive to become more spiritual and less materialistic by the forces of light. Spirits, such as Kathleen, are toiling tirelessly to open our hearts.

This is the spiritual revolution that is happening before our very eyes. The spirit realm has abandoned communicating to the high priests and religious orders; for they hid the messages or worse, miscommunicated them to make them appear to give the priestly class more power over the masses. Spiritism is bringing the message that we, each individual, are responsible for opening a channel to the higher realms.

Via near death experiences, out-of-body experiences, visions, meditation, and most importantly daily prayer the spirit world encourages all of us to begin a daily dialog with the other side. It will take time and effort. Start small, speak from the heart, calmly listen to your conscience and heed what it tells you. After time, your will become proficient in discerning the signs to guide you.

Chapter 29 – Why Does God Allow People to Not Believe in God?

If there is a God, why doesn't God manifest a great demonstration of divine power and close, forever, any doubt of the existence of a Supreme Intelligence, a First Creator? How could people be allowed to blindly ignore their spirituality and pursue temporary material happiness, when the cost is lost time and misery in many lives? The rewards of heaven are so obvious, why prolong the suffering of those in ignorance? This was a lingering doubt of a high spirit from the tenth level of heaven.

This high spirit, who was sent on a mission, with his group, had stopped on the fifth level of heaven. While there, he took a rest to meditate. He laid upon a field of small red flowers, surrounded by trees and the sounds of nature. During that blissful moment, he wasn't thinking about why evil was even permitted to exist by God.

Whereupon, a man sat beside him:

"His mantle was of rich purple, and underneath he wore a tunic of gossamer through which his flesh shone like sunlight reflected from the heart of a crystal. His shoulder-jewel was of deep green, and the one upon his forehead was of green and violet. His hair was brown, but his eyes were of no color of which you know.

So he sat there looking before him and I looking upon him and his great loveliness for a long time, and then he said, 'My brother, this seat is a very cozy one, and pleasant to rest upon, think you?' And I replied, 'Yes, my Lord,' for I had no more

174

words than those.

'And yet,' he said, 'it is a bed of flowers on which you set your mind to lie upon.' And to that I could not give any answer. So he continued, 'Think you, friend, that these little red beauties of the flower family which are filled with budding life and comeliness, such as little children have, were made for such purpose as this to which we put them?'

And all I could reply was, 'I had not thought of it sir?'

'No, that is after the manner of most of us, and it is strange, too, seeing that we be, every one of us offspring of One Who is thinking all the time, and Who does naught that is not in agreement with reason. And it is within the ocean of the Life of Him we swim from age to age, and never out of it. It is strange how we can act unthinkingly, who are children of such a Father as He.'"[146]

The high spirit, ashamed at crushing the glorious flowers, got up and started to walk with the Lord who had sat next to him. The high spirit was part of the group that used the spirit Kathleen to communicate with the Rev. G Vale Owen, who wrote of this account in *Book Three – The Ministry of Heaven*, in 1917.

The high spirit told the Lord who had sat next to him:

"'This is my favorite walk,' I told him. 'It is hither I often come to think out matters which perplex me.'

'Yes,' he said thoughtfully, 'this is a sphere of perplexity beyond its fellows. And, coming hither, you often sit down upon some bank and think things out – or do you rather think yourself deeper into your perplexity, I wonder? But let that rest awhile. Where sat you last when you came hither to think?'

He stood still to ask the question, and I pointed to the bank before him and I said, 'It was here I sat when I came hereabouts last time.'

'And that but recently?' he asked, and I said, 'Yes.'

'And yet,' he said, 'I see no mark of your body's shape upon this moss or its blossoms. They have very soon recovered themselves of any untoward pressure they received.'

...

But he continued, 'Yet this is the concern of the All-Creator equal in value and appraise with the bruising of the souls of men. For whatever work is His is His indeed, and His alone.'"[147]

The high spirit was deliberately shown the red flowers fully restored. They had been crushed under his weight, but now had no outward sign to mark them as once almost destroyed. The Lord wished to impress, that the blistering furnace of suffering, after a time, leaves little or no outward mark upon us. After throwing out that little nugget, the Lord embarked on the next step to enlightenment.

The Lord led the high spirit to a hill, in order for him to experience a vision, which would expel his doubts about God's method of progress for spirits. The vision unfolded:

"At length there arose in the midst of the dome the figure of a Man, Who ascended until He stood upon the top of it. It was the figure of Christ, clothed all in white. The garment He wore came from His shoulders to His feet, but did not hide them. And as He stood there, a rosy hue began to flood His garment, and this deepened in tone until, at length, He stood there enrobed in deep rich crimson, and upon His brow a circlet of rubies, too. And when He held His hands stretched outward I saw that on the back of each one great red stone sparkled, and I knew what the vision meant to me. He had been lovely in His whiteness. But now He shone with crimson loveliness, and rich deep beauty which made me gasp for ecstasy as I looked upon Him."[148]

The high spirit realized that Christ came to earth as a pure white light of love and blessings, but for the true message to sink deep into the hearts of the believers – suffering had to sear - like a

176

red-hot glowing knife, that had laid in the fire, to close an open wound - the goodness in, so it could never be removed.

Then he saw Christ's effect upon His flock:

"Out upon the plain below we saw the people thronging to get a sight of this glory. And upon their faces and their robes there shone the light projected from His body, and it seemed to breathe some call to sacrifice and service which needed trust to undertake it, inasmuch as those who should offer themselves for work must go forth and suffer, yet without knowing quite all the mystery of suffering."[149]

Then, as if it was the first time, the high spirit looked upon the Lord beside him and he saw the inner suffering and the faint lines that revealed themselves in the Lord's face … which did not detract from his handsomeness, but made him glow with love all the more.

Then the high spirit told us what was said next:

"But I could not speak to him, and so stood by in silence. And then he said, 'My brother, I have come from a place much brighter that this sphere of yours to bring you hither that you should see the Man of Sorrows in His glory. Those sorrows He came forth freely to gather to Himself and make them His own. Without them He would lack some loveliness which is His today. And those sorrows which give to Him so much of gentleness are they which, in their crude and undeveloped state, flood earth with pain and the hells in torment. These are but for the moment for each who passes beneath their shadow. We cannot penetrate, my brother, into all the great Heart of God. But we can, as we even now have done, get at times a glimpse of the reason shining through it all, and then perplexity loses some of its more sinister aspects, and the hope arises that someday we may be able the better to understand.'

'But till that days dawns for me, I am content to know that He Who came forth of the Father's Heart came white and pure, and with steadfast purpose, faced the task ahead where His path lay amidst the turgid clouds of sin and hatred which gathered about the planet of earth. Nay, into the very hells He went and sought out those who suffered there, and because of their anguish He suffered also; so the Man of Sorrows returned to the Steps of His Father's Throne, His task accomplished. But not as He gone forth did He return. He went forth white in purity of holiness. He came back again the Crimson Warrior Prince and Conqueror. But the blood He shed was not that of another, but only His own. Strange warfare this, and new in the world's stranger history, that the warrior meeting his foe should turn the blade towards his own breast, and yet come forth conqueror by reason of his blood he shed.'"[150]

Hence, we all must find our own path to purity. For some it entails ages of suffering and for others, only the vision of love itself serves as the catalyst. God, in His effort to promote free will in all cases, has provided multiple paths to the same destination. There is no one road, there is no one direction, and there is no set time – only freedom to explore.

It is up to us set the pace … to determine how close we should hold the lessons learned … and move beyond our pettiness into the world of love and light.

Chapter 30 – Inspiration and Communication from Heaven – How it is Determined and Delivered to Mediums

Many mediums have written how they have received communications from the spirit realm. Some say they channeled a certain spirit, others a collection of spirits of various levels. The information they share with us is often interesting and enlightening. But, do you ever wonder how the spirit realm manages the process of sending us new and vital information … revelations that are meant to change our lives? They don't rely on a single spirit to a medium channel, they organize a group of spirits and insure their collective message reaches the mind of the medium in the correct fashion, character, and style.

While there are many mediums and groups of mediums that communicate with individual spirits (spirits at many levels) for a variety of reasons; when the message is important to the spirit world to be delivered clearly and accurately there is a more complex process at work.

To understand the care and effort undertaken to facilitate the successful delivery of a message, one must first understand the difficulties of any communication from spirits to humans. The spirit Kathleen, communicated with the Rev. G Vale Owen in November, 1917 concerning this very subject.

"By reason of many intricate complications we find sometimes, when we read over what message we have given, that much which we tried to impress is not apparent there, and some lesser quantity of what we had not in mind appears. This is but a natural consequence of the intervention of so thick a veil between the sphere from which we speak and that in which the recorder lives his life. The atmosphere of the two spheres is so diverse in quality that, in passing from the one to the other, there is always a diminution of speed so sudden and so marked that a shock is given to the stream of our thoughts, and there is produced, just on the borderline, some inevitable confusion. It is like a river tumbling over a weir into a lower level where the surface is a span of ruffled water. We try to get in beneath, where the stream is not so disturbed, and then our message comes through more clearly. But this is one of the many difficulties we find."[151]

We should take two truths from what Kathleen tells us. First, we are infinitely slower of mind in a physical form than in spirit form. We are like the baby who hurts his hand, he looks at the hand, then his lips begin to quiver, only after a lag of seconds does he begin to cry because he realizes he is in pain. His mind and body are just beginning to be connected, we realize why he is so slow and love our child all the more for it.

The spirit world looks at us in the same manner – they know we are sluggish and not all there – hence complex discussions will take time or be abandon altogether. Just like we wouldn't dream of discussing algebra with a five-year-old.

Secondly, and this pertains to the allusion that Kathleen made of trying to flow into calm waters. What she is actually saying, in a nice manner – I will state it plainly – is that our minds are so full of conflicting and disorganized thoughts; finding a few brief moments of clarity (space not filled with what we want for dinner that night, the movie we just saw, the friend we are mad with) is quite an effort! This is why a constant message from the spirit world to mediums is to practice meditation. They are hoping for a medium to wall off other thoughts so their message can sneak in.

Before the process as revealed by the spirit Kathleen is exposed, two other major personages who were responsible for delivering messages from the spirit world, should be analyzed.

180

Francisco (Chico) C. Xavier

I was listening to a speech, in Portuguese (confession: without my wife helping me to translate, I would be lost), by Geraldo Neto Lemos, one of the people who worked closely with Chico. He discussed how the series of books by the spirit Andre Luiz were written and psychographed by Francisco (Chico) C. Xavier.

Geraldo told us that a committee of 12 high spirits helped write the Andre Luiz books. He would only reveal one of the names of the spirits - Socrates was one of the authors.

Geraldo further explained that the series of books just gives us a hint of the truth of the spirit world. The curtain was lifted enough to allow us a peek of what lies beyond.

Chico Xavier psychographed over four hundred and fifty books from various spirits. They brought us a fountain of information of how the spirit world is organized and how we are helped and guided. Chico continued on the work of Allan Kardec, the man who codified Spiritism, with the help of many mediums throughout Europe in the 1850s.

Allan Kardec – The Great Codifier

Allan Kardec, in his *The Mediums Book*, surveys different types of mediums. Not all of us, in fact a tiny percentage of us, has the ability to communicate with the spirit world. But, he does say that we are all inspirational mediums. Meaning, that unbeknownst to us, spirits send their thoughts to us and we believe they are our own creations, or inspirations.

Allan Kardec never thought of himself as a medium who could communicate directly to spirits. He never professed that he had any mediumistic ability other than being inspired. Spiritist literature tells us that we are unconscious receivers of thoughts, some more powerful than others. Spirits who desire to influence our actions, speak directly to us, giving us ideas. Higher level spirits send us edifying messages to help us onto the path of performing a service to society, such as charitable acts or help us create new inventions to benefit the human race. We are also sent moral guidance to reinforce what our conscience tells us.

The spirit realm sent Allan Kardec on a mission to earth to fulfill what Jesus had promised – He would send us a Consoler – The Spirit of Truth – to explain further what the Kingdom of God is and our place in it. The spirit realm realized this job was key for the future of mankind. Hence, they left nothing to chance.

There is an article in the book, *The Spiritist Review, Journal of Psychological Studies of 1859*, which contains the entire contents of that year's magazines, edited and partially written by Allan Kardec. The article is about an errant spirit who is on the cusp of determining whether he wishes to pursue a better path. A medium talks to him about Allan Kardec and Spiritism.

The spirit decides to visit Allan Kardec to see for himself what type of person he is. In the second session the spirit reports back what he saw.

The medium wrote out the transcripts and sent them to Allan Kardec, which he read and confirmed as accurate. I start at Question 47:

"47. Let us return to Mr. Allan Kardec.

I went to his house yesterday. He was busy, writing in his office… He was working on a new book… Ah! He takes good care of us, poor spirits. If we are not known it is not his fault.

48. Was he alone?

Yes alone – that is, there was no other person with him. However, there were about twenty spirits around him, whispering above his head.

49. Has he heard them?

He heard them so well that he looked around to try to establish the origin of the noises, trying to see if they were not coming from thousands of flies. Then he opened the window to see if that was not coming from the wind or rain.

NOTE – Allan Kardec wrote – The fact is absolutely correct

50. Do you recognize any of those spirits?

No. They are not those in which company I pleased myself. I had the impression that I was an intruder. I remained in a corner of the room, observing.

51. Have the spirits given the impression that they were observing what he was writing?

I believe so. Two or three in particular whispered what he was writing, giving the impression that they heard the opinion of the others. However, he strongly believed that the ideas were his and seemed happy with that."[152]

I particularly love the last sentence, since we have all been at the place where we are pleased with ourselves after we had thought of something quite brilliant. I wonder how many times that was our own thinking versus thoughts whispered into our heads.

As with Chico Xavier, who was directly in communication with a group of spirits, Allan Kardec too, had his spirit handlers, supplying him with inspiration to organize and write his books.

Nothing is left to chance, when the stakes are high, and when the future of the earth and our collective spiritual future is in balance, by the vast number of spirits who are tasked with charting our path to enlightenment.

The Group Supporting G. Vale Owen

First the group of spirits - who worked with G. Vale Owen from November 1917 to February 1918 – studied how he communicated with previous spirits:

"We therefore studied and analyzed your mentality and what you had stored there in the years of your earth-life, and your soul – that is your spirit-body, so we employ the word here in these writings – and its health, and in what members health required perfecting the more; and also, so far as we could, the quality and the character of the facets of you, the spirit himself.

183

These we put through the spectrum which we use – not much like the one of which your scientists speak, but which is applied by us to men and their emanations as your scientists do to a ray of light. Thus were you, unknown to yourself, searched and tested with much care and closeness. We made our diagnosis, carefully writ down in details, and then we compared it with that one which was made when my lord Zabdiel used you, and also the more crude, but fairly full, record used when first your mother came to you and with her companions impressed on you their thoughts."[153]

As a football scouting combine weighs and tests potential players, so does the spirit world measure potential mediums to be utilized for the task of conveying vital information. Next the team is formed. The organization of the team is told to G. Vale Owen, by the team leader through Kathleen:

"There are many things to hand for humanity's help which are committed to us as our own peculiar task in the sphere from which we come. These duties are divided and a more especial task allotted to bands of workers. Of these bands we here present, to the number of seven, form what you would call a section or detachment. We have been deputed for this work we have now in hand, which is the giving a series of messages through Kathleen, your little friend, and then through you in order. The band to which we belong varies in number from time to time, as new members are initiated or progressed members are called into the sphere next above. At the present time the total number of the band is thirty-six, and we work in detachments of six with a leader, in ordinary, but sometimes less, according to the nature of the work we have to do. The reason why we work in numbers and not singly is not alone for reinforcement of strength and greater power, but also for the combination of influences to be exerted as a blended whole. This we have already explained to you. The blend, to be effective, must harmonize with the personality or personalities through whom we work, otherwise the effect would be of uncertain quality and liable to error of greater or lesser degree."[154]

Detachments, rotating workers, groups of six with a leader – none of this comes to mind when thinking of a medium conversing with the spirit world. Imagine the small army of spirits who surrounded Jesus when he was on our planet in human form. Like a play with intricate scenery changes which looks smooth to the audience, while backstage ordered chaos occurs. A mass of workers, moving large objects quickly to prepare for the scene ahead.

The spirit world isn't an ethereal mist where we float for an eternity in total bliss. The spirit realm is a place, where people go about on their business, cities are full of people, and everything must be organized. Around the earth, one of the main, if not the primary function of the heavenly government is the training of immature spirits, incarnate and discarnate. Hence, the teams that descend to earth to pass on their messages are following a process that has a well-worn trail. They have been speaking with humans on earth since before the time of Moses.

From the Group to the Medium

Seven spirits surrounding the Rev. G. Vale Owen don't all direct their conversations to his mind. They work to meld their story together and then use the spirit most attuned to the medium to focus the final product into the thoughts of the medium. They tell us the process in detail:

"The chain extending between the composite of our mentality and the pencil and paper by which you hand on this stream of thought-matter to others is now growing towards completion. Having searched in regard to you own personality and traits peculiar, we had to find a link between us and you – one who could receive this same stream of our minds united, refract it, in certain measure transmute it, eliminate from it those elements which in a spectrum are not of utility to the human eye, nor with effect on the retina, and transmit the residue to you. What comes to you from us, therefore, is not the sum total of what we send initially. It is analogous to what you call the visible part of the spectrum, that is, it is all that can be made visible to the human eye – that light made up of the ray –

185

vibrations which are not ultra either end. This in itself is an explanation of many difficulties of communication which seem often so unreasonable at your end of the chain. Now, all laws cohere and have certain points of likeness. It is so in the present. For as that white light by which you see is not unity, but unification, so it is with us. The white light unifies in itself more colors than one which, combining, produce a stream of light of one color, and that one a neutral, So we, our minds combining, produce to you, not each its own element separately, but one stream coherent as if from one mind alone. This illusion is helped also by reason of our transmitting this stream through our most excellent little friend and medium of transmission Kathleen. Mark also that these elements must be blended in due proportion, and each in its proper quantity, or that effect would be marred, even as the light would be not white, but tinted, were one color to predominate over its due proportion of them all."[155]

As compounds that are baked together form a new element, for example a stronger fiber, so does the workings of multiple spirits that arrange the ideas, the feelings, the symbolisms, the background of the words to be delivered into a complete sentence. Then, as if straining through a filter, the words are channeled through the spirit next to the medium for placement into the correct stream of thoughts.

All of this effort is but for one purpose … to elevate the human race. To place in front of our eyes and ears wisdom which would be useful for our spiritual advancement, if we would only pick it up. We live life after life, often missing completely the opportunity to remake our character into something good, something higher than what we were before. And in each life, there are books we didn't read, people we didn't believe, and signs we ignored – each small event – a door to enlightenment.

Open your eyes and heart to what the spirit world is laying at your feet. Start to analyze the little gateways which seemingly open at random, but in reality are planned at just the right moment. Follow the path to love.

Chapter 31 – Inspiration and Guidance from Heaven – How it is Determined and Delivered

The spirit Kathleen tells us, directly and in plain English, that our lives are predestined … that we on earth follow a plan that has been created from the higher reaches of heaven. Read her words:

"Know you, therefore, you who dwell in one of the uttermost of these Spheres, that such duties as are assigned to you have all been worked out as to their class, and the end to which they tend, by those who dwell in realms far above you. These schemes of allotted service are transmitted downward until they reach you, and are made known to you sometimes in one manner, sometimes in another, and to one more plainly, and to another less watchful, not so plain. Nevertheless, all who run the race of the earth-life may read the scroll if he choose, and persevere still to will that light be vouchsafed to him as to what his life shall be and to what end he has been guided."[156]

I was one of the not so watchful, until I was told of a future event that was so specific as to be unbelievable. Yet it did occur. From that seed I embarked on a discovery to understand how and why are our lives are predestined. I found the answer in Spiritism.

In fact, after learning and reading everything I could get my hands on about Spiritism, I wrote a book detailing how my life was guided by spirits above. The book is titled: *7 Tenets of Spiritism - How They Impact Your Daily Life*. In examining my life I found I had many signs and signals that I had blissfully ignored, like a five-year-old who doesn't understand he is being manipulated.

188

In essence, Spiritism lays out the reason we are here on earth and what is our destiny. We are here to learn to become civilized spirits – to utilize our vast potential power for good. All of the chaos and hardships on earth are the direct result of past wrongs we have committed. The spirit world expends great effort to show us the effects of those hurtful and wrongful past deeds.

We are immortal souls who will travel through life after life until we learn that love, charity, fraternity, and honor should be the keystones of our everyday life. Sounds simple and direct, but extremely difficult in practice! I fail in some way every day.

The spirit Kathleen, communicated with the Rev. G Vale Owen in November, 1917 about how we are guided and inspired by spirits to follow the path predestined for us. She revealed that we don't follow a set plan that is known to all – the spirits directing us are only allowed a short foretaste into our future. Only at the highest levels is everything known. Kathleen goes into detail what is revealed to us and what we can and can't do against our assigned destiny:

> "But to few is given to know or glimpse the future far ahead, 'Sufficient unto the day' is the rule, as He once said, and this suffices, so your trust be firm and quiet all the time. Not because the future is not known, but only because it is competent alone for those of high capacity and estate to view the distant course of life's grand purpose; and our capacity is sufficient for just a little view, and that of man in average scarce for any view ahead at all. As such schemes are given through so many spheres descending, it is therefore of natural consequence that they be tinctured by the dominant character of each of those spheres through which they filter downwards, and, by the time they reach you, they partake of a nature so complex in design that the ultimate issue is very hard to discover, even to us, times oft, who have some practiced skill in the matter. This is one purpose and use of faith, to be able to realize one's duty and no more, and on that conviction to go forth and do valiantly, never doubting that the end is seen by those who compassed the design."[157]

Kathleen is telling us that like good soldiers, spirit obey orders, even though they are not sure what is the intent and objective of the command. The knowledge that their superiors above are aware of the situation and are focused on the ultimate goal keeps their dedication steady. Spirits realize by their interaction with superior spirits, that these high souls are in a position of leadership because they have earned it. They have passed test after test and arrived at their present level on merit alone. And having arrived they do not lord over inferior spirits, but treated everyone with humility and respect.

Even more is revealed to us. As one descends in the levels of heaven, all the way down to earth, the span of future sight narrows, until it reaches ground level, where the present is all that is exposed. We on the receiving end are following an invisible script, unknowingly acting on cue and speaking our lines, until we make choices that draw us off course. Kathleen elaborates:

> "For every man is free to choose, and no man's will is overruled in the matter of his choosing. If he choose to go faithfully onward and with trust, then the end is sure. If he choose to go out of the way designed, then he is not let nor forced. Guidance is offered then and gently. If this be refused, he is left to go alone – yet not alone, for others will be his companions, and that in plenty."[158]

The choice is always between one of love, charity, fraternity, and honor against flight from responsibility, selfishness, greed, envy, and revenge. We would not need any external guidance if we learned to follow our inner voice, our conscience. Nevertheless, the spirit realm fully understands our infinite capacity to rationalize away our baser decisions and attempts to supply us with a reminder.

Mostly, certainly in my case, we make the mental gymnastics to convince ourselves of the rightness of our decision and overrule that nagging voice inside which incessantly tries to light the way to the true path. The argument that other people are doing it too, was always one of my trusty standbys.

Fortunately, for us, Spiritism, brought to us by Allan Kardec, describes the rewards for delaying immediate gratification against the immense benefits of a heavenly reward - a hundred times more than what we could ever experience on earth. The loving atmosphere of heaven ... from the first level to the top is a goal worth denying yourself of any ill-gotten gain on earth. In the physical world all states are temporary, in the spirit realm, all is eternal.

An Example of Guiding the Human Race

When one reads the Bible or compilations of messages from inspired authors by spirits, the information is interesting, but one is not able to grasp the process behind the concept. Kathleen tells us we are guided, but what does that mean? How does that work?

The spirit Kathleen supplies us with an example. This is what makes the book, *Beyond the Veil*, so unique, so wonderful. Information is given, explained, and then we are also provided with examples. Everything in textbook style is there to satisfy our urge to uncover every last nugget of information.

Kathleen delivers a detailed explanation of the process of influencing events and progress of the human race on earth. She begins:

"In order to illustrate our meaning. A book will be projected whose need is seen. We will say that those in a sphere whose dominant note is that of science will conceive the outline of the book. This is handed on to another sphere whose note is love. Into the scheme will be infused a softening, rounding-off effect, and the scheme handed on. A sphere where beauty rules will add some illustrations which will give harmony and color to the theme. Then it will come to such a company as they who study the different traits dominant in the races of mankind. These will study very carefully the theme itself, and look for the nation most fitted to put the venture forth in the world. This decided, they will carefully select the next sphere to which it shall be entrusted. It may need an infusion of historical precedent, or a poetical vein, or romance perchance. And what

191

started out a framework of hard scientific fact may issue into the earth-plane as a scientific treatise, and historical resume, a novel, or even a poem or hymn."[159]

Nothing is done on a whim by a higher spirit, all is thought out, each possible outcome is mapped, and each option is analyzed. Multiple departments examine the plan and add, subtract, or modify the details. There is no Supreme Intelligence determining our every move. It doesn't work that way. God provides the grand structure, the noble goal, and spirits, at many levels (who have all started out like us), create and work to implement the plan. All along the process, during creation, implementation, and delivery each phase is monitored and possible slight alterations made.

There truly is an army of spirit benefactors working to move our herd of slow-thinking humanity onward to a better world. Imagine what the earth could be like today if we actually cooperated!

Kathleen reiterates that the method to achieve assigned goals are flexible:

"For you will readily understand that such schemes are originated not all in one sphere but in many, and do not pass all from one sphere into another in identical order. Also, what may originate as a book may, before it reaches you, have been so much transfigured as to become an act of Parliament, or a play, or even a commercial enterprise. There is no finality to the ways and means. Whatever eventually seems to commend itself to the group of companies concerned in the production of any scheme in the service of God and on behalf of man is pressed into service. Thus it is that men work out the work of those who watch and guide them from on high. Let such, then, realize what great host of helpers they have behind them, and go forward bravely, nothing doubting, never faltering in their way, for they are not alone."[160]

Under the leadership of Christ, we, once and future earthly humans, who have experienced the pain and joys of physical existence, are core to the day-to-day efforts to guide those who are on the planet under a cloud of ignorance.

We, the incarnated, travel through our life under the impression that we can find bliss at some future point. If we just plan ahead and save for a rainy day, we could amass the required savings to find a peaceful sanctuary and live as we wish. Spiritism smashes this fallacy. We are on earth to change, to learn, to grow, and that is next to impossible without stimuli. We aren't allowed to retreat, we must be present in the class and participate.

There is a legion of former incarnates, who are back in the spirit realm, whose job is to move us, as a collective and individually, forward. We are nothing but a grain of sand on the beach as powerful and incessant waves pound us. Each wave imperceptibly transforming our character to the better.

Chapter 32 – We are Truly Blessed

We are truly blessed. The spirit realm is watching over us in a manner that we could never envision. Our life, each life of every one of us, is so much more significant and rich than we can imagine.

When we are at our lowest point or the highest point in our life, remember that each stage serves nothing more than to teach us. Often the successes we have are the most dangerous, because then we forget to be humble and grateful. We become too full of ourselves. We think we are invincible gods.

Whereas in reality we are an actor in a play, with the scenes all scripted. The audience is waiting to see how our character reacts to each successive challenge. Behind the curtain, there is an assistant, whispering our lines to us, in case we forget. Reminding us to stay on track and not to lose focus.

The audience is evaluating our performance. They await to see each denouement of each distinct episode. They long to see the character grow. To rise out of any previous misconceptions, to emerge a better person. They laugh and cry with us, and they are ever hopeful.

The audience well knows that when the play is finished, the actors will go home; back to the real world. The actor is the same person, but positively slightly altered by what part he or she played.

Each of us is the actor, the spirit world is the audience, and the assistant gently guiding us is our guardian angel.

Everything about us has been built for one express purpose. To create an atmosphere where we may learn to improve. To eventually become a productive member of spirit society. To take our place as a responsible spirit who has acquired the personality to weld god-like powers.

Nothing else matters. Not how much money you make, not the car you drive, not the exotic vacations you take, or the house you live in. All that is just scenery to place your character in context for your lesson.

An army of educators and care-takers stand-by at your request. And that is the most difficult obstacle. To acknowledge, that we are not masters of our own fate, but students who need help and don't always know when to ask for it.

Spiritism tells us to not hesitate to request assistance. It is far better to ask for guidance and attempt to follow the righteous path and fail, than to reject our conscience and forge ahead on our own. For then, failure and our response is actually a victory. We proved that we shall not alter our path to achieve a goal by nefarious means. That material sacrifice is nothing in regards to our spiritual growth.

Hence, know well, you are surrounded by kind and loving guides, who are always ready and willing to provide love, fortification, and advice. You are never alone, no matter how it may seem to you. You are never abandoned. You are an important young soul, who one day will be a great spirit and a benefit to the entire universe.

Section 3 - Future Events

The earth <u>will</u> become a planet of regeneration. Famine, wars, economic devastation, and poverty will be eradicated. Hate, selfishness, and jealously shall become greatly reduced or eliminated. Christ, following the commands of God, to raise the earth to the next level, will not fail. The earth will become a paradise.

But, this does not mean that all of us will rise with the planet. A portion of incarnate and discarnate spirits, who have ignored and resisted the urge to follow the light and instead have held on to their material leanings and use their brethren for their own selfish desires … they will be removed from the earth and sent to another planet; befitting their character and attitude. They will be given another chance to learn. While those remaining, will reside in a just and equitable society; free of the fear and chaos we have today.

This is the future. It will occur. When and how it will unfold is the subject of the communications analyzed in this section. The time frame was not revealed to us. How many more centuries do each of us have to earn a ticket for the transition is unclear.

Many Spiritist, myself included, believe that we are now in the beginning of the first phase of transition. Forces are being marshalled to begin a spiritual transformation of the planet. Past enlightened emissaries of Jesus, such as Socrates and Buddha, will return to earth, in physical form, to lead us.

The pendulum swinging from spirituality to materialism is close to reaching its apex. The emptiness of life based upon consumerism and relative morality will contribute to a longing to fill a void of the soul. As humans, programmed by the spirit world to seek out a greater meaning to our lives, we can't withdraw forever from the concept of God.

Therefore, our culture will undergo a dramatic transformation, which is required for the coming physical transformation of the earth. The arc of the pendulum will begin to move back to spirituality, but without the ignorance and prejudices of the middle ages. Sans the rigid dogma and ceremonies which served to limit the intellectual curiosity of those who seek others to give them all answers.

This is the major difference between most visions of earth's future which end in monumental catastrophes, either by asteroids, climate change, massive famine, or a combination of earthquakes and volcanic activity or legions of spirits fighting between good and evil. According to Spiritism, the earth doesn't change in a flash, but over a long extended period. What is required for the transition isn't physical but spiritual. The contours of the earth may stay steady (and evolve over time), but the harmonic vibrations from collective humanity will rise together to cause drastic changes. Alterations measured in hundreds, if not thousands, of years.

While the earth may seem to be a giant mass with a molten core, mantles, and crust – hard, heavy and unchangeable … it is in reality created and held in place by the force of will of high spirits. The earth is susceptible to dominating vibrations and thoughts. As billions of humans raise their awareness and are in tune with the spirit realm and all that implies, the earth (and humans too) will become less dense, more ethereal. Only then shall the first phase of the future be attained.

Hence, the visions of the future brought to us by different spirits communicating with the Rev. G. Vale Owen aren't images of tidal waves and lost cities, but of new ideas, new cultural norms, and new structures and organizations which will be the identifiable results of a sea-change in human society.

197

Chapter 33 – Cycles of Progress – Material and Spiritual

The spirit realm guides us individually and collectively. Unbeknownst to us, there is a grand plan for all of humanity. But it is not a straight line, or an upward curved line of progress. We move forward on a spiral. We who live in the present, and see our path behind us from a narrow perspective; we see progress, decline, and progress again. We see movement ahead and at times, whole cultures declining into dark ages. We believe that a span of thousands of years is practically an eternity.

We must broaden our field of view and see that what we take as sliding into chaos is a form of progress and renewal. A gathering point to make humanity ready for the next great leap forward.

To peer into the future, we must analyze the past. But our analysis is flawed, for we aren't able to peer into the entire past of humanity, for such destruction was wrought to cultures long ago, that we have only distant myths to enlighten us.

And we must realize the earth is but one point in the universe. That our destiny and trajectory is connected to the entire physical universe and the will of the spirit universe.

All of this was contained in the message to the Rev. G Vale Owen from the spirit Arnel on Friday, March 22, 1918, concerning progress on earth, in the universe, and how the Great Lords of Creation had attempted to shorten the path to perfection:

"There were at that time, so long ago, some who had in mind to take a shorter path to perfection and others who chose a longer one. These two groups did not clash exactly, but the variety of their endeavors overlapped somewhat, and the confusion which ensued has caused all that men today call evil. All things are working towards perfection, but so great is the field of activity that the period must necessarily be long, if you count it in days and years. As viewed by those who stand in God His Presence it is neither short nor long, but one continuous event, as a river when considered as a unit embraces the whole from source to sea."[161]

Arnel tells us that the earth's evolution has told the story of the remnants of quick evolutionary species which proved, in the end, to be inadequate manifestations. On the other hand, they were useful in setting the stage for the next great leap. Therefore, the spiral shape of progress, one species or an entire ecology progresses and dominates, but can only reach a certain plateau, whereupon, they must be discarded.

Arnel supplies the example of the growth of dinosaurs and even the extremely large mammals that we uncover as ancient fossils, as proof of the destruction and subsequent rise of a superior replacement.

We, as humans stand upon the platform of all animals that have come before us. Only by experimentation, learning through failures and successes, were we able to be thusly constructed.

Darwin, in his book *Origins of the Species*, saw this struggle and deemed nature to be the guiding hand. But, there is also the invisible orchestration by the spirit realm, in facilitating our planets major periods and making subtle changes in DNA to push natural selection to perform its duty.

Twofold Paths

Arnel didn't limit his thesis to attempts to shorten the evolutionary ladder of intelligent animals; he included the grueling climb of our spiritual perfection as well. He tells us:

"Now, the further principle of which I speak is this: The course

200

of development shall take a twofold line of direction. That direction shall be first outward, from unity into diversity of expression, as we have already explained. But also along with this line of movement shall go its twin, which is, that progress shall take the direction from the spiritual ever toward the material. It is like two runners running their course side by side. The one is named 'From Unity into Diversity,' and the other is named 'From Spirit into Matter.' These two must keep pace together. Neither must be allowed to outstrip the other; for they run not to win except they win the outward goal together."[162]

Hence, from the seed of a microbe, the diverse life of the planet was hatched. Different insects, plants, wild animals, and higher intelligent mammals were constructed. As soul bearing dominate humans progressed in form, so should they progress in spiritual knowledge.

"From Spirit into Matter" isn't the final objective – it is an important goal. One that must be reached when the level of the body and civilization is ready. It is the connection of mankind's fascination with materialism with the expansion of the spirit willed physical universe.

Arnel explains further:

"There were those who schemed to shorten this course by arresting the tendency untimely, before the whole outward course had been run, and turning again the urge of creative life inward toward spirit before the outermost post had been reached and rounded. That post is the material expression of an inner manifestation of a still deeper cycle of development behind which there are those Lords of Creation who by their willful energizing guide the great fleet of sun-systems in their constellations on its voyage through the space of matter towards the port where they shall bend their course round and homeward once again."[163]

This is where the logic and speech of high spirits becomes difficult to penetrate. Arnel speaks of the general universe, yet at the same time, he is speaking of our progress on earth.

In the spirit realm, everything is tied into everything else. As we make progress as an individual spirit, so does humanity progress, so does our solar system, so does our galaxy, and our universe. There are spirals within spirals within spirals, and so on.

To those learned and wise spirits in the upper reaches of heaven circling the earth, they see us as one small part of an intricate mechanical pocket watch. With small gears gating larger ones, and hands spinning at different speeds, but when looked upon from the front – all makes sense. While we, humans locked in our bulky physical bodies, are imprisoned in one of the gears, peering out observing an indescribable complexity.

Arnel explains that providing material progress to humankind and human-like souls in other planets too early in their progress has unforeseen consequences and that civilizations have had to be reset to put in harmony the physical and spiritual journeys of immature spirits.

Arnel tells us that we have been too technically advanced in relation to our spiritual progress in the past. The destruction of Atlantis and Lemuria attests to that. He implies that at some point in the far and distant past humans reached a material plateau, but they weren't ready to embark on the road to reclaim their spirituality. But now we may be ready.

"To clear my meaning for you: The Ocean is the realm of Being expressed in outward expansion of the Mind of the Infinite and Ultimate One. The fleet is that Universe which was brought into existence at His command and by the Creative Lords of whom I spoke. The port to which the outward course is that to which you find yourself today. The homeward course is that to which you are now tending; for the outermost point has been reached and is just being rounded. It is the rounding of that point, it is the turning of the vessels out of the harbor of material inertia towards the more active element of the open sea, which is the cause of much unrest in all directions at the present time. Soon the sails will fill and set steadily athwart the hulls, the vessels will settle down to their homeward course, and both officers and crews, now homeward bound, will be of cheery disposition, and ever, as the fleet ploughs through the ocean of being, nearer and nearer will it come to the port from which it set out so many ages ago, and gladness and peace will gather about them as they go for the welcome which awaits them aport far away ahead into the east where the light is already breaking and the smile of God is seen."[164]

This message was sent to us in 1918. The First World War was ending, the Second World War, was only twenty-one years in the future, the beginnings of the age of the internet was only a little more than sixty years ahead.

The entire collective humanity on earth went through massive destruction, illustrating the capacity of the dark side of technology, then one more push, starting in the fifties, of invention and material wealth. All the while, a large portion of humanity have had a sense of something lacking. A hole, a missing spiritual component to our lives. The sixties were a reaction to the consumer tidal wave, but, being based upon no firm foundation, other than freedom from everything, it eventually succumbed.

Parallel to material growth, our culture has rejected even the tiniest demonstration of faith, of a set of Divine Laws from God that should govern our moral compass to always point to love, charity, fraternity, and honor. Instead, we have relative morality, based upon a wholly material world, with no sense of an immortal spirit. Hence, we only live to seek pleasure.

Counterintuitively, our very advances carries the seeds of shaking our materialistic platform and awakening the world to the existence of another plane – the spirit world. The internet, that device which spreads opportunities to buy instant gratification, also serves to gather together like-minded people to discuss: their faith, their spirituality, their near death experiences, their stories of unexplained phenomena, and the ability to plan collective efforts to help others in need.

The great Brazilian medium, Francisco (Chico) C. Xavier, told his acquaintances that the World Wide Web will open up the Doctrine of Spiritism to the planet. People will discover Allan Kardec and other Spiritist writers, so they may fully understand their place on earth and the meaning of life.

Arnel is placing us at the apogee of materialism. He believes we are leaving that port – that place of buying and selling goods – and embarking onto a different ship which will lead us to balance our material with the spiritual.

Examples of Spiral Progress

While the sinking of the continent of Atlantis provides a good example of a culture with advanced technology, but not the spiritual maturity to manage it, there are more recent demonstrations of entire societies allowed to practically disappear in order to rise up once again, but with a different perspective.

One can detect the hand of the spirit realm in the collapse of civilization in the thirteenth to twelfth century B.C., also known as the Late Bronze Age Collapse or the Invasion of the Sea People. Entire cultures were wiped out – Minoans, Mycenaeans, Trojans, Hittites, and Babylonians. Only the Egyptians survived intact, but even it declined after the experience.

Historians are still attempting to piece together what could have caused such a general rout of ancient empires. The simple explanation of an outside invasion doesn't do the practical erasure of long living societies justice.

The spirit world also took a hand in the destruction of Rome, as reported in a book, psychographed by Francisco (Chico) C. Xavier in 1939. Emmanuel, Chico's spirit mentor and author of the book, *On the Way to the Light*, explained what happened to Rome:

"The Roman Empire could have effected the founding of a sole State on the planet due to the marvelous unity it achieved and thanks to the efforts and watch-care from On High; but instead, it disappeared in a sea of ruins after its wars, aberrations and circuses filled with wild beasts and gladiators.

204

The enormous organism began rotting away in the open sores opened by the negligence and impiety of its children, and when the palliative of mercy from selfless and compassionate spirits was no longer possible due to the galvanization of the overall sentiment on the broad table of earthly excesses and pleasure, suffering was called in to reestablish the fundamentals of the truth in souls.

Nothing was left of the proud city of the emperors except piles of stone. Under the lash of expiation and suffering, guilty spirits changed their garments in order to evolve and redeem themselves in the infinite scenery of life; and while many of them continue to weep in redemptive suffering, the sad and lamenting winds of the night mourn over the ruins of Vespasian's Colosseum."[165]

The theme of the above paragraphs is that raw power, with the backing of technology and superior organization can and will dominate other groups, but that power without kindness and compassion for conquered subjects or allies will – eventually – cause the spirit world to withdraw its support, thereby initiating a decline. That advanced technology without the guidance of spiritual maturity in its use will result in tragedy.

But tragedy can be looked at as but one curve of the spiral. A society climbs to the pinnacle of civilization, proves inadequate in softening its approach to all humans – chaos commences – out of the ashes are chastised spirits who will make a better attempt the next time.

While history can be viewed as invention and loss of intellectual property, the intermediate growth of spirituality by the waves of reincarnations by spirits, who once led great empires, now toiling on a farm, sets up a subsequent growth, better grounded in morality.

One can see from Rome, where slaves outnumbered freemen, to the rise of European powers; where slavery was eventually abolished. Certainly, there were still cruelties and injustices, but on the whole the successive government organizations were more inclusive and just to its citizens.

In the nineteenth century, Europe made great strides in governments and institutions, but their history of colonization was a black mark. Emmanuel, again in the book, *On the Way to the Light*, states:

> "Condemned to irreversible sentences for its social and political crimes, European dominance will disappear forever like the Roman Empire, handling over to the Americas the fruit of its experiences with a view to the civilization of the future."[166]

The spirit realm had already planned the destruction of European power even before World War II had begun. The spiral of history continues on.

Eusebio's Lecture

Arnel told the Rev. G Vale Owen that we are headed back to a renewed spirituality that is in harmony with our progress. It won't be done under the leadership of Europe. Emmanuel has told us the baton has been passed to the Americas.

In a book psychographed in 1947, by Chico Xavier, written by the spirit Andre Luiz, Andre reports on a lecture by a learned spirit Eusebio. He tells us of our collective path to become better souls:

> "How long have we done and undone, finished and started over on the reparative journey, only to return, perplexed, once more to the beginning? On the terrestrial stage, we are the same actors of the evolutionary drama. Each millennium is a short act; each century, a brief scene. Even though we inhabit sacred bodies, we act like carefree children who are entertained only by child's play and we lose the sanctifying opportunities of our existences. Thus, we become reprobates of the sovereign laws, ensnared in the ruins of death like shipwrecked pirates, who, for a long time, are unworthy of sailing the seas once again. While millions of souls enjoy good opportunities of correction and readjustment, once more involved in regenerative efforts in earth's cities, millions of others mourn their defeat, lost in

206

dismal disillusionment and suffering."[167]

Hence, the entire student body of the campus called earth has had to take and retake the same courses. Each time the expectation is that we are to learn to become a bit more empathetic, a little more loving, and expanding our caring and fraternal instincts.

Eusebio asks the audience:

"How long will we be masterminds of destruction and wickedness? Instead of loyal servants of the Lord of Life, we have been soldiers of the armies of illusion, leaving behind millions of tombs opened under a torrent of ash and smoke. In vain, Christ has exhorted us to seek the manifestations of the Father within us. We nurture and expand only selfishness and ambition, vanity and fantasy. We continue to incur onerous moral debts and enslave ourselves to the sad outcomes of our deeds, lingering indefinitely in a crop of thorns.

In such a state we have reached the modern era, in which madness is widespread and men and women's mental stability is on the verge of disaster. With an evolved brain and an immature heart, we hone our art of wrecking our spiritual progress."[168]

Eusebio has notified us that we shall stay on this merry-go-round until we deserve our way off. We go in an elliptical orbit in life after life, on a spiral upward trend … it is up to us when we make the decision to exit. We just have to earn it.

But, we can't do it alone and not think of the multitude that would be left behind. We must do our part to improve our culture; to bring the knowledge that we never die, that we exist again and again in a great endeavor – to become a perfect spirit. Only by raising our collective harmony can we earn the right to ascend.

The future isn't just a cataclysmic event ordained by God. It is a series of waves of changes brought to us by painstaking planning of individual lives, cultures, and nations. In the chapters ahead, the spirits explain to G. Vale Owen how we as individuals are watched and guided to concrete destinations and how much is known and what could be random about our individual future.

They also explain how directives are handed down from on high and followed by the massive legions of spirits in the realm above and outside of our physical universe. Think not of the future as being a specific date or occurrence, but a journey, a long transformation – which may last a thousand years.

Chapter 34 – Waves of Emotion – Call to Action Sent by the Spirit Realm

Have you noticed that groups of people on earth tend to share the same longing, the same urges toward a common goal? The Renaissance was one collective gasp of intellectual freedom from the bounds of the Catholic Church. It seemed to occur organically.

Unbeknownst to humanity, the spirit realm sends out signals – subtle pushes to our minds and emotional state to begin to move us in one direction or another.

As an example, according to the spirit Emmanuel, in the book *On the Way to the Light*, the Renaissance was planned by the spirit realm to set the human race onto a new path:

> "At the dawn of the 15th century, when the medieval era was about to end, large assemblies of spirits met in the vicinities of the planet to direct regenerative movements, which, in light of Christ's determinations, would lead the world into a new era.

> This entire regenerative effort took place under his merciful and compassionate gaze as He poured out his light on all hearts. Devoted messengers reincarnated on the orb to carry out loving and redemptive missions."[169]

According to a message from the spirit Arnel, a similar event occurred around the turn from the 19th to the 20th century. The message was dated March 8, 1919 to the Rev. G Vale Owen.

Arnel has told G. Vale Owen, in previous messages, about the long journey of mankind toward material progress; now he presented a new journey that shall begin. It will reawaken spiritual forces and emotions that have been lost for thousands of years:

> "The trend of human development had been downward and outward, toward and into matter. That was God His purpose, namely, that He manifest Himself in detail of form phenomenally. Because this way was downward set, the elements of error increased in greater measure than the reservoir of spirit into which they were poured from earth was able to absorb, assimilate and transmute. It was, therefore, necessary that on our way to earth we clarify these spheres. And this we did preparatory to our more intensified operations on earth itself."[170]

Arnel and other spirits describe the progress of humankind, as well as individuals, to be a spiral. Progress is made, but sometimes, through a dramatic event, an invasion for a country, or a rancorous divorce for a person – it seems that all forward movement was lost. But, it wasn't, for the episode actually created a firmer foundation to launch the next round of progress.

When Arnel speaks about the elements of error, not just on earth but in the surrounding regions, he well knows that psychic emanations affect discarnates and incarnates alike. That sometimes, the rays flowing from our thoughts need to be tuned.

In this case, the entire human race had been pushed to advance their technology, which for the short-term, meant that a material outlook pushed out the spiritual side of life. This is an unbalance that was allowed to exist, so earth's society could reach where it was guided.

Now, and by now, it could mean starting hundreds of years ago, for the changes are subtle indeed, the human race is being herded back to experience a collective longing for spirituality. Think of moving the humans on earth like a mile long supertanker; from the moment the helm is turned the noticeable change in direction is extremely lengthy. We, living for around eighty years in our physical bodies at a time, do not have the field of view long enough to decipher alterations in course.

Arnel tells us this guiding is constant and unrelenting:

"Always earth is operated on from these realms. This was to be an intensification of those operations, an access of dynamic urge of such degree and impetus as should serve to send the hoop spinning safely down the lower slope and give it a good start on the upward turn on its way toward the peaks across the valley. This has now been accomplished, and the ascent is well begun."[171]

Something large was started. Arnel enlightens us more:

"This commotion increased and extended as we pressed more closely round the sphere of earth; and ever more and more they mingled in earth's life and policies until they at last burst through the encircling envelope ethereal altogether and became of the economy of the world of men."[172]

A new purpose is starting to anchor itself on earth. I believe it starts with a sense of lacking, a feeling that something is missing. Like the sixties generation who attempted to believe in love and all that implies. But we must realize these are only skirmishes, a battle takes place, and then society pushes back with all of the weight of the entropy of hundreds of years. Although, after the dust settles, a little progress was made.

The Rev. G. Vale Owen wished to know was the Great War, as World War I was known at that time, was the climax. Arnel tells him:

"Of that as climax. But ever in increasing force, as I have already said, this war has gone on for these ages past. Its martyrs have been many, and many phases has the war passed through. You would count it strange were I to table for you all of these in total. I name but a few of these phases: the phase religious and theological, artistic, political and democratic, scientific, the warlike phase which took such vogue this last millennium as to absorb well-nigh all dynamics into its wide-open maw."[173]

The good Reverend, like all of us, tends to localize great events

211

around themselves. While Arnel is speaking of centuries, we think in terms of years or decades.

Arnel is preparing us for our future. Our future as humankind. We like to think of prophecy as boiling down to a distinct occurrence. Sometimes that is true, but the stronger, the irresistible prophecy is a vision of the human collective ... the spirit realm is guiding us to this future. As sure as the rain falls, we shall arrive there.

Arnel gives a glimpse of the destination:

"For you do dwell upon the earth widespread and with large spaces unpeopled. So you in total are still but few. We encompass earth about on every hand and our ranks spread back upward through the steppes and stories of the serried heavens. So we be many, and each one of us of power greater than the most of you. Ah well, the dawning light will send its rays aloft and search us out in our hiding-places amid the light and brightness of the spheres. Then earth will feel less lonely as it rolls along the meadows of the void. Earth will know in that day that all about those meadows fairies plays and elves besport themselves in their merriment and that earth is not lonely but at one with the myriads of the redeemed of earth who have linked up humankind with those afar who dwell on planets some of which you see of a clear night and others which are not visible to you of earth. Nor will they be until you put off from your low-lying shores and sail your boat toward the open sea, toward the great expanse, toward the western region of the sun."[174]

We are being alerted that we – humanity on earth – will join other planets who have attained a balance of technology and devoutness, materialism and spirituality, wisdom and faith. As we approach these goals, we shall be assisted by other races from other planets.

In fact, this prophecy dovetails with the prophecy stated by Francisco C. Xavier in the 1970's when he told us that if the earth could live through the next fifty years, starting from 1969, when men went to the moon, that sometime after 2019, the earth would be openly visited by aliens who would render us assistance.

The help from these other worldly visitors won't only be in the form of wondrous gadgets and applications, but also of spiritual knowledge. We shall be exposed to what they have learned long ago – that we are immortal souls, who reincarnate to learn and to improve, and that we began in the spirit realm and shall ever return.

I go into more detail in Chapter 40. I explain what the prerequisites for an open visitation are and the benefits entailed. Remember, there is no certainty in the exact timing of future events determined by the spirit world. Each depends on the state of mankind, and most probably the state and choices of key individuals in possession of power.

Chapter 35 – "And God Wrought Special Miracles" - How the Spirit Realm Implements the Word of God

We think of God and heaven as a place where our Supreme Lord has everything ordered. Perfectly ordered. A machine with gears and cogs that run for infinity without any required maintenance. A utopia, where there is no need for improvement.

According to Spiritism, earth is an imperfect representation of heaven. From this, we are to understand that there are organizations, learning centers, work, architecture, etc., all of the required components that we need on earth to run a large city or a nation which also play a role in heaven.

Hence, nothing is static, like a time-lapsed video of a busy city center, the higher celestial spheres are constantly in motion. This motion must be orchestrated by a sophisticated organization. A command and control structure is a requirement in order to accomplish the directives of management. In other terms, the Word of God.

I have written about the organization of certain sections of the higher planes, but I have not detected a good explanation of the process of decisions being turned into actions through multiple layers of management in the spirit world. The nuts and bolts of the structure to lay out general guidelines and the method of control of an army of spirits to act upon a set of orders has, until now, been a mystery, at least to me.

There are many gems of knowledge exposed in the book

Beyond the Veil. In one section where the spirit Zabdiel is expounding on the theme of unity and diversity, he succinctly lays out the process whereby orders from above flow down the chain of command and presents the width of freedom to interpret general directions. Additionally, he notifies us of the rules of engagement, when the actions of one group overlaps another.

When Zabdiel discusses a soul's power, whether in a spirit or a physical body, he states that a person's attunement to Divine Will enables an individual enhanced capabilities to accomplish great deeds. Hence, to be an effective member of the spirit hierarchy, a spirit must be aligned with the spiritual direction of his or her spiritual superiors. Zabdiel illustrates his point with the following:

> "For instance, there are here such as have charge of the elements which condition the earth and those things which grow upon the earth. Let us take one example which will serve to illustrate the others: Those who have charge of vegetation.

> These are under one Mighty Prince; and are divided and subdivided into departments, all in perfect order. Under these again are others of lower estate who carry out their work under direction, and in conformity to certain unalterable laws laid down in higher spheres."[175]

In the paragraphs above, we aren't told anything new. In Spiritist literature there are numerous examples of the structure of directors of certain functions and their support organizations. In fact, the spirit Emmanuel, in the book *On the Way to the Light*, reveals that Christ was a member of the "Community of Pure Spirits" who directed the establishment of our entire solar system.

Therefore, we on earth, incarnates and discarnates alike, are led by Christ. The earth was created under his direction, the billions of years of evolution it took to form mankind in a vessel for spirits to inhabit and who need to learn by multiple trials, and the building and destiny of nations and whole societies, have all been decreed by Jesus.

Given all this, exactly how did Jesus give commands and have them followed in order to produce the flora and fauna we live with today? Zabdiel supplies the details through an example of the group of spirits which guides the evolution of plant life on earth:

> "It would seem, then, that one rule they must observe in their work is that, having planned out any scheme of development for a family of plants, that scheme must be pursued, in its main elements and essentials, to its natural consummation. All their armies of subordinates are kept within the limits of that unalterable law of evolution. If an oak family is planned, then an oak family that must remain. It may evolve into subdivisions, but these must be subdivisions of the oak. It must not be allowed to branch off into the fern family, or seaweed. These also will be developed along their own line."[176]

From the example above we see that a path is planned, there are definite guiderails in place to keep the workers moving forward. The main objective must be held in sight and no wild tangents are permitted. While the road is set, the exact lane within both curbs is up to the spirits toiling toward the goal mandated by the higher powers.

Next Zabdiel discloses what happens if two teams work at cross purposes:

> "Another law is that no department of spiritual workers shall be able to negate the operations of another. They may not, and often do not, work in conformity; but their operations must be along lines of modifications, rather than absolute negation, which would mean destruction.

> Thus we find that if the seed of two plants of the same family be mixed the result will be a mule plant, or a blend, or a modification. But the seed of one family being mixed with that of another is without effect. And in neither case is effect annihilation.

> A parasite may entwine itself around a tree. But then ensues a fight. In the end the tree is usually worsted and pays the penalty of defeat. But it is not suddenly laid low. That fight

216

proceeds, and indeed sometimes the tree wins. But it is recognized here that those who invented and carried out the parasitic idea have in the main won the battle of forces."[177]

The Supreme Intelligence has set up a system of positive conflict between teams. Whereby, different groups could be in competition with one another, on the other hand they both serve to improve the quality of the products they created. No group is allowed to utterly destroy what the other developed. If a defect is found, then time is granted to modify the affected creation to strengthen it.

Darwin was right about the Theory of Evolution, what he didn't know is there are spirit teams subtlety influencing modifications to DNA to achieve their desired result. Each group has a plan and sometimes they work in concert and at other periods they are in competition. No matter what, their work always follows Divine Will.

Positive Competition Creates Diversity

Disparate teams working for an overall goal, but with freedom of action to advance to their target, while in a friendly rivalry with others create a myriad of ways to reach a common destination. The genius of the Supreme Intelligence has created a machine to never fail to reach whatever is desired; and to arrive at the goal via the optimally efficient and beautiful path.

Zabdiel explains how unity of purpose, orders from on high, facilitate diversity in execution and results:

"And now I must tell you something which I have hinted already, and which you may find difficult of acceptance. All these main principles, even when diverse in action, are planned in spheres higher than my own by high and powerful Princes who hold their commission secure under others still, who hold theirs from others above them.

I use the word 'diverse' in preference to 'antagonistic,' for among those High Ones antagonism does not find a place, but diversity of quality in wisdom does, and is the cause of the wonderful diversity in nature as it works out in its procession from those higher heavens outward through the lower spheres into that what is visible to you on earth."[178]

We, in our current time on earth, believe wholly in science without spirituality. Science is correct, there are natural laws, there are mathematical models of how the universe operates, and yes there is evolution. Yet, behind all of it, is a foundation of Divine Laws upon all that we see, hear, and touch is based upon. While species compete and fight with each other, there are spiritual teams that sit above, determining when a branch of a family tree should be allowed to fall or to impose a slight transformation to carry on the experiment.

The Spirituality guides the earth and we are here for a purpose. We are part of a larger plan. We live on a planet made for us, so we can acquire the wisdom we so sorely need. There are spirit teams who plan our lives and evolution, just like the teams which plan the arc of all vegetation on earth.

The central lesson for attempting to read between the lines for any prophecy of the future, is that our transit from present to beyond is always dynamic. Hence, while the target could remain the same, the path is influenced by multiple factors and by many departments in heaven, and as such, we must be ready for events to not unfold as first presented, but to come in mysterious ways. Through it all we need to retain our faith that the journey will end up at the selected location.

Analyze what Zabdiel communicates to us about our globe:

"And yet, when you consider the stars of different size and complement, and the waters of the sea, naturally still but by the motion of the earth and the gravitation of bodies at a distance allowed to have no rest; and then the more rarified atmosphere which, also responding to the pulls and pushes of the forces which impinge upon the earth, whips into motion the heavier liquid; and all the diversity of form and color of grass and plant and tree and flower and insect life, and life more evolved, the birds and animals, and of the continuous movement among

218

them all; and the way in which they are permitted one to prey upon another, and yet not to annihilate wholly, but every species must run its race before it pass away – all this and more; then will you not, my ward and friend, confess that God is indeed most wonderful in the manner of His working, and that the wonder justifies most fully the measures He has permitted His higher servants to adopt and use, and the manner also of their using?"[179]

The spirit realm works according to the set of rules laid done by God, while we think that He works in incomprehensible ways, He really doesn't. He works in ways which allows us free-will. Not perfect freedom to perform dangerous acts of destruction on a cosmic level, but on a level suited to maintain our interest and self-satisfaction. On a level which entices us to want more and more responsibility. To plant the seed within each person the desire to complete our training, on earth, on other worlds, on multiple levels of heaven, so we may take part in the excitement of creation. Creation of beautiful objects, tangible living things that reflect back on us the love that we gave in their construction.

Chapter 36 – The Future of Science

There is an interesting section of Book Two of *The Highlands of Heaven* on the topic of science. Zabdiel, the high spirit, discussed the cyclical nature of science. He communicated the following:

> "Science, as history, repeats itself, but never in exact duplicate. Broad principles govern, from time to time, the search for knowledge, and are succeeded by others in their turn which, having served, then also fall behind into a secondary place in order that other principles may receive the more concentrated and undivided attention of the race. But from time to time, as the ages go by, these principles return again – not in the same order of sequence – to receive the attention of a new race. And so the march of human progress goes on."[180]

While history is thought of repeating, due to the constancy of human nature, our greed, our thirst for domination, our hubris, science is generally seen as a line. A line that starts out on an almost imperceptible upward slope, from the first discovery of fire, then in the Renaissance begins to increase in altitude, with greater upswing beginning in the 17th century to the hockey stick slope of today.

The spirit Zabdiel, tells the Rev. G Vale Owen, that:

> "Items of discovery also are lost and found anew, often in other than their original guise, and with some strange features added, and other old features lacking."[181]

When one thinks back on the knowledge lost during the Dark Ages, Zabdiel's thesis that science flows in a cycle has some strong evidence supporting it. But if one looks at the world, where India and China, for instance, didn't experience a great social disintegration, scientific discoveries didn't regress.

But, this isn't what Zabdiel meant at all. To the modern world science means, at the base, following scientific methods, facts must be presented, experiments must be reproducible before any theory can be accepted as fact. In essence, the approach to science inspired by Aristotle and brought further along by the efforts of Roger Bacon. Science today is only what can proved and is purposely devoid of any spiritual essence.

Zabdiel had a different point of view than what we mean as science:

"There was a time when science did not mean what it means to men today: when there was a soul in science, and the outer manifestation in matter was of secondary interest. Thus it was with alchemy, astrology, and even engineering. It was known in those days that the world was ruled from many spheres, and ministered to by countless hosts of servants, acting freely of their own will but within certain strait limits laid down by those of greater power and higher authority. And men in those days studied to find out the different grades and degrees of those spiritual workers, and the manner of their service in the different departments of nature and of human life, and the amount of power exercised by each several class.

And they found out a considerable number of facts, and classified them. But inasmuch as these facts, laws and regulations and conditions were not of the earth sphere but of the spiritual, they were fain to express them in a language apart from that of common use."[182]

Zabdiel speaks about the science of spiritual exploration. The attempt by men and women to decipher the processes of the spirit world and how we on earth are affected by the spirit realm.

In the book *On the Way to the Light*, by the spirit Emmanuel and psychographed by Francisco (Chico) C. Xavier, Emmanuel, in laying out the history of the world and how it is guided by the spirit realm, talks about ancient science:

> "The psychic sciences of today were familiar to the mage priest of the temples.
>
> The fate of the dead and the communicating with them, in addition to the plurality of existences and worlds, were for them problems that had been solved and understood. A study of their pictorial arts is evidence for the truth of our statements. In a large number of frescoes, earthly humans are portrayed accompanied by their spirit double. Their papyri tell us of their advanced knowledge in this area, and through them modern Egyptologists have recognized the fact that initiates knew about the preexistent spirit body that organizes the world of things and forms. Their knowledge regarding the sun's energies with respect to human magnetism was far superior to that of today. Such knowledge gave rise to the procedures for mummification, whose formulas were lost in the indifference and apprehensiveness of other cultures.
>
> Their kings attained the highest degree of initiation and they held all the spiritual powers and all the sacred knowledge in their hands. That is why discarnation triggered the magical concentration of all wills in the sense of surrounding their tomb with veneration and utmost respect. This love did not only manifest in the solemn act of mummification – the ambient of the tombs was also sanctified by a strange magnetism."[183]

Hence, the quest for learning was for the broader picture of the meaning of life. Once the meaning was discovered, then the entire complex process of how our lives are organized and directed were explored. The ancients wished to understand everything they could about the spiritual realm, for they realized that our physical time on earth was but temporary and all of us would return to where we belong. The Druids called it the "Other World".

Zabdiel tells us that the fairy tales of Europe and the stories of magical wonderment coming out of the East were derivatives of knowledge lost from ancient sources. That knowledge from eons ago about the spirit realms has metamorphosed from exact definitions and descriptions into mythical stories and fairy tales. Zabdiel presents us with an example of the lost science:

"There is the story of Jack and the Beanstalk. In the first place, look at the name. Jack is the colloquial for John, and the original John was he who wrote the Book of Revelation. The Beanstalk is an adaptation of Jacob's Ladder, by which the upper, or spiritual, spheres were reached. Those spheres once attained are found to be real countries and regions, with natural scenery, house and treasures. But these are sometimes held by guardians not altogether in amity with the human race who, nevertheless, by boldness and skill of mind are able, by natural quickness of character, to prevent those guardians from regaining possession of these treasures of wisdom and depriving the human race of the right won by the conquest of the bolder sort.

Now, this is picturesque, and is made to assume a quaint and even ludicrous guise by reason of its being handed down from age to age by those who did not understand its deeper import. Had they done so most certainly they had not nicknamed the original as Jack. But, as his customary attire of dress will show you, this came about in an age when things holy and spiritual were had in light esteem by reason of the inability of men to realize the actual presence of spiritual beings among them. So, also, they garbed a demon, and gave him spiked ears and a tail, and for a similar reason – that his actuality to them was mythical. The personality they made of him was mythical indeed."[184]

It is as if the spiritual teachings of the Druids, were handed down from generation to generation, and for each cycle slight transformations were made. Then when the Romans had successfully eradicated the Druids, the stories persisted, but changed according to the influences of the Roman gods and then Christianity.

The Passing of Materialism

The Supreme Intelligence and the governor of our planet, Jesus Christ, has seen worlds and species like ours before. They know well the necessary phases humankind must travel through to reach the goal to progress from a planet of atonement, where we are now, to a planet of regeneration. From a planet where immature souls must pay for past wrongs and learn to live as civilized humans to a world devoid of hate, envy, and wars between nations.

To reach that goal, one aspect is the attainment of the Spiritist doctrine. It has three aspects that work together to provide the scaffolding which encompass the ever growing pool of knowledge.

First is philosophy. *The Spirits' Book* laid the foundation for the relationship between the spirit world and the physical world. The eternal questions of our creation, our creator, our destiny and our soul are all covered within Spiritism.

Second is science. This is the area which certainly would have the most doubters. Rightly so, for nothing has been proven to date. Modern society accepts people's belief in God, but only as a nod to those that need it.

Third is religion. To be clear, Spiritism does not consider itself to be a religion. Spiritism is a Doctrine. A way of life. There are no rites, no churches or temples, and no one who would function as a priest.

There is a moral code. A set of Divine Laws that is implanted into each us so we may instinctively sense the right path. Whereas, our desire for material goods often masks our good intentions, we do realize what we should or should not have done. And this is precisely the basis for our struggle on earth.

Once we are able to follow the road of love, charity, and selflessness we shall leave this period of our education and begin the next.

Thus, the culture of materialism, which denies all but what we can see and touch and possess is due to be modified over time.

Modern science, an example of the absolute materialistic purity demanded by our times, needs to balance physical experiments with spiritual. Zabdiel tells us what will occur:

"Thus, in other guise outwardly, but inwardly more akin, the broad principle which governed the Egyptian astrologers, and the wisdom which Moses learned and used to such effect, is returning today to lift men up a little higher and to put a meaning into that dead materialism of the past which, handling things produced of the energizing of life – shells, bones and fossil stones – denied the Author of Life His place in life's grand arena. It spoke of the orderly working of natural law – and denied the One Source of all order and all working. It spoke of beauty – and forgot that beauty is not unless the spirit of man perceives it, and that spirit is because He Who is Spirit is forever."[185]

Hence, we see and study the object, but never acknowledge the force behind the object. We refuse to notice that nothing is created or persisted without the will of the Spirituality. Yes, there are natural laws which we can interpolate, but there is a will and a meaning behind each, and we spend no effort in deciphering the background for creation.

Zabdiel tells us that the spirit world is not idle, that they are pushing us toward the goal of cementing science and spirituality:

"We are watching, and we are guiding as we may and opportunity is given us. If men respond to our prompting there is an age to come more full of light and the beauty of love and life than that just passing away. And I think they will respond, for the new is better than the old, and from behind us we feel the pressing of those of higher wisdom and power as we look earthward. And so we do what we are impressed is their intention and desire."[186]

According to Zabdiel, progress is being made. Zabdiel communicated this message to G. Vale Owen on Friday, November 21, 1913, although the books weren't published until the 1920s.

The same message was later delivered to Francisco (Chico) C. Xavier, by the spirit author Andre Luiz, in the book *In the Realms of Mediumship*, published in 1955. I have previously referenced a quote from that book in Chapter 27 explaining how we are all uniquely tagged and that someday scientists working on expanding our knowledge are fulfilling the plan to discover other planes, dimensions, and universes.

In essence, Emmanuel is telling us, that no matter what a scientist believes as regards to a higher power, he or she is working toward the day, when the existence of the spirit world can't be doubted. Which, *The Spirits Book*, by Allan Kardec, tells us will occur one day.

Our world is on a preplanned flight path, it may take longer than planned, due to our obstinacy, but we shall arrive at the destination. Science and spirituality will be coupled, along with philosophy, and out of that shall emerge a better world. A world where the terrors and uncertainties of past existences are left far behind.

Chapter 37 – The Spirit World Knows What is and What Will Happen to You

The spirit realm is always near, even when your guardian angel may be millions of miles away. They are continually informed of your actions, what you said to others, your thoughts, your feelings. Everything about you is exposed. Your future too.

Zabdiel reveals the extent of spiritual surveillance in Book Two of the book *The Life Beyond the Veil* called *The Highlands of Heaven*. He tells the Rev. G. Vale Owen how the different levels of spiritual spheres track and interact with us:

"Moreover, friend, it is a good thing and a helpful to bear in mind our presence at all times; for we are near, and that in ways both many and various. When we are personally near at hand we are able to impress you with helpful thoughts and intuitions, and to order events that your work may be facilitated and your way more clear than otherwise it would appear to you.

When in person we are in our own spheres, we still have means whereby we are informed not alone of what has happened in and around you, but also what is about to happen, if the composition of circumstances pursue its normal course."[187]

Read the last part of the last sentence once again, let it sink in that the spirit world knows our future: "but also what is about to happen, if the composition of circumstances pursue its normal course." We are told the future is known, but not one hundred percent accurate at any given time.

Why is that? Because we have been given free-will, we still can make choices that alter the sequence of events. Once events deviate from the planned path, a new future is formulated and that becomes our destiny. Our lives are predetermined, but preset with required course changes to fit the environment and choices we have made.

Dates are Still Hard to Pin Down

While the episodes we must travel through are predetermined, the exact timing is not. Variables can change causing the needed factors to not be aligned. Hence, an event should have occurred may have to be put off, or even cancelled. It all depends.

Therefore, when people expect specific dates from spirits, they are unable to answer with confidence. Instead, they try to anchor an event with another event. This plus the added factor that time is different, or actually non-existent in the spirit realm, makes the job of pinning down a time on earth extremely problematic.

As an example of the complexity of referencing time on earth to the spirit world, there is an interesting segment from a book, *A Wanderer in the Spirit Lands*, by the spirit Franchezzo. The medium who transcribed the book was A. Farnese. The book was published in 1896. My Spiritist friend in Brazil, Geraldo Goulart, sent me the PDF.

The spirit Franchezzo asked his spirit mentor how long a task would take him to finish. He wanted to know the length of time in relation to earth time. This is what he was told:

"No, it will last but a short time—two or three weeks of earth time—for behold as I shadow it forth to you I see following it fast the image of your returning spirit, showing that the two events are not separated by a wide interval. In the spirit world where time is not reckoned by days or weeks or counted by hours, we judge of how long an event will take to accomplish or when an occurrence will happen by seeing how near or how far away they appear, and also by observing whether the shadow cast by the coming event touches the earth or is yet

228

distant from it—we then try to judge as nearly as possible of what will be its corresponding time as measured by earthly standards. Even the wisest of us may not always be able to do this with perfect correctness; thus it is as well for those who communicate with friends on earth not to give an exact date for foreseen events, since many things may intervene to delay it and thus make the date incorrect. An event may be shown very near, yet instead of continuing to travel to the mortal at the same speed it may be delayed or held in suspense, and sometimes even turned aside altogether by a stronger power than the one which has set it in motion."[188]

I haven't seen a better explanation of the difficulty of dating events to earth time than the one above. Imagine living in a world where time doesn't move forward, only change of status. In other words, things do happen, people learn, people meet new friends, and people go on missions to earth; but the clock doesn't move forward. It doesn't move because time doesn't advance, plants don't decay, houses don't fall down over time, and bridges don't rust. Objects are altered when a spirit wills them to change. Not because years have passed.

Then, you toss in that a spirit must determine the current approximate time on earth, at the moment someone is asking for a future date, the event must be correlated with a future event that may or may not occur, which then must be translated into another time and date on earth. One then begins to understand the complexity of supplying an answer, that we on earth think should be relatively easy.

Different Levels of Predetermination

Spiritist recognize that we are put on earth to travel through a predetermined set of trials. We also have free will in how we chose and react to these trials. While at the same time, the spirit world is busy planning the forward motion of our planet.

The spirit realm has set many souls on the earth to perform vital tasks, missions with a purpose to advance our society. The complexity of planning is beyond our imagination. Try and visualize the number of factors that goes into just one life, not to mention the order of magnitude variables when you add in intersections with other lives.

There is a small hint of the stratification of complexity when it comes to different types of spirit reincarnating.

In the book, *In the Greater World*, psychographed by Francisco C. Xavier, the spirit Andre Luiz, encounters his grandfather in a low spiritual plane, in the Lower Zone. He seeks to help his grandfather and realizes that a new life is required to help repair the psychic damage that has been wrought by the grandfather's past actions.

Andre is told that his grandfather will be reincarnated, and Andre asks if he can count on help from his spirit friends. He is told:

> "Of course. Since it will be a reincarnation merely for reparatory activities and no involvement in communal interests, our personal cooperation can be more decisive and immediate. There are many benefactors in this area who provide for a large number of reincarnations in regenerative circles. Let's see if we can examine our brother's future situation."[189]

Andre's grandfather will be reborn into extreme poverty so he can experience hard work in order to "reeducate his aspirations".

I believe there are two salient points. The first is the reference to "involvement in communal interests". This implies that whenever anyone interconnects with an incarnated spirit who has been sent with a purpose, the ramifications of that person's physical life must be analyzed at a higher or more detailed level.

Second, is that for anyone who is planned to enter society at its fringes or at the unseen working class stage, the planning is less centralized. Probably, the number of factors and events are not as laid out in detail or possibly less precise in execution, since a greater amount of variability is perfectly acceptable. In other words, the confidence interval for successful execution is allowed to be lower.

Room for Error

When accidents occur, then plans must be reformulated, or the damage must be undone in order to maintain the original plan. The spirit world has spun an unbelievably complex web of events, where one act affects another and so on. It is as if each thread in a grand tapestry had its own life and it had to be perfectly fitted with all other threads that touch it, and to those that touch the threads once removed, and so on. The complexity is beyond our capability to manage, but not beyond the Creator of our universe.

There is an example of the spirit world undoing the effect of an accident. It lies with a fascinating near death experience. Michael was a boy who, like boys everywhere, was where he shouldn't have been. Michael was climbing on a limestone cliff on a frozen day, when part of the boulder he was hanging onto suddenly broke free. He and the large rock both fell, with the boulder landing on top of him. According to Michael's recollection, the stone weighed 400-500 pounds. He felt that he left his body and seeing himself, he knew he was dead. Next Michael encounters a spirit guide:

"He told me this was an accident and I <could> go back, IF I wanted. I told him by my thoughts there was no way to make that body work. It was squashed flat. He basically told me that he could make it work again. Did I want to go back? I wanted to know my options. What would happen if I chose to go back and what would happen if I didn't. No sooner did I think these thoughts and BOOM, I was hit with a package of images. It showed in brief what would happen if I didn't go back. I saw my sister get into alcohol and drugs and her life spin out of control ... BECAUSE I wasn't there. I saw my Dad commit suicide because of my death shortly after my mom divorced him over the matter of my death. I saw my paternal grandfather wither away and die, his heart broken over my death and my dad's suicide. There were twin blows that destroyed all the joy he had left in life. The effects went on and on, my mom was sad and heart broken the rest of her life and so very lonely ... And I saw a parade of faces of people I would never meet and whose lives I would have impacted and whose lives would have impacted mine but now I would never know any of them

231

and they would never know me. The man in the white robe had me with my sister. I've always loved my little sister and for her alone I would have chosen to come back but seeing all that pain it would cause everyone else ... mom, dad, grandparents, friends, cousins, aunts, uncles ... man I HAD to go back." [190]

Michael's spirit guide, or guardian angel as many call them, was right there in an instant. People who have had NDE's recognize that we live close to the spirit world. They are all around us, watching, guiding and trying to lead us to become better souls. But for most of us, the thought that spirits, or worse ghosts, inhabit the same space is a primitive notion and should be discarded, otherwise we would demonstrate to the world our ignorance and naivety. What if, these uncivilized people, who lived closer to nature and by no choice of their own, possessed little material goods, detected a truth about our sphere and the spirit realm that we have lost? Could we, who must be presented with absolute proof of everything, be missing something important, right before our eyes?

An alternative future was shown to Michael. How could this be? Allan Kardec, in his *The Spirits Book*, describes the power of a high spirit. He likens it to us, here on earth, walking through a trail in a canyon, not knowing what the next bend will look like. Whereas, the spirit, sitting on the mountain top, sees our path, where it will lead and other paths that may be offered to us. Still, this is easy to say, but how could this be in practice? What type of instantaneous mathematical calculations of probability, combined with moving pictures of those possibilities must be processed to present in life-like simulation a series of future options? Only the presence of a computing apparatus so complex as to make our super computers seem like simple calculators can explain what Michael saw.

Next, Michael was shown what would happen if he chose to return to his physical body:

"Then came a second package of images, those of what would happen IF I went back. I skipped over the obvious. Dad DIDN'T commit suicide. My sister turned out Ok. Mom ended up happy. My grandfather went on to beam with pride over his first grandson to attend a university. My grandfather was a legal immigrant from Italy who never made it past the 4th grade and he treasured education beyond EVERYTHING. He crowed like a proud rooster when his kids graduated from high school and I became the first of his grandkids to attend a prestigious university. But what I focused on in this second package was what I would pay as a price for going back. I knew that I would walk again, that all I had lost would be restored but only temporarily. In my later life, perhaps 10 to 15 years after the accident, I would suffer pain, extreme pain and it would affect me the rest of my life.

I chose to come back. He smiled, as if he KNEW I would pick the harder path because of how I felt for my family and friends. There was a snap and a pop and I was back in my body. It was FILLED with crackling electricity like sounds and feelings. I had no breath, no air and this huge rock was choking off all air. I grabbed the small end of the tear near my nose with my one free left hand (my right arm was pinned under the rock) and rolled the thing off me like it was made of paper mache`."[191]

Michael's perispirit, the connection we have from our spirit to our physical bodies, was re-attached to his broken body. From the second option presented, one can see how positive influences have far-reaching and significant effects on other people's lives. We should never underestimate our power to help. While things may appear to us to be small and unimportant, one never knows how our action could be translated into helping or harming another person's life and the relations of that person.

Michael was next transported to the hospital, where he experienced his second phase of his NDE:

"The next thing I know I'm back in the operating room where the surgeon is working frantically to save my life and as he works at massaging my heart I found myself drifting away and the further I drifted the darker the room got and the further away his voice sounded, Found myself well above the operating theater where I should have been on a floor above that room or outside looking on a roof, but I wasn't. Instead I was floating in the entrance to a tunnel or vortex. I was sucked into it and then was when my adventure REALLY began.

I ended up with a life review, and was escorted around "the other side" by a being who was my guardian angel/teacher whom I came to call "professor" but he had an incredible sense of humor. I say "he" with tongue in cheek because "he" was neither a he or a she."[192]

Michael suffered an accident, a true random event, the Spirituality determine that it could repair the damage done and set the train of future events back on the right track. Therefore, they used their considerable power to heal Michael; to bring him back to the state of health before a large rock fell on top of him.

State of Watchfulness

Michael's guardian angel came to him almost immediately after the accident. Zabdiel tells us that we are never out of sight:

"Thus preserving contact with you, we maintain and ensure our guardianship that it be continuous and unceasing, and our watchfulness that it shall in nowise fail on your behalf. For here, and through the spheres between us and you, are contrivances by which intelligence is sent on from one sphere to those beyond and, when necessity require it, we enjoin others to carry out some mission to you, or, if the occasion so requires, we come to earth ourselves, as I have done at this time."[193]

Not only is a spirit able to come to his or her assigned student on our physical plane, but Zabdiel also speaks of other methods of guiding us remotely:

"But further still, and in addition to this, we are able each to come in contact with his own charge direct in certain ways, and to influence events from our own place. Thus you will understand that the whole economy of the Creator, through its manifold spheres of light, is unified in action and correlated. So that no part is but influenced by all those other parts, and what

234

you do on earth not only registered in the heavens, but has effect on our minds and thoughts, and so on our lives."[194]

Everything is connected, everything flows from thought, while we may think we are unable to receive feelings and ideas from others, we certainly do. Some of us are more affected than others, but deep within our frame of mind alters through the radiant power of others around us, and from afar.

Our actions, our inner most feelings has force as well. For as others send out waves that penetrate us, we do the same. Spirits pick up the signals that pour forth from our mind, and spirits connected to us pay attention to our changing states. Zabdiel alerts us of the importance of controlling ourselves, our thoughts:

"Be, therefore, of very careful mind and will; for your doing in thought and your doings in word and your doings in act are all of great import, not alone to those you see and touch around you, but also to those around you unseen and untouched by you, but who see and touch you constantly and often. Not these alone, but those who go about their business in their own spheres are so affected. It is so in my own, I know, and how much higher I do not hazard to say. But, were you to ask me I would reply that your doings are multiplied by transmission through the spheres of light by seventy times seven; and that no end is found to their journey within the ken of man or angel. For I little doubt, if that at all, they find out at last the very Heart of God.

Be ye, therefore, perfect, because your Father Who is in the Heaven of the Heavens is perfect; and no imperfect thing can find acceptance and approval to enter where He is in His awful Beauty."[195]

Zabdiel has laid out our mission on earth in no uncertain terms. We must better ourselves and rid our minds of harmful emotions and thoughts. Let no one think this isn't a tremendously difficult task, for everything around us conspires to stop us from making progress. Like an addict who is surrounded by others of the same addiction, who is constantly reinforced to stay stoned with the crowd, because the mob can't conceive of any alternate lifestyle. To pull away from the group takes enormous effort and discipline.

Starting with small baby steps is the correct process. The spirit world doesn't demand a drastic alteration overnight, but a little progress, forward motion in the path to love and light is appreciated. In fact, when the desire of a person, who fervently wishes to improve their spirituality is detected, the spirit realm reaches out and assists. Help is always around the corner. One just has to commence trying.

Chapter 38 - Spirits Tell Us the Hardest Spiritual Battle is Beginning - Fighting Materialism in the West

A new stage, a new battle is forming – it is one that will change our culture and have ramifications to our society. At the end of a message from the spirit Kathleen to the Rev. G Vale Owen on November 17, 1917, concerning the difficulties of reaching out to us on earth, Kathleen tells him of the coming challenge:

> "The time is well-nigh here, and much that is helpful may be looked for and expected. For we have seen that the hardest battle before us is to conquer the materialism of the West, and we rejoice in a hard fight, as you do, and moreover we do not weary so soon."[196]

The spirit realm sent this message in 1917, a time that we do not see as an overwhelming consumerist culture such as ours. This is because from our vantage point - the twenty-four hour per day exhortations to buy, borrow, spend whatever it takes for that one more item wasn't present. The technology to bombard commercial propaganda into every aspect of our lives wasn't yet developed.

The spirit world has a different point of view; they look at us over centuries. They have seen the corruption of the Roman Empire, the intellectual darkness of the Middle Ages and the lapse into superstitions. Their plan has and continues to be to promote technological advances and spiritual development for the world. They utilized western civilization to make a great leap in technology which effected the entire planet.

Now they are trying to swing the pendulum back to a balance between materialism and spiritualism. They recognize that to place one completely over the other creates disharmony.

For people to be able to hear the voice of higher spirits we must open our hearts and ears. Kathleen points this out when she tells G. Vale Owen:

"It is easier to speak to a Hindu than to you, because he gives more entrance to spiritual matters than you do. To you here in the West the science of organic things and inorganic things – as you suppose them to be, and wrongly – the things of substance and also the science of exterior organization, which is the business of your state politic, are the things which have seemed of more urgency. And that work you have done very well, and it was a necessary work to do. It was necessary also that your greater efforts be concentrated on that aspect of the world's affairs. But now the thing is almost complete, so far as this present age is concerned, and we await your turning your mind into a higher channel upward towards the spirit-life." [197]

Hence, a force unseen to us, is moving the West and other countries to a different axis. One where buying the latest fashion is not the primary goal … spiritual reflection and maintenance of love and harmony between all is prime.

We may not see how this transition will occur: but it will. The spirit Emmanuel, dictated the book *On the Way to the Light*, to Francisco C. Xavier, which details how the spirit realm, under the leadership of Jesus has guided the destiny of Earth since the beginning of its formation, reveals the extent of the meticulous planning of our progress by our undetected superiors.

Spiritism was introduced in the 1850's to commence the transition back from an age of material dominance to one more balanced. Allan Kardec, the codifier of Spiritism, under the guidance of The Spirit of Truth, brought to us what was promised by Jesus – new knowledge of our true life as an immortal spirit and comfort about our role on earth.

In essence, Spiritism lays out the reason we are here on earth and what is our destiny. We are here to learn to become civilized spirits – to utilize our vast potential power for good. All of the chaos and hardships on earth are the direct result of past wrongs we have committed. The spirit world expends great effort to show us the effects of those hurtful and wrongful past deeds.

Therefore, as you detect more discussions in the WebSphere about the messages of near death experiences, visions, communications from high spirits, know that these are not random events, but planned by a higher power to slowly prepare us to refocus our culture on what is important.

Chapter 39 – The Future of Womanhood – A Message from the Spirit World

The spirit Arnel, sent a message to the Rev. G Vale Owen in 1919 about the future of womanhood. In the early 1900's the woman's suffragette movement was in full stride; in England there were arrests and hunger strikes by women demanding the right to vote. The communication is remarkable because it foretells where the movement will be going, the phases, and the results. In summary, women will lead in the future, but not as men lead, but at a higher level of caring and kindness. Essentially, what we are told is that the world will be governed by love, not by force.

The message, dated Monday, March 24, 1919, starts thusly:

"Write what we give you and do not stay to question it. When the whole is written then read it whole and judge our message whole and not in part. I say this to you, my son, because we have that to give you which will not conform to the mind of many. Write it down notwithstanding, for we have to say what we say; and there you have it in brief."[198]

In the entire collection of the four books that make up the compilation of the *Life Beyond the Veil*, I have not read a similar declaration. This message is almost at the end of Book Four – The Battalions of Heaven. The content of the message begins:

"Until the time of the coming of Christ in Jesus of Galilee evolution had proceeded on the lines of dominance of intellect and force of a man's right arm. That was the masculine element

240

in the progress of the race of mankind. Where other notions prevailed these were exceptional to the general trend of evolution, like small runnels tributary to the main stream. We speak now of the general and not of the particular.

Jesus came and into the maelstrom of human activity He threw His flask of oil. He explained to those who would listen to Him that ultimate victory was not to the strong, either of arm or of intellect, but that the meek shall inherit the earth – inherit, not take it. You note that He spoke of the future.

Men took up His teaching and acknowledged it to be both beautiful and true, if practicable. For two millennia nigh they have been striving to blend the two together; to graft the meekness on to the dominance, to mix the two together in affairs national, international, social and other. The two have failed to blend together; so much so that some have said that Christianity is not possible in public affairs. They are wrong in their conclusion. The teaching of Christ is the only durable and perpetual element in the life of earth.

So men, therefore, have confessed that violence and force have been proven fallacious. Their remedy hereto has been to retain the fallacious element and to try to soften it with the softer element of meekness. They have endeavored to retain to the man in his dominance, while trying to soften that dominance with the feminine element of meekness. The resultant is failure. Do you see the inference, my son? The one course left is the abjuration of the fallacious element and the gradual emergence into the premier place in the world's life of the element of meekness, which is feminine."[199]

Arnel, on behalf of the spirit world, speaks about all of the progressive movements that have ended in violence and bloodshed. From the mass purges of the old communist Soviet Union to the concentration camps of North Korea and the prisons in Cuba, which house dissidents, who only wish a voice in running their country.

Even the lighter forms of socialism, turn into static regimes,

241

incapable of providing sustainable employment in the face of mountains of rules and regulations, all directed by a hidden bureaucracy, which knows no master but its own endless quest to mandate even the smallest detail of daily life for millions of people.

Each form of government eventually evolves into a quest to sustain their dominance over an increasingly restive populace. When power has such great rewards, men will find a way to retain their advantages for as long as possible … no matter the consequences for their constituents or the nation.

Arnel next begins describes the future:

"The past of the world has been man's past; the future of the world will be woman's future. The woman has felt this stirring within her as a new thing to be brought forth for the salvation of her sex. That is an unworthy thought, because partial, and therefore inadequate. When a woman brought forth a Savior aforetime He came as a Savior not of a sex but of the whole human race. Such will be the outcome of woman's present throes."[200]

The spirit world is speaking about women, who in their dedication to be free of any dominance, completely reject all men. We are being told that all of mankind needs the influence of women, not just other women.

Now comes the part, which I believe, describes the current state of the women's movement … a period where women desire to be not only on par with men, but to take on their baser attributes as well.

"Feeling this new thing stirring within she has set herself about preparing for her offspring. She has been making his clothes. I say "his" clothes, for the garments she has been making are for a man-child. For them she has gone to the same mart where men buy and sell their wares and has challenged them in barter. 'We can do your work,' says she. But she does not understand that she is putting new wine into old wineskins thus. Well, they both shall perish together. Meantime woman must learn her lesson as man has had to do. Man has learned where failure lies, yet does not know where to turn for success. With one hand he holds fast to the past; the other he holds out to the future. But that hand is empty yet, and no one has taken hold, nor will do so until he let go of the past with the other.

The woman now is doing as he did; she is seeking to join with him in his dominance of affairs. Her future lies not that way. Woman shall not rule the race, neither solely nor with man conjointly. She shall guide the race hereafter, not rule it."[201]

No better description could be written of the current state of affairs in the beginnings of the 21st century, than that what was written almost one hundred years ago. In women's quest for equality and justice they are pursuing absolute parity with men in all things … such as demanding outrageous pay as CEO's, squeezing employees to increase the price of their stock, stabbing others in the back on their way to the top. All of the grosser attributes of an animal who only wishes to take and dominate others. This is what Arnel means when he says putting new wine into old wineskins.

If the equality of women means they will be just as corrupt, petty, and mean as the men at the top, then all of this means is that we will have a greater pool of selfish and driven people to pick from. Whereas, respect and equal rights for all is a noble goal, the push for a different approach to regulating our organizations, running global and small businesses, and outreach to communities is of vital importance to altering our society to improve its moral quotient.

A great percentage of men and women realize the moral sacrifice to climb the organizational ladder. While, some accomplish it in an honorable manner, this is a rarity. One would hope that women would lead the way to retain one's humanity while in possession of great responsibility, so decent and caring men and women could influence the levers of power for the good of all, not just the self-selected few.

243

The spirit realm is telling us to realize there is a better way and that is for women to retain their caring and kindness, that they demonstrate to their families and loved ones, to carry that forward to guiding organizations and society as a whole.

Arnel ends his message with these closing words:

"My son, it is very difficult, as I find it, to make in any way clear to you what this future leading of the woman shall be. For all such leading hereto among you has a dual content in the human mind, namely, the governing and the governed, the dominant and the subservient. This duality has no place in the future leading. Even this word 'leading' has a sense of one company going on before the other company following after, and that of compulsion. That is not the leading we have been shown as that which awaits the human race.

Let me put it in this wise. It is manifest in the Christ of Jesus. In Him you see all the excellences of the man without their accompaniment of traits unlovable and unlovely. And in Him also blended you see all the sweetness of the woman without the weakness. So in the future shall the two, the man and the woman become, not two sexes, however perfectly assimilated the one to the other, but two aspects merely of one sex sole.

Where force rules the word is 'I lead; you follow.' Where love rules there is no word needed, but heart beats out to heart the message, 'We go on together, beloved.'"[202]

When will we reach this wonderful plateau? Arnel tells us that the change shall not come suddenly but slowly as a glacier moves it weight down from the mountain to the ocean.

As with other prophecies in the chapters in this section of the future and the possibilities of the future, the road shall be long. Most likely longer than our span of human vision takes us. The exact path will not be straight or smooth … but it will lead to the objective eventually.

At some time in the future the earth will become a fair and impartial sphere, where all men and women are respected. Where those in positions of authority, weld their baton lightly and only in the interest of love and justice.

—————————— ·◆· ·◆· ——————————→

Chapter 40 – The Spiral Course of Progress – from Atlantis to the Future of Earth

The spirit Arnel talked to the Rev. G Vale Owen on Friday, March 15th, 1918, about the spiral path of human civilization. How the spiral of progress moved as the sun's meridian hit the earth, over the span of centuries. He mentioned the technological progress of Atlantis and Lemuria and the subsequent downfall as representative of the cycle of human achievement.

First, Arnel spoke about the principal of the spiral which is set in motion by the Will of God. That progress doesn't come in straight lines but in an ascending upward movement, with different velocities to maximize the perfection of what is being created. He gives us an example:

"The first motion of sensation is seen in the plant, and there you see clearly illustrated the spiral principle. The bean climbs spirally, as do other climbing plants, some more explicitly and others less perfectly. The veins of the trees also tend to incline from the perpendicular as they traverse the trunk in its length. The plants which climb by tendrils support themselves by a spiral hook. Seeds float afield, or fall to the ground, in a similar curve. All these are consequent on the principle, active as the vibrations proceed through the sun and reach the plant life on earth. These reproduce in miniature this motion along the heavens of space, and, in themselves, mimic the orbits of the constellations."[203]

Therefore the spiral is a central concept in the creation and evolution of mineral, vegetable, and animal life. It goes even further; we learn in spirals as do the entire human race.

"On the other hand, where man is concerned, the principle is seen operative most in those matters where his individuality is less apparent than is the general guiding Mind of his race. Thus: civilization proceeds from east to west, from time to time encircling the earth. It obeys the lead of earth's Central Sun. But the sun's meridian does not travel in a right line along the equator, but inclines, now to north, now to south, as earth leans one way or other. This motion of earth is a remnant of the ancient rule, and shows earth's origin from the nebular state, wherein the same spiral movement, obtains. Even so, the path of civilization, encircling earth, never crosses over the same region twice in succession. By the time the civilizing wave reaches the point of longitude which marks its former revolution earth has inclined itself at its poles, the north southward and the south northward, some degrees. As the path of the impact of the sun's radiation upon the earth is thus varied, so also is the path of the onward march of civilization, which, by the way, is but another way of saying 'revelation.' If you think of the location of Lemuria and Atlantis, and their successors in the progress of human experience, you will see my meaning."[204]

In Spiritist literature there is also mention of the Atlantis and Lemuria civilizations. I have read where Atlantis reached an advanced stats of technological understanding. Unfortunately, the level of technology did not meet the level of spiritual progress; therefore, the spirit realm reset the base of knowledge for the human race.

A similar occurrence, but on a smaller scale, happened to Rome. Whereby, the institutions of Rome were stellar in their organization and effectiveness, Roman society was bent on conquest and enslaving populations, not enlightening them. Therefore the collective citizenry of Rome were sent back to the fields to toil in the Dark Ages, to find their connection with nature and to set the stage for a spiritual re-awakening.

If we march back from where Arnel talked about the wave of civilization, from Europe in the north, then to the Mediterranean, owned by Rome, backwards in time to Mesopotamia, India, China, and Egypt. One can detect a slight northwards step to the dominate civilization. Hence, if one takes India, Egypt, and China as the lowest point in our ancient history – then Atlantis and Lemuria were probably located closer to the equator.

Arnel explains that each civilization reached an apogee and then could go no further, due to their lack of spiritual advancement. He supplies an example:

"The utilization of the molecules of ether for the service of mankind is illustrative of this. You will note that the present advanced state of this branch of science was worked up to very gradually. We will start with the process of combustion by which gas was liberated, heat was generated, and, from this heat, steam was produced. This was followed by the application of this same gas, but discarding the intervening medium of steam. Then a finer system of etheric vibrations was pressed into service, and electricity now is fast supplanting steam. But another step forward has been taken, and what you call wireless waves are beginning to be found more potent still.

Now, all this has been done before, in varying degrees of perfection, by scientists of those long ago civilizations, which have to you become almost a mythical memory."[205]

Historians strive to explain the bitter downfall of the Roman civilization and all of the learning that was lost with it. In our modern world, we think we are immune to such a fate. We have great industry, computers, and a world-wide web connecting everyone on the planet.

Arnel even foresees the overall installation and use of electricity and the utilization of radio waves for more than communication. And yet, Arnel tells us, in 1919, that all of this has been done before. Arnel is speaking to us in eons, not merely in thousands of years.

248

What would we find if we ever dug deep enough in the lost continent of Atlantis? What marvels of technology would be unearthed, destroying our conceit that only our level of sophistication could have produced the gas engine, radio, television, and cell phones.

This demonstrates the power of the spirit realm, to take collective humanity of earth to where they must be in order to learn to first become spiritually civilized.

What comes next is truly astonishing:

"The next step is also seen ahead. It is the substitution of mental waves for the etheric waves. This also some few of the highest and most progressed of those your forerunners compassed in their science. They were not allowed to give forth their knowledge to their fellow-men, who were not progressed enough morally to use it aright. Nor will it be given to the present race of men to perfect this as an exact science until they have further progressed in spiritual competency. Otherwise harm would accrue to the race, and not benefit."[206]

Again we are told that we shall only be allowed that which we can morally handle. This was the message in 1919. Then in 1969, men went to the moon.

A Brazilian program, Data Limites, on YouTube, details a prophecy for earth by Francisco (Chico) C. Xavier.[207] Chico spoke about this prophecy to his friends and on a Brazilian television program. He relayed what he was told by the spirit realm to warn mankind. I will summarize:

1969

In 1969 when astronaut's first landed on the moon. The coming meeting of "The Community of Pure Spirits" as promised by Emmanuel, in the book, *On the Way to the Light*, in 1939[208], occurred. This was the third meeting, the first was at the formation of the solar system and the second when Christ came to earth.

They met because they were worried about men traveling to the

249

moon, while our spiritual growth was immature. At a time when the world was on the constant brink of a nuclear war, the Community of Pure Spirits wanted to take the earth back to another dark age to allow time for our collective spiritual maturity to take hold.

Christ interceded and asked for time. It was decided to give the earth fifty years. Hence, if the earth didn't have any nuclear war for fifty years we would be allowed to continue to progress. The end date is July, 2019.

Dark Age

If nuclear war occurred during this time period, the damage would be immense. Besides the nuclear fallout, the earth itself would rise up and pay back for all of the harm done to it over the centuries. The Northern Hemisphere would be devastated. Most land would be uninhabitable and the military of the surviving countries would invade the Southern Hemisphere in order to have arable land. For instance, the US would invade Latin America, as would China and Europe. Brazil itself would be broken up into parts, shared by the occupying powers.

New Age

If the world manages to reach 2019 without nuclear conflict then wonderful events will unfold. Aliens will come to earth and help promote dramatic improvements in medicine and technology. These aliens have been nervously watching earth for some time. They have the capability to transport themselves through great distances.

What has not been known to us is that conflict on our planet sends out destructive negative waves which affect the entire galaxy. Hence, more advanced races are watching our progress.

The aliens are cognizant of the power of the spirit world and they work with the spirit realm in their endeavors. Just like us, the aliens are immortal souls, who reincarnate, perish, and reincarnate again. In fact, some of the aliens may have had a life on earth in human form in the distant past.

The Present

In 1919 Arnel ended his message to G. Vale Owen with this:

"But the present cycle of progress will, in this matter, go beyond that of the cycle last preceding, for at this point in those days they stopped and went no further. Their decline set in, and what they had come by gradually became absorbed into the spiritual spheres, to be conserved there until the next race had been prepared and brought to such a state of perfection as should qualify them to receive it back again with added momentum inspired into it by its guardians during the ages in which it has rested quiescent in their charge. Call the spiritual spheres interior, and the earth sphere external, and you have the same principle of movement reproduced which we have already attached to the atom of ether."[209]

Therefore, we have a choice, we can move forward into a land of technology from aliens and of harnessing mental rays, or we can be forced to repeat a whole grade ... all of humanity. The entire world set back a couple of levels so we may rethink our intransigent stance, that our wants, our selfishness always outweighs love, charity, and fraternity.

Arnel notifies us that our destiny is in our hands. Our collective actions and character determine our future. If we demonstrate responsible government, formulate peaceful solutions between countries, and live to care for our fellow humans, we shall be deemed worthy of graduating to the next level.

The reward for all of us is to become a planet of regeneration. Where there is peace between all nations, people are led by those who have shown superior morality, and the Golden Rule is mainly followed by all races and cultures.

Chapter 41 – Infusing Spirituality into Science

The Spirit realm guides the human race. We are led on an upward spiral trajectory. Great leaps forward, followed by seemingly catastrophic retreats, but which are, in fact, required to build a solid foundation for the next stage of progression.

This has happened to the human race multiple times. The spirit Arnel spoke to us about a great mission to bring more spirituality into science and he mentioned how technological progress has been destroyed before:

> "So we did not destroy your science by cataclysm, as has happened in the past ages of earth not once nor twice. No. For, cramped and limited as it was, it ministered to progress as a whole, and so we held it to that degree in reverence. So we transmuted it by expansion, and are so continuing today."[210]

I have written before how spirits have told us about the fall of Atlantis and Lemuria. In the book *Edgar Cayce On Atlantis*, by his son Edgar Evans Cayce, communications reveal the breakup of Atlantis wasn't just a single event but happened in waves over a long period.

In Edgar Cayce's readings for people, he explored their past lives, in some cases, their past lives during the period of Atlantis was exposed. Edgar Evans Cayce cites readings which mention advanced technology as far back as 50,000 B.C.

There is an instance of a gathering of leaders from different nations to combat the problem of being overrun by animals. Here is one such reading:

"In the period when this became necessary, there was the consciousness raised in the minds of the groups in various portions of the earth, much in the manner as would be illustrated by an all-world broadcast in the present day of a menace in only one particular point, or in many particular points. And the gathering of those that heeded, as would be the scientific minds of the present day, in devising ways and means of doing away with that particular kind of menace.

As to the manner in which these gathered, it was very much as if the Graf [Graf Zeppelin?] were to start to the various lands to pick up representatives, or those who were to gather, or were to cooperate in that effort. And, as this, then, was in that land which has long since lost its identity, except in the inner thought or visions of those that have returned or are returning in the present sphere, the ways and means devised were as those that would alter or change the environs which those beasts needed, or that necessary for their sustenance in the particular portions of the sphere, or earth, that they occupied at the time. And this was administered much in the same way or manner as if there were sent out from various central plants that which is termed in the present the Death Ray, or the super-cosmic ray, that will be found in the next 25 years."[211]

The reading dates the meeting of the Atlantians to have taken place in the year 50,722 B.C. The reading itself was given on February 21, 1933. Approximately twenty-five years later, the microwave and lasers were being actively worked on.

Edgar Evans Cayce dates a second large continent shaking event at around 28,000 B.C. and the final breakup of Atlantis at around 10,000 B.C.[212]

Edgar Cayce wasn't a Spiritist medium, hence I do not know the accuracy of what was revealed as he communed with spirits. I state his readings to present a possibility of what the spirit Arnel referred to when he spoke of resetting human civilization.

What is interesting is the time frame mentioned by Cayce. Certainly, in our present time, we have not detected concrete signs of an advanced civilization, although there have been hints and objects uncovered which are unexplainable.

In our current cycle of history we usually cite the beginning of written history at around 4,000 B.C. And yet, for Arnel to be correct, there must have been much earlier cycles of human development. Therefore, for past advanced civilizations, with technology on a par with ours, as it was in the beginning of the twentieth century - going back fifty thousand years is not an unthinkable starting point. Between that time and the beginning of what we note is the start of civilization, multiple rises and falls could indeed occur.

Humans – 40,000 Years Ago

Books psychographed by the great Spiritist medium Chico Xavier may help with placing previous possible epochs of human history. Reading the books inspired by Andre Luiz, and psychographed by Francisco (Chico) C. Xavier, there are references to interesting information divulged to us during conversations or lectures recorded by the spirit Andre Luiz. In the book, *Liberation*, first published in Portuguese in 1949, Andre tells us of a lecture, about the need to assist spirits in the Lower Zones and the Abyss, in which the following statement is made:

> "We know today that the human spirit, taken as a whole, has had the ability to reason for exactly forty thousand years ... Nonetheless, with the same furious impetus with which Neanderthals killed one another with hatchet blows, humans of modern times - regarded as the glorious era of world powers - exterminate their brothers and sisters with firearms."[213]

This didn't sound right, we have been told that humans have been on earth for around 350,000 to 400,000 years. But then I looked up modern humans in Wikipedia and this is what I discovered:

> "Anatomically modern humans evolved from archaic *Homo*

254

sapiens in the Middle Paleolithic, about 200,000 years ago. The transition to behavioral modernity with the development of symbolic culture, language, and specialized lithic technology happened around 50,000 years ago according to many anthropologists although some suggest a gradual change in behavior over a longer time span."[214]

Hence, our brains must have evolved to a state around 40,000 years ago to where the spirit realm determined was the minimum level of reason. Then I looked up more information:

"Loren Cordain contrasts the anatomical and behavioral perspectives on this question: 'for two million years until ... the agricultural revolution of roughly 10 000 years ago our ancestors were hunter-gatherers, so the adaptive pressures inherent in that environmental niche have exerted a defining influence on human genetic makeup. The portion of our genome that determines basic anatomy and physiology has remained relatively unchanged over the past 40,000 years ... Although anatomically modern humans first appeared perhaps 100,000 years ago, modern human behavior first becomes recognizable in the fossil record of about 50,000 years ago ... between 50,000 and 40,000 years ago their creative and technological innovation increased dramatically ... During this period skeletal robusticity decreased somewhat suggesting that less muscular force was required for daily tasks."[215]

Here is the key sentence, "The portion of our genome that determines basic anatomy and physiology has remained relatively unchanged over the past 40,000 years." A book that was published in 1949, before carbon dating, before DNA sequencing, before computers were anything other than used by governments, pegged the beginning of our ascent into the world of reasoning and increased use of technology in the same time period as our modern genetic science.

One more little piece of evidence that we are being guided along a path. The spirit realm created the conditions so that basic humans could evolve and then, most probably, subtlety modified our DNA to give us that next mental boost. A physical brain which could be powerful enough to connect to our perispirits and process the exchange of information between our spirit and our bodies. Between fifty to forty thousand years ago, one of us started our first reincarnation on earth. Beginning the long climb from primitive to civilized behavior.

Given the span of time described, Edgar Cayce's reading of over fifty thousand years ago may not be too far-fetched. After all, we believe that only hunter gatherers were present on the earth about five thousand years ago, and within seven thousand years we have attained our present level of technology.

Hence, if humans achieved our present state of evolution approximately fifty to forty thousand years ago, there would have been plenty of time for sophisticated civilizations to rise then fall, to rise and fall again.

Current State

The high spirit Arnel who communicated with the Rev. G Vale Owen, who wrote of this account in *Book Four – The Battalions of Heaven*, in 1919. Arnel told G. Vale Owen of a great endeavor to herd humanity to a higher level of spirituality, so that science and its application to destructive possibilities could be tempered by moral judgement to allow humanity to continue progressing, without the need for a step backward.

According to Arnel, this great push forward had been going on for centuries, the objective is to introduce an aspect of spiritual wisdom to the pure intellectual reasoning demanded by science. Arnel describes the process:

"Under our pressure thus applied it expanded until the boundary of the material was reached. But the impetus we had given to this material science could not there be stayed. It gradually pressed outward on its own bounds and began to emerge here and there beyond. So that the sharp line, so arbitrarily drawn between material and spiritual, began to sag and to bulge, and here and there a small breach was made - small at first, enlarging later. But small or large, mark me, no such breach was ever repaired. The dyke once gapped, the steady irresistible pressure, all-encircling without, found inlet and, from that time, a steady stream of spiritual content flowed increasingly into your science of earth, and is today continued."[216]

While it may seem that all scientists adhere to a strict agnostic or atheist creed – since that is the current state of peer group pressure – the truth is different. In a Rice University study by Elaine Howard Ecklund, she found a significant percentage of religious scientists:

"The study also found that 18 percent of scientists attended weekly religious services, compared with 20 percent of the general U.S. population; 15 percent consider themselves very religious (versus 19 percent of the general U.S. population); 13.5 percent read religious texts weekly (compared with 17 percent of the U.S. population); and 19 percent pray several times a day (versus 26 percent of the U.S. population)."[217]

These percentages may not include those who declined to reveal the extent of their spirituality, due to fear of being ostracized for holding significantly different views from the group at large. Or from individuals who don't associate themselves with any organized religious groups but are spiritual persons.

Hence, what Arnel was describing in 1919, which must have taken place at an earlier time, is still having an effect today. Science has not erased God or the spirit realm from all consideration. Nor will it ever, for with wisdom deriving from a faith in a better moral destiny, comes a more certain future, where new devices and discoveries will be utilized for the common good, as opposed to dominance or profit over weaker groups.

The Triple Aspect of Spiritism

The future of science combines and intersects with knowledge about the spirit realm and what it means to us on earth. Spiritism does not ask you to possess blind faith. In fact it discourages it. According to Spiritism, miracles don't occur. All phenomena has an explanation.

Do we have absolute proof that God or spirits exist? As of yet no, but Spiritism tells us that one day it shall occur. For Spiritism is not meant to be a fossilized dogma but an ever-expanding pool of knowledge.

Knowledge that will be brought to us by our scientists and by the spirit world. As we grow morally and technically, more will be presented to us.

Spiritism is a dynamic doctrine. It has three aspects that work together to provide the scaffolding which encompass the ever-growing pool of knowledge. Which I covered in Chapter 36, but will touch upon once again here.

First is philosophy. *The Spirits' Book* laid the foundation for the relationship between the spirit world and the physical world. The eternal questions of our creation, our creator, our destiny and our soul are all covered within Spiritism.

Second is science. Science will someday walk hand in hand with philosophy and science. It will prove the existence of the spirit realm and the plurality of multiple dimensions with intelligent life.

What is not in question is the ground swell of studies about Near Death Experiences (NDE) and the retention of thought after all physical brain activity has ceased. The internet now allows people to compare their stories of premonition, talking with spirits and mediums who have knowledge about personal facts which would be improbable for them to know.

Combine the accumulation of personal accounts which are a mystery and can't be absolutely proven to be false, with the machinations of the spirit world to influence our scientific leaders to expand their horizons into unseen realms – a seed has been planted which will grow.

Thus, while many of us are aware of and comfortable that there is a world beyond our senses, others scoff as nonsense any unexplainable event. At the least doubters must mark these strange occurrences down to one more data point that promotes our feeling that our knowledge is limited and there are many things that are still unfathomable by science.

For now, Spiritism leans on the information provided by mediums throughout the world. Books, such as the ones psychographed by Chico Xavier, are continually being created, with the help of the spirit world. Books which little by little reveal more about the earth, our destiny and the complex workings of the spirit realm which looks over us.

The third leg of the stool is religion. Religion will transform from places of worship to be places of education, assistance, and healing. In the future the basic precepts of the Spiritist Doctrine, such a reincarnation, will be absorbed by the religions of earth.

Eventually, all will realize there is a universal moral code. A set of Divine Laws that is implanted into each us so we may instinctively sense the right path. Whereas, our desire for material goods often masks our good intentions, we eventually realize what we should or should not have done. And this is precisely the basis for our struggle on earth.

Once we are able to follow the road of love, charity, and selflessness we shall leave this period of our education on a planet of atonement and begin the next stage as the earth transforms to a planet of regeneration – a paradise where wars, hate and jealousy are vastly diminished or eradicated.

Chapter 42 – Future of Religion

The future will not only alter our culture and technology, but also philosophy and religion. That which has been set in stone for thousands of years, whether Hindu, Zoroastrian, Islamic, Christian, Buddhism, or any other type of philosophy or religion or sect will be modified. The fact that a spirit world exists will reawaken our spirituality. When we know with certainty that we are immortal spirits under the guidance of the spirit world – Everything will change.

The high spirit Arnel who communicated with the Rev. G Vale Owen, delivered this series of messages in *Book Four – The Battalions of Heaven*, in 1919. In essence, Christianity shall be torn down and rebuilt. Arnel tells us why:

"Some buildings there be badly reared by not very skillful workmen but capable of reconstruction and repair as they stand. Some be so bad they must be broke up and scattered and new material be brought together that the house may be built anew. The only part left is that of the foundations below ground. This latter house is earth's Christ. I say not the Christ, but the Christ of earth's creeds, the dogmatic Christ of Christendom. Such Christ as appears in the accepted Creed of Christendom today is unworthy of Him as He is. That must be pulled down, its material scattered – all but the deep-down foundations. Then new materials will be brought together, and a shrine resplendent and beautiful will rise, a shrine worthy for Him to set His Throne within, worthy to cover His head as He sits within His Throne"[218]

Christ of the loving countenance is true, but so is Christ the leader of all physical and spiritual bands around the earth. Jesus isn't only a figure sitting on His Throne dispensing love and wisdom, He is a dynamic executive organizing tremendous initiatives and motivating His billions of subjects to achieve the goals He sets. He is a Father, a Son, and an Executive.

Everything He does, has a reason. And He doesn't merely channel the power of God to conjure His wishes from thin air. He plans, He gives orders to hierarchies of spirits to attain the goals He sets under their own initiative. He tracks, He analyzes, and He holds his managers accountable to the targets He allocated.

Most important of all, Christ started out just like us. An ignorant spirit, who had to live life after life to learn, to eradicate bad characteristics and attitudes, to finally, after billions of years, reach the level He is at now. And there are spirits at the same level and even higher than Jesus. They too have traveled the same road to purity and greatness. We can too.

Although, the exact majesty of His power and capabilities, and standing in the spirit realm is still a mystery to even those relatively high in the spirit realm.

This is what Spiritism has brought us. This knowledge of our place, of the spirit world around us and how we too can ascend to a spectacular life of love and creation.

Resetting the Image of Christ

Spiritism, the Third Revelation, was the first salvo, which put in motion a reassessment of the relationship of God, Christ, and humankind. And as Jesus becomes thought of in a new light, His ministers, those He sent to earth to spread His message, such as Buddha, Mohammed, Confucius, and Socrates, will also be seen from a different perspective.

Arnel spoke to G. Vale Owen about the difficulty of the transition:

"Much pain is caused to many when they hear their Savior spoken of in terms of seeming irreverence. This is because of their love for Him. I hesitate to say it, my son, yet I will say it, for I am constrained to do so: It were well for them if their knowledge of Him were great as is their love. For much of their devotion is paid to Him through clouds of mist and vapor which are not part of Him but are the result of their own imaginings. However sincere these be they are imaginings still and their effect on the devotions of those who create them is to dilute those devotions until their bulk is much reduced. This worship does reach Him, yes, but there is a fear blended with it which weakens it. It were, therefore, well if these devout ones could cast aside that fear out of their love and could love Him so truly as to be assured that He would not be displeased by them if they would think about Him bravely, albeit with humility, even if they should, in some small details, chance to err. This we do ourselves, yet we do not fear Him, for we know we are not yet competent to understand Him whole, and that, so it be with humility and with good intent, we may search out the truth as it is in Him without disaster or reprimand.

My son, do you this also. And be assured that, as He is of larger majesty than Christendom has ever dreamed of, so is He also far beyond all your dreamings in the perfection of His love."[219]

Hence, starting with Allan Kardec, the codifier of Spiritism, presenting the stark reality of why we are here, to learn to become perfected, to other voices bringing news of the land beyond, all of this shall eventually lay the foundation for the day when science proves the existence of a hidden dimension and religion accepts the facts of our immortality and purpose of repeated incarnations. When all the world internalizes the truth of karma, that every action in our lives has a reaction. This is one of the steps required for earth to become a planet of regeneration.

The Spirit World is Getting Us Ready for the Big Leap

All of this won't happen in a big bang. Like the tide moving slowly up the shore, the spirit world is preparing us for the time of the grand realization.

In the book, *In the Greater World*, by the spirit Andre Luiz, psychographed by Francisco C. Xavier, Andre Luiz documents some of the assistance which is provided for people who are trying to learn and evangelize Spiritism. This is only an example, for there are other lectures and assistance given to those who are on their exploration for greater spiritual knowledge.

Once a person discovers Spiritism, the breadth of its doctrines soon become clear. Instead of a casual relationship one has with going to a local place of worship, where you are able to meditate and recharge your spiritual batteries on a once a week basis, the knowledge that every action we take is judged, that we are surrounded by other spirits, that we have a duty to spread love and our awareness, can make our discovery seem, at times, a heavy burden. The Spirit world recognizes the difficulties of balancing our spiritual lives while living in a materialistically dominated world. Andre Luiz, in the book, *In the Greater World*, is told about the assistance given to Spiritists:

> "Through their diligent efforts in spiritualizing work, they are the future instruments for the endeavors that lie ahead. In spite of the clarity of the rules they live by, they still suffer disharmony and afflictions that threaten their incipient stability. Even so, they aren't left without the assistance they need. In our spheres of action, institutions for restoring their energies open their welcoming doors to them. Freedom from the body during sleep is the direct resource of our manifestations of fraternal support. At first, they receive our influence unconsciously; then their minds are slowly strengthened and they begin recording our concourse in their memory as we give them ideas, suggestions and opinions along with beneficial and redeeming inspirations by means of imprecise recollections."[220]

Andre Luiz is introduced to one such method of aid. His instructor takes him to a lecture given by the spirit Eusebio. Instructor Eusebio presents a lecture to those incarnated souls who have the desire for learning more and becoming active Spiritists, but are daily facing the obstacles we all encounter and still have that element of doubt in the absolute reality of our immortal soul. Andre is told that every person who is able to promote Spiritism is vital. The importance of the training is explained by Andre's companion, "Chance doesn't perform miracles. Any undertaking requires planning, execution and completion. The miracle of changing a physical person into a spiritual person requires a lot of collaboration on our part."[221]

The Lecture for Spiritists

Eusebio begins the lecture by clarifying how his talk will affect each individual at the meeting, "Of course, because the deficiencies of the brain render it incapable of supporting the burden of two lives at the same time, you will not retain a full recollection of this hour upon reentering the corporeal envelope. Nevertheless, the memory of our meeting here will linger in the depths of your being, guiding your higher inclinations toward lofty purposes and opening your intuitive portal so that our fraternal thoughts may assist you."[222]

Eusebio explains to his audience how humanity has arrived at this precise moment. He recounts the sacred reading of the Old Testament by the Jews, who then would go out and fight the Philistines, the reverential praise of the writings of Marcus Aurelius, while at the same time his Roman government ordered the murder of innocents. He closes his point with, "In such a state we have reached the modern era, in which madness is widespread and men and women's mental stability is on the verge of disaster. With an evolved brain and an immature heart, we hone our art of wrecking our spiritual progress."[223]

Stressing the significance of maintaining our energy and increasing our self-enlightenment, Eusebio acknowledges the importance of such activities. But, as his warms to his subject, he notifies his listeners that individuals who strive to focus on themselves in their quest for purification is not good enough. He throws out the challenge, "If you wish to be pioneers of the living faith in the world, from now on, in spite of the difficulties, a complete demonstration of your convictions of divine spirituality will be required of you."[224]

At this point Eusebio reveals the mission, "Modern spiritualism cannot confine God within the walls of an earthly temple, for our essential mission is to change the whole earth into the majestic temple of God."[225] Eusebio is telling us that adding a Spiritual center next to the local church or temple, for those select few that will take the time to drop in, is totally inadequate. Our job is to change the world. Change from a materialistic centered society to a balanced one. Where, yes, scientific advancement is encouraged, new goods can be developed, but where the culture understands the importance of fraternal love and that all actions have a consequence. Where each individual recognizes they have past penalties to pay and they have mostly themselves to thank for when they must endure difficult times as they pay off their debts.

After the call to change the world, comes the command to organize ourselves for the task, "For our vanguard of determined and brave workers, the phase of futile experimentation, disorderly investigation and peripheral reasoning has passed."[226] We are being asked to actively evangelize the doctrine of Spiritism. Set up gatherings to bring people into the fold and to seek out ways to publicize our message to others so they may, at the least, have the option to be exposed to the truth.

The importance of this is stated in Allan Kardec's *Genesis*, where the future of Spiritism and the transformation of the earth to a higher status is heralded by the gradual transition of more spirits which will be reincarnated with a *propensity for the good*.[227] For the good spirits amongst us, they need to hear our message, because these spirits will be, according to *Genesis*, "Charged with the founding the age of moral progress, the new generation is distinguishable by an overall precocious intelligence and reason combined with an *innate* sentiment of the good and spiritual beliefs – an unmistakable sign of a certain degree of *previous* advancement."[228] Focus on the word *innate*, meaning in this instance, "Coming directly from the mind". An external trigger must exist for this feeling to come to the surface and be acted upon.

This task will not be without difficulty, pain or sacrifice. Eusebio puts our efforts in context, "Jesus did not reach the culmination of resurrection without climbing Calvary, and his lessons refer to the faith that moves mountains".[229] Next, to emphasize his point, Eusebio throws out a litany of advice to surmount the impediments:

"Do not go looking for miracles: yearning for them can become addictive and lead to your loss."

"Your burdens on the earthly landscape, however rough or displeasing, represent the Supreme Will."

"Do not jump over obstacles or try to go around them in a deliberate attempt to escape: conquer them using will and perseverance, providing an opportunity to develop your growth."[230]

As well as supplying the reason, the method and the hurdles of promoting Spiritism, Eusebio lays out the context of our struggle in today's environment, "The powerful winds of the evolutionary wave are sweeping the earth. Every day we see the collapse of conventional principles held inviolable for centuries. The perplexed human mind is forced to make distressful changes. The subversion of values, the social experiment and the accelerated process of selection through collective suffering perturb the timid and inattentive, who represent the overwhelming majority everywhere." [231]

The lecture given by Eusebio was not a homily filled discourse on how we can grow as a Spiritist. This was a, "get out of your chair and do something about it", speech. A call to arms, where we are told the objective, the terrain, and the difficulties that we should expect on the way. If it wasn't clear before, it should be clear now, being a Spiritist is not an easy task.

The Lecture for Catholics and Protestants

A more subtle lecture is delivered to a group of incarnate Catholics and Protestants. Later in the book, *In the Greater World*, Andre Luiz is invited to hear a lecture, again by Eusebio, to a mixed group of Catholics and Protestants, albeit a less dogmatic and more likely to be persuaded types of persons. Andre Luiz was surprised that the lecture was being held, he was told, "It's

266

important to understand that Divine Protection shows no privileges. Heavenly grace is like the fruit that always results from earthly effort: wherever there is human cooperation, there too will be Divine support."[232] This information leads us to believe the tone and substance of lecture will be similar. A call to action, a request to get with the program.

As in the first lecture, Eusebio opens with what it meant to be a Christian in ancient times and reviewed the sacrifices they underwent. Next, Eusebio offers a challenge, "However, as heir to those nameless heroes who lived in affliction, of minds built up in the promises of Christ, what have you done with transforming hope, with unwavering trust? What have you done with the living faith that your forbearers acquired at the price of blood and tears?"[233]

Eusebio then delves into his opinion of exactly what these institutions of faith have actually accomplished:

"You have erected barriers against each other that are difficult to cross. Dogmatism poisons you; schism corrupts you. Narrow interpretations of the divine plan darken your mental horizons."

"What delirium has taken you as you involve yourselves in a mutual competition for the imaginary obtainment of divine privileges?"

"In times of old, Christ's disciples competed for opportunities to serve, whereas today, you look for every little opportunity to be served."[234]

After a devastating review of their faults, Eusebio arrives at his request, "Therefore, do not limit your demonstration of trust in the Most High to the ceremonies of outward worship. Get rid of the indifference that chills your ornate cathedrals. Let us make ourselves each other's true brothers and sisters. Let us transform the church into the sweet home of the Christian family, whatever our interpretations might be."[235] This is a plea for a less bureaucratic and more involved practice of their religious principles, and an appeal for less infighting and more focus on the fraternal family under Christ.

Whereas, the goal for Spiritists is to change the world, the request for the souls at the lecture is to return to their Christian roots and stop fighting each other. The Spirit world is not expecting the audience to transform the world, but to outwardly demonstrate the teaching of Christ as revealed in the New Testament. The spirit world is first attempting to steer the ship of the large religious organizations back onto a truly fraternal course. Without this correction, the ability and the required openness to accept the Spiritist doctrine would be absent.

The work by the spirit world to motive us, is but one step in the plan. The road ahead is wide and sure. Not only is our personal beliefs being shaped, but our spiritual institutions will also be significantly altered.

The Future of Religious Organizations

In the book *Missionaries of the Light*, inspired by Andre Luiz and psychographed by Chico Xavier, there is a passage commenting on the future uses of religious establishments.

In the book, Andre Luiz is attending a Spiritist center, located in a home in Rio de Janeiro. Andre's mentor, Alexandre, comments on using a home as a religious gathering point:

> "You mustn't forget that great lessons by the Master himself were given in family settings. The first visible institution of Christianity was Simon Peter's humble home in Capernaum. One of our Lord's first manifestations in the presence of people was the multiplication of family joys at a wedding party in the comfort of the home. Jesus often visited the homes of confessed sinners, switching on new lights in their hearts. The last meeting with the disciples took place in a home setting. The first center for Christian service in Jerusalem was in the simple house of Peter."[236]

In Alexandre's comments, he is attempting to remind all of us that our faith is important, not where we demonstrate it. The home is a sacred piece of earth, a place where children are raised and

268

family are loved and looked after. It is the actual living as a Spiritist that is vital, not the outward expression of faith.

Next he goes on to tell us what will be the future of Churches, when we drop our need to worship God publicly and learn to practice our worship as our daily mode of living.

"In the future of humankind the material churches of Christianity will become church-schools, church-orphanages and church-hospitals, where the leaders of the faith will not only convey words of interpretation, but where children will find support and instruction; the youth, the preparation needed for achievements worthy of character and sentiment; the sick, health-giving remedies; the ignorant, learning; the elderly, support and hope. Evangelical Spiritism is the great restorer of the loving and hardworking apostolic churches of the past. Its faithful followers will be valuable helpers in transforming theological ministries into schools of spirituality, and stone cathedrals into welcoming homes of Jesus."[237]

Hence, there shall come a day, when the organized religions will primarily turn their focus on providing services to their community, rather than mainly facilitating religious events. For, while religious ceremony can certainly be comforting to many, the act of charity and fraternity takes precedence.

Chapter 43 – Future of Earth

The earth will transition – from a planet of humans paying off debts from previous lives – to a planet of learning and peace. It has all been planned out by the spirit realm. The future is absolutely certain … the timing is not. That is up to us.

The high spirit Arnel spoke about the future of our planet with the Rev. G Vale Owen, in a series of messages in *Book Four – The Battalions of Heaven*, in 1919. He was and most probably still is part of a great endeavor to move the people of earth to begin their spiritual journey to cast off their ties of excessive materialism. He and other spirits were shown the impending destiny of earth in order to illustrate the goal they are working toward. A large globe appeared:

> "As it went round upon its axis there appeared shapes of lands and waters upon its outer circumference. These were not coterminous in outline with those of earth as they are today. We were now being shown our future sphere of work, and these were changing as they are now changing on earth's surface, but more quickly. The ages ahead of you were foreshortened for us and we read them as a moving model.
>
> There appeared also the cities and their peoples and animals also, and the engines which the people made for their several uses. And as the globe turned its surface to us, continually revolving, we were able to see the progress of it all.
>
> I mean this; take, in token of other lands, your own islands. I noted then first as they will be a few years hence. Then they sailed round out of view. When they came before us again they

had become changed a little in configuration of coastlines, and as to their cities and people. So, as the globe revolved, these lands, and the whole human race and their works of building and engines of locomotion and all their handiwork progressed in their ages, but condensed from millennia into hours. I must suit my words to you way of thinking, my son. Years have not the same significance to us as they have to you.

Now it would not be permitted to me to fish for you in the deeps of future ages. You of earth must net your own supper. That is as it should be. Nevertheless, it is permitted to me to tell you where the fishing-ground are like to be. Then those who will think of me as a good admiral will set their sail to my chart, and out upon their quest. So.

Now, the earth became more beautiful as it sailed round upon its voyage of the ages. The light increased upon its surface, and its mass became more radiant from within. The peoples also hurried not so greatly here and there, for nature had become more at one with them and yielded more genially to their abundance. So their lives were less fevered and more given to meditation. Thus they became ever more in harmony one with others, and all of them more nearly attuned to us who were able, in our turn, to spend upon them a larger degree of our power and of our sweeter pace.

As this attunement advanced it enthused us with a largess of happiness to know we had gained for ourselves, after much stress of warfare, these younger companions of our ancient race. It was very sweet to us, my son.

And gradually earth itself was changed."[238]

Thus spoke Arnel about earth. He saw the British Isles change as the centuries progressed. He witnessed the world, the technology, the people all transformed as millennia after millennia flew by in a simulation of that which will occur to earth as dictated by God and carried out by legions of spirits following commands from Christ.

Spiritist Revelations and the Bible

Before and after messages were delivered to the Rev. G. Vale Owen there has been communications about the transition of our planet from Spiritist mediums. The primary message is always the same ... we are in a time of transformation. Where our planet will become a regenerative world. Hence, this change, this modifying of the human race, our culture, and our technology is the Apocalypse.

For Christians the Apocalypse is a series of calamitous events. Disasters that would affect the entire planet. But according to Spiritism, the earth will change, yes, disasters will occur, but overall our planet will convert gradually.

To understand the coming changes to our world, one must first know the present and past state of the earth. Where has it come from and where is it going. For we are all passengers and are locked into our seats until we reach the final destination.

Levels of Planets

In the book, *The Gospel According to Spiritism*, by Allan Kardec, in Chapter Three, there is an explanation of the different worlds that spirits will inhabit during their long trek toward purification.

1. Primitive World - Intended for the first incarnations of the human soul. The beings that inhabit them are, to a certain extent, rudimentary. They have the human form but are devoid of any beauty. Their instincts are not tempered by any sentiment of refinement or benevolence, or by any notions of right or wrong. Brute force is the only law. With no industry or inventions, they spend life in conquest of food. The earth was once a primitive world.

2. World of Trial and Expiation, also called Atonement - You are living on this world. There is more evil present than good. This is why life is not easy; because it is not supposed to be while you are reincarnated on the planet earth.

272

3. Regenerative World - Where souls still have something to expiate (pay off the debt of a past wrong) and may absorb new strength by resting from the fatigue of struggle. There is still evil, but much reduced, the good outweighs the evil, consequently there is no motive for hatred or discord.

4. Happy Worlds - On Happy Worlds, we still retain our human form, although the senses are more acute. Where people who are in power are placed there for their dedication to others, not themselves.

5. Heavenly or Divine Worlds - Where good reigns completely, all inhabitants are purified spirits. There is no evil. Humans are lighter, less dense, and life span is longer.

The New Testament Apocalypse

Given that the earth is a planet of expiation or atonement, the spirit realm is actively involved in moving us to a better spiritual plane. The spirit Emmanuel, who was the spirit guide for Francisco C. Xavier, and who inspired many books psychographed by Francisco, wrote in his book, *On the Way to the Light*, about the reasons for the spirit world to send the Apocalypse revelations to John:

"A few years before the end of the first century after the coming of the new doctrine, the powers of the spirit world made an analysis of the dreadful situation of the world in view of the future.

The Divine Master called to the higher spheres the spirit John, who was still being held prisoner by the bonds of the earth, and the astonished, afflicted Apostle read the symbolic language of the invisible world.

The Lord told him to deliver his knowledge to the planet as a warning to all the nations and peoples of the earth, and the old Apostle of Patmos transmitted the extraordinary warnings of the Apocalypse to his disciples.

All of the events posterior to John's life are foreseen therein.

Certainly, the Apostle's description frequently enters the obscurest terrain. One can plainly see that his human language could not faithfully replicate the divine expression of his visions of remarkable interest for the history of mankind: the wars, the ideological struggles of western civilization are all foreseen in minute detail. And its most dreadful image, which even today is still offered to the eyes of the modern world, is that of the deviant Church of Rome, symbolized as the beast clothed in purple and drunk on the blood of the saints."[239]

Let's look at a summary of part of the New Testament Apocalypse, Chapter 13, and then analyze it through the eyes of the spirit Emmanuel:

"Chapter 13: A Beast comes out of the sea. It has ten horns, seven heads containing diadems and blasphemous names. Like a leopard, but paws like a bear and mouth like a lion. It is given power, throne and authority by the Dragon. One head was mortally wounded and healed. In wonderment, the whole world followed after the Beast. People worshiped Beast and Dragon. Their authority to last only forty two months. Granted authority over all people, nation and race. Worshiped by all those who do not have their names in book of life.

Let him who has ears *heed these words: If one is destined for captivity, into captivity he goes! If one is destined to be slain by the sword, by the sword he will be slain! Such is the faithful endurance that distinguishes God's holy people.* A Second Beast comes up out of the Earth. It used the authority of the first Beast *to promote its interests by making the world worship the first beast whose mortal wound had been healed.* Performs great miracles, leads astray Earth's inhabitants by telling them to make an idol of first Beast. Life is given to the image of the Beast, and the power of speech and the ability to put to death anyone who refuses to worship it. Forces all men, rich and poor to accept a stamped image on right hand or forehead. No one allowed *to buy or sell anything unless first marked with the name of the beast or the number that stood for its name. A certain wisdom is needed here; with a little ingenuity anyone can calculate the number of the beast, for it is a number that stands for a certain man. The man's number is six hundred sixty-six."*[240]

First we are told the authority of the beast will last forty-two months, according to Emmanuel, the correct interpretation is:

"The Apocalypse states that the beast would stay great and blasphemous for 42 months, adding that his number would be 666 (Rev. 18:5,18). By examining the importance of symbols at that time and following a certain course of interpretation, we can take each month as being 30 years instead of 30 days; hence, there is a period of 1,260 years, which is precisely the period 610-1870 of our era, when the Papacy was consolidated from the time of its appearance with the emperor Phocus in 607 to the decree of papal infallibility by Pius IX in 1870, which marked the decadence and absence of Vatican' authority in light of humankind's scientific, philosophic and religious evolution."[241]

Therefore the beast is the Catholic Church, which became corrupted over time, forgetting that it is the church who is to serve, not the populace to serve the church. Emmanuel tells us of many occasions when the spirit world attempted to bring the church back to its beginnings. One such effort is when one of Jesus' apostles reincarnated as Saint Francis of Assisi. Saint Francis tried to demonstrate, by his example that the church was meant to go out and help people, not to just collect money or to remain isolated in monasteries.

What about the famous number 666? If the Catholic Church was the beast, what does the number 666 signify? Again, Emmanuel has the answer:

"As for the number 666, without referring to the interpretations using Greek numerals, but rather using the Roman numerals because they were the most widespread and well-known, we must keep in mind that the Supreme Pontiff of the Roman Church uses the titles "VICARIVS GENERALIS DEI IN TERRIS", "VICARIVS FILII DEI" and "DVX CLERI", which mean, respectively, "God's Chief Vicar on Earth", "Vicar of

275

the Son of God" and "Captain of the Clergy." All one needs is a little game of patience, adding up the Roman numerals found in each papal title, and one will find the same results of 666 in each one of them."[242]

Hence, the beast were the Popes who contributed to the churches journey from simple gathering places, where people congregated to discuss the teaching of Jesus and to assist those in need, to the builder of wealth for the religious class at the top, by siphoning the hard-earned money of millions of peasants. To the present day Catholic Church's benefit, many of their priests and branches have reformed themselves into a more benevolent organization, performing many good services for their flock.

The Spiritist Apocalypse

So, how will the Apocalypse, according to Spiritism, occur? The end will come, but it will come for those low spirits who did not care to learn from their successive lives on this planet. As more spirits understand what it means to be selfless, charitable, and honorable in all circumstances, thereby shedding the constant striving for material goods, they will remain within the earth's sphere, whether in spiritual or physical form. The good spirits will vie for the honor of assisting the transformation of the planet.

The last question of the one thousand and nineteen questions in *The Spirits Book*, tells us exactly how the Apocalypse rolls out:

1019. Will the reign of goodness ever be established upon the earth?

"Goodness will reign upon the earth, when, among the spirits who come to dwell in it, the good shall be more numerous than the bad; for they will then bring in the reign of love and justice, which are the source of good and happiness."[243]

Hence, as more people are truly good, the weight of the culture will influence others to follow their example. Those living will have some time to improve themselves, to turn away from the pursuit of coinage by any means. Others will not be so lucky; The Spirits Book tells us their fate:

"The spirits of the wicked people who are mowed down each day by death, and of all who endeavor to arrest the onward movement, will be excluded from the earth, and compelled to incarnate themselves elsewhere; for they would be out of place among those nobler races of human beings, whose felicity would be impaired by their presence among them. They will be sent into never worlds, less advanced than the earth, and will then fulfill hard and laborious missions, which will furnish them with the means of advancing, while contributing also to the advancement of their brethren of those younger worlds, less advanced than themselves."[244]

The people who continue to behave badly will have a surprise waiting for them when they expire. Waking up in the spirit world and then expecting to return to spread more chaos, they shall instead be whisked away to another, less advanced planet, to live among those who are on a lower level.

Imagine dying after residing in a beautiful mansion by the sea, bought by systematically stealing the wealth of others, then landing into the midst of a city with the reek of an open-sewer, no modern technology, where luxury is having hot water boiled for you once a week. This is the punishment awaiting all who resist modifying their behavior and attitudes that celebrate robbing innocents, violence and feeling superior to those that don't stoop to their level. Even then, under God's benevolence, they too, shall have a chance to redeem themselves and re-ascend to a better planet.

The weeding out of the reluctant spirits and the populating of the planet with good spirits will be a gradual conversion. We are being groomed to attain the state required for us to inhabit a non-expiratory world. In Allan Kardec's book *Genesis*, the Apocalypse will not occur in a big bang but will be; "According to the Spirits the earth will not be transformed by a cataclysm that will suddenly wipe out an entire generation. The current generation will disappear gradually and the new one will follow it in the same way, without there have been any change in the natural order of things."[245]

So what happens to us who remain? The Spirit of Truth, as

277

promised in the New Testament John 14:15-17, as the Consoler sent to Allan Kardec to reveal the Doctrine of Spiritism, tells us in *The Gospel According to Spiritism*, what will be:

> "The time is near for the fulfillment of those things proclaimed for the transformation of humankind. Blessed will be those who have worked in the Lord's field selflessly and with no other motive than charity! Their workdays will be paid a hundredfold more than what they expected. Blessed will be those who said to their fellow men and women, "Brothers and sisters, let us work together and combine our efforts so that the Master may find the work accomplished at his coming"; for the Master will say to them; "Come unto me, you who have been good servants, you who have known how to silence your jealousies and discords so that no harm will come to the work!"[246]

Our hundredfold reward will be life on a Regenerative planet. Where good outweighs evil and we can thrive in an environment relatively free of discord. With no fear of war or other violent ends. A place, a safe haven, to continue learning how we can progress to become a pure spirit.

Arnel Describes the Transition

Psychometry is the inherent vibrations infused into matter, from simple car keys, to articles of clothing, which tell the story of all that intersected with that particular slice of matter. Arnel tells us that cosmic psychometry are the vibrations of entire planets.

And it is more than that. Not a mere receptacle of vibrations. But a process of accumulated vibrations which infuse an object and transforms it. Our collective vibrations work to modify the vibrations of earth. Arnel describes the process:

> "And so it came to pass that as the people of earth progressed spiritually higher, so earth itself gradually but faithfully answered to their influence which was registered upon the substance of which earth is built up. Matter became less gross and more ethereal. That is why it became brighter with

radiance from within as we saw it revolving. It was no more nor no less than cosmic psychometry in mass, but essentially identical with you at present know manifested in detail.

As earth and its peoples became more and more etherealized, so the hosts spiritual were able with greater ease to consort with those peoples, and their conversation was both more frequent and more free than it is today. And, to shorten my story, we came to that period when progress had been made to such a degree that the communion of spirits with people of earth was normal and continual."[247]

Hence, we and the planet, become less dense. Just as a higher spirit is composed of more energy and less matter than a lower spirit, our entire globe shall fade away from view in our current dense solar system and appear as a planet, in the same orbit, in a solar system composed of higher worlds.

Arnel tells us that our current level of science may be able to understand the proportions of matter of different planets, but we are unable to discern their spiritual level. At the same time, there are worlds that have progressed and have become ethereal.

The civilizations which reside on those planets are able to detect our dense planets. And they interact with us without our knowledge. There is more, Arnel tells us:

"There are others which are not visible to you of earth for they are those which have progressed in their etherealization beyond the material, and have become ethereal. They may be seen by those who live on planets of like substance. They are not spiritual, but between the material and the spiritual estate. Their inhabitants are cognizant of the other planets of which earth is one. And they act upon these planets very powerfully, being at the same time more progressed than earth people, and yet nearer in estate than the spiritual people are.

These of which I speak are true planets of themselves. But there are other ethereal planets, so to say it. One of these encompasses earth. For it is of the engrossened ether of which this ethereal planet is composed that earth is suffused. This is not merely a belt of ether solely for service of earth. Most of these have lived on earth in bygone ages, and some have never been earth-dwellers, never having reached material manifestation in body of flesh and blood."[248]

Therefore, we live in a multi-dimensional universe, within multiple universes. Our current science knows our layer of visible matter isn't enough to account for the universe we live in. Arnel exposes the truth, that we are mere children playing at science compared to the higher spiritual civilizations.

The complexity of God's creation is unfathomable to us. But it may be helpful to think that we are swimming in a sea of numbers. Ponder that each one of us sends out encoded messages – constantly, our thoughts, our feelings, our current status, and our location, to name a few. That our planet, our matter, has all been created by force of will, and is kept in place by the faith and force of high spirits. Visualize a dense matrix of numerals, strings, and structures, in which a multivariate analysis would expose that all numbers, all data within any table, are all related to all other pieces of information.

Slice the universal library of everything anyway you choose and another whole ecosystem of spiritual, ethereal, and material is discovered. Add that all is fluid and all is connected to everything else. That a thought can change a data point, hence all other relationships are reset. Only then can one get a small inkling in the true state of the universe we reside.

It is difficult to visualize the truth, when we see density, thickness, and stability all around us. When only children believe that a thought can conjure an object. Our physical limitations are for a purpose. The spirit world has deliberately held all other variables steady, so we may live on earth and concentrate on one primary task … transform our character. Once that is done, we can be safely exposed to a realm beyond the imagination.

The Ultimate Manifestation

Arnel described the revolving globe and the future of mankind on earth. He told the Rev. G. Vale Owen how each one of us, those who have chosen the path to the light, will accompany the earth to a higher state. Next Arnel speaks of the finale - the last act of the earth as it became wholly transformed:

"Earth, as we beheld it before us, had come to that stage when the ethereal and the material had almost equal place in content. The bodies of men were still of matter, but purified and more readily co-responsive with the heavens of spirit life than in former times – these same times in which you live today.

Earth had responded to the upliftment, and the vegetation which it produced lay upon its bosom almost sentient as a babe upon his mother's breast.

No kingdoms were upon earth, but one confederacy of peoples whose colors were not so diverse, each from other, as they are today.

Science also was not the science of Europe as it is now, but the powers of ethereal dynamics being understood, the whole life of men was transformed."[249]

In the future, we are lighter, we easily communicate with the spirit realm, we are at peace and we live together as one, in harmony. But is wasn't just humans that were changed – everything else was too.

Minerals, which made up the earth were charged to be in harmony with our planet. Plant life was given the ability to respond to our thoughts. Animals had increased sensations and personalities. The ethereal intelligence of the universe inundated all of earth, giving each division of inorganic and organic life a boost. A little more awareness, an increased sense of connectivity, and a place within the vibrations and harmony of the earth.

Arnel describes the earth as radiant, with living entities covering the surface. He tells us that "Earth now shone like one great and very beautiful pearl, but with veins of green and gold and crimson and amber and blue upon it. And within it shone its native light aglow with fire of worship about its heart, which throbbed with life and happiness as the impulses of the Creative Lords and their myriads invaded it and wooed from it this responsive and shimmering loveliness."[250]

Paradise awaits us. It is not something we have to travel towards. It doesn't entail a physical journey. To arrive at paradise takes an arduous mental trek, a trip to re-wire our personalities. To cut off ties from excessive material desires. To rid ourselves of primitive emotions – hate, envy, and selfishness. To step forward toward the light, in all humbleness, open to learn that which we have resisted for so many lives. That love is the greatest force in the universe, that kindness and respect for all is the foundation upon which paradise shall be created.

Watching the earth's globe spin, Arnel hears a hymn that arises from earth, a song of love and expectation:

"What lies beyond you in the deeps of space we know not yet, and earth is but a mote in the rays of your Heavenly Sun. But this we know, since we have seen this Province of your Kingdom, Christ of the Father, that what is there beyond is wholly good.

What comes to meet us out of the eternities ahead of us, on the road we go, what peoples there abide, what sort of Princes rule – these too, we know not now. Yet we go forward fearless, for we follow you, O Christ. Upon your shoulders sit twin power and love embracing each other in your crown of majesty.

Who the Father is we know, for we have seen you His Beloved, and we have loved you also. So our love meets with the Father's love in you as trysting place. We know Him in you, and we are content.

You are very wonderful and beautiful, Beloved, yet all your beauty cannot be shown to us so great.

But in that future emprise we adventure forth all strong of heart and buoyant and unafraid. And you still lead us we will follow you, Christ Consummate of wisdom, of strength and of creative love.

We pay you our due worship, ordered and arrayed in our degrees. Content us with the benediction of your Peace."[251]

Chapter 44 – The Future

The future is written. We shall move from a planet of atonement to a planet of regeneration. There will be a paradise on earth for those who have demonstrated the intellectual and spiritual maturity to be allowed to ascend with our planet.

How we get there is the only question. Is it fast, is it slow, is it painless, or is it torturous? It is all up to us – the collective humanity.

The probable path is slow and torturous – given the obstacles – which are the number of souls on earth and spirits in the Lower Zone and below who are still tied to the material bonds of physical life and their dedication to achieve material pleasures by any means at their disposal.

Individual lesson plans for each person will have to be created to lead them to the realization that life on earth is temporary and useful only for the purpose of character improvement. Situations must be manufactured whereby entire nations, societies, and religions will be force to learn that grasping for power and mindless intolerance are not the path to happiness or to salvation.

The trek will be hard for those who understand the problem. They will have to assist where they can and promote peace and love in whatever manner they are able to perform. Even the good of heart will be buffeted by the upheavals and political cataclysms which shall be coming our way.

The battle will be on two fronts. The physical world and the spirit world. Incarnates will be swept up in events and the discarnates residing in the Lower Zone and the Dark Abyss will fight to keep their cruel kingdoms.

The lower and unrepentant spirits understand well that when earth transitions, they will be removed. Sent to undesirable locations where they will land at the bottom of the totem pole. They will have to fight for eons, once again, to regain that power they had while on and below the earth.

A planet of regeneration has no place for spirits who are not on the path dedicated to love, fraternity, and honesty. Pollution of the spiritual atmosphere will not be allowed by those who have not made or actively striving for progress. Spirits who have rejected the light, made the conscious decision to select themselves for removal.

While there is still the presence of bad influences by spirits who have not yet totally let go of negative characteristics and there are still some debts to pay for past wrongs, on the whole the amount of chaos, inequality, violence, and corruption is greatly reduced. Reduced to the extent that these should be rare occurrences, not the daily litany of bad news that we live through today.

And this is just the next step. Beyond that is the goal of being a happy world, where there is an even greater level of love and understanding. Next is the ultimate destiny of a heavenly or divine world where there is no hint of evil and our physical form approaches that of a spirit.

Hence, as we collectively make the long and arduous journey toward a future where we shall be in greater communion with the spirit world – where guidance is at hand as we need it, where people are in harmony, where race is not a factor, where nations work together – look to that vision to carry you through each hurdle, each tragic episode in your life – to a beautiful state to a paradise on earth.

Glossary

Term	Description
Abyss or Dark Abyss	The Abyss begins just below the surface of the earth and extends downwards for an unspecified distance. This is the term for a type of Purgatory or Hell for spirits who are unrepentant and still intent on staying attached to worldly goods, baser emotions (such as hate, envy, and revenge), or other criminal intentions. There is no concept of eternal damnation in Spiritism; all spirits are able to leave when they change their character and beliefs. All will eventually rise to heaven, but it may take multiple lifetimes.
Allan Kardec	Known as the codifier of Spiritism. Many Brazilians believe he later reincarnated as Francisco (Chico) C. Xavier to carry on the presentation of Spiritism. His first book is *The Spirits Book*. He presented Spiritism to the word in the 1850s.
Andre Luiz	Spirit Author of a series of books, starting with Nosso Lar. All books were psychographed by Francisco (Chico) C. Xavier. Highly recommended reading for anyone interested in learning about Spiritism.

Term	Description
Camilo Branco	Camilo Castelo Branco wasn't just an ordinary suicide. He was a commanding figure in Portugal's literary scene in the late 1800's. He was known as the Portuguese Balzac and was awarded the title of Viscount of Correia Botelho. In despair over his son's insanity and his own ailments that would certainly lead to blindness, he ended his life in 1890.
Discarnate	A spirit in the spirit world, they do not possess a physical body.
Emmanuel	Emmanuel was the spirit mentor of Francisco (Chico) C. Xavier. Emmanuel has since incarnated in Brazil in the year 2001 or 2002. It is said by some Spiritist mediums that Chico Xavier, will be the spirit mentor for Emmanuel.
Errant spirit	I have seen two slightly different uses of "errant spirit", the most used one is a spirit who is wandering in the Lower Zone, between heaven and the Abyss. The other usage is when a spirit is not assigned a region, and is free to wander onto different spirit worlds (where there is no physical life).
Francisco (Chico) C. Xavier	A Brazilian medium, who psychographed more than 450 books, dictated to him by spirits. His spirit guide was Emmanuel. Chico Xavier was a Spiritist and did much to spread Spiritism throughout Brazil.
Heaven	Heaven, in Spiritist books, including mine, usually refers to the higher regions above the earth. There are different heavens around

Term	Description
	other planets for those souls who live there. Heaven is where people in physical bodies return to, if they have demonstrated love, kindness, fraternity, charity, and honesty toward their fellow humans. Being a member of any one type of religion or even a belief in God is not a requirement to ascend to heaven, according to Spiritism.
Hell	Called the "Abyss" or the "Dark Abyss" in the books by the spirit Andre Luiz
Incarnate	An incarnate is a spirit who is inhabits a physical body. The spirit can still roam in the spirit world during time of sleep.
James	A high spirit, but one who advanced rapidly after his modest incarnation on earth, but spiritually very profound. He was rapidly advanced to sphere seven and given responsibility over the colony of the Glade. This is the colony composed of the souls rescued by Shonar after they were massacred by another faction. The colony resides on sphere four.
Jesus	According to Spiritism - Jesus is the governor of Earth. It has been reported by Brazilian Spiritist that Jesus is also in charge of four other planets, one in the forming stage, one primitive, one a planet of atonement (Earth), one a planet of regeneration, and one a happy planet.
Levels of Heaven	As Jesus said in the New Testament, "My mansion has many rooms", there are many levels of heaven. As one increases their spiritual and intellectual ability one

Term	Description
	graduates from a lower level to the next higher level. In the book, *Beyond the Veil*, a numbering system is used. Level 1 being the lowest. Spirits have said they are using that system just for convenience sake, as a tool to explain the demarcations of heaven for us here on earth.
Lower Zone	Also called the Umbral in Portuguese, which you may find in some of the English translations of Chico Xavier's book. The Lower Zone is the area at the surface of the earth and slightly above it where spirits who haven't yet released their ties to material goods on earth and/or have not yet accepted the need for love and fraternity toward all humans. All will eventually rise to heaven, but it may take multiple lifetimes.
NDE	Near Death Experience – People who have had NDEs are those whose were close to or in an actual death state.
Nosso Lar	The first book dictated to Francisco (Chico) C. Xavier by the spirit Andre Luiz. A movie was made using the first book (of the same name) by the spirit author Andre Luiz. It is called Nosso Lar, or Celestial City. The movie is in Portuguese with English subtitles. I highly recommend this movie, excellent production values and true to the Doctrine of Spiritism.
OBE	Out of Body Experience – This includes people who were not classified as being in a near or at a state of death, but still were transported into another plane.

Term	Description
Perispirit	Connects the spirit to the physical body. You are composed to three key items – Your spirit (which is immortal), perispirit (which is the link between the spirit and the physical body), and your physical body (which is mortal and will be destroyed after each life).
Reincarnation	Reincarnation is the concept whereby a spirit, the entire personality and character, is deposited into a physical body. According to Spiritism, when a spirit is place inside a physical body, they retain their basic character (which gets revealed around the age of 15 to 18), but they do not have any memories of past lives. This is for the purpose of allowing that spirit to learn the lessons assigned to them. Incarnates (spirits in physical bodies) do retain their conscience – the mechanism to determine right from wrong – and their instinct. Once a spirit sheds their physical body, at the proper time their memories return.
Rev. G. Vale Owen	An English Rev. in the Anglican Church. He received messages from the spirit realm in the 1910s and 20s. Four of his books are in the compilation book, *Beyond the Veil*
Shonar	A high spirit. He works in the Lower Zone, helping souls who have not yet found the path to heaven and has been incarnated on earth for vital missions. "He has many centuries of service to his name and has been especially active during eras of disturbance and revolution on Earth – as, for example, in the reign of Ivan the Terrible in Russia, during the French

Term	Description
	Revolution, and in the time of Henry VIII of England."[252]
Spirit / Soul	I use the word interchangeably – but I do realize that many do not. For simplicity sake I use spirit to denote all of us, we all have or are spirits and we all have a soul. For those not on a physical plane I will put either their name or put "spirit" before their name to denote they currently reside in the spirit world.
Spirit World, Spirit Realm	The spirit world was created before our physical universe. We come from and shall return to the spirit realm. The world of spirits is where we shall spend the vast majority of our eternal life.
Spiritism, Christian Spiritism	A Doctrine codified by Allan Kardec in the 1850s, revealed to the world by the Spirit of Truth, as promised in the New Testament (John 14:15-17, 26). Spiritism follows the precepts of Christianity and updates them with new revelations from the spirit world.
Umbral	Also called the Lower Zone in English. The Lower Zone is the area at the surface of the earth and slightly above it where spirits who haven't yet released their ties to material goods on earth and/or have not yet accepted the need for love and fraternity toward all humans. All will eventually rise to heaven, but it may take multiple lifetimes.
Universal Fluid	From this, flows all forms of matter. It is the basis for everything in the spirit and physical universes.

Term	Description
Wulfhere	A high spirit. Mother of Shonar in one of his incarnations. They are still close. She was in charge of a group of workers in sphere seven. She is very intelligent and has a strong personality, but and sweet and caring woman.
Yvonne Perreira	A Brazilian medium who psychographed books from spirits. She has many books published in Portuguese. Presently there are two books translated in English

Your Exploration Continues . . .

Learn more about Spiritism in my blog at:
http://www.nwspiritism.com.

To assist you in understanding more about Spiritism, I have eleven other books to support you in your spiritual exploration:

- Heaven and Below – Book 1 of Spiritism - The Spirit World Revealed to a Anglican Vicar
- Spirits and the Spirit Universe – Book 2 of Spiritism - The Spirit World Revealed to a Anglican Vicar
- Spiritism 101 – The Third Revelation
- The Spirit World Talks to Us
- 7 Tenets of Spiritism – How They Impact Your Daily Life
- Explore Your Destiny – Since Your Life's Path is (mostly) Predetermined
- The Case for Reincarnation – Your Path to Perfection
- 51 Disclosures from Spiritism – The 3rd Revelation
- What Really Happens During Near Death Experiences According to Spiritism – 12 NDEs Explained and Explored
- The Problem is the Solution
- Spiritism - Everything is Connected

Below are brief introductions to all my books concerning Spiritism.

Heaven and Below – Book 1

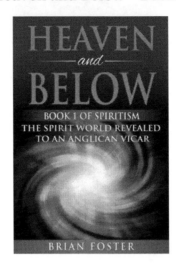

This book covers communications that pertain to three main themes:

- Life in heaven
- Lower regions
- Appearances of Jesus in the spirit realm

Many religions offer pictures of life after our spirit leaves our physical body. Most descriptions are hazy and prone to numerous interpretations. Spiritism, via communication from spirits who have been selected by high-level spirits, supplies us will real and actionable knowledge. Revelations in Spiritist literature presents an exciting picture of the bands of heaven and life therein. While a fuller explanation is extended about aspects of life and the organization of the regions below heaven.

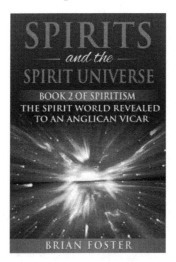

This book covers communications to the Rev. G. Val Owen that pertain to five main themes:

- Spirit Education – Lower levels of heaven
- Spirit Education – Higher levels of heaven
- Spirit Attributes
- Power of Spirits
- Knowledge of the Universe(s)

Imagine a fantasy world where, if you apply yourself, you can travel from sphere to higher sphere, accumulating new attributes and powers after graduating from each level. Nothing could stop you, for there are no limits, promotion is based solely on merit. Within each stage your mind is fully engaged in comprehending the most extraordinary knowledge; all within an atmosphere of supportive and congenial friends. If this sounds like heaven to you, then you are correct – it is heaven.

Something wonderful has happened. It occurred in the middle of the 1800's and it caught the attention of the world. It grew quickly in popularity, so fast that many in positions of power went on a crusade to stamp it out.

Why? Because it provided answers to questions that we all have been searching for. Questions that have been posed by philosophers since the beginning of time were asked and the results fully described.

Like other messages of love, charity and fraternity before; this one was met with strong opposition. Ideas are hard to stamp out and this one is growing again. The world is re-awakening to Spiritism.

Learn what Spiritism is and how it can positively shape your life and happiness. Available at Amazon Kindle for $0.99, and in paperback - *Spiritism 101 – The Third Revelation*

The Spirit World Talks to Us

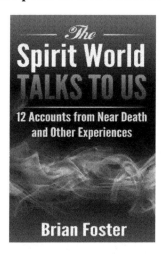

The spirit world is talking to us ... each and every one of us. Most of us are unaware of the subtle signals and soft voices that draw us to listen to our conscience. But they are there, ever hopeful that we may discover the truth about our sojourn on this blue planet.

The experiences reviewed in this book layout exciting disclosures about the spirit world and ours. We are told about heaven, the different spiritual zones around the earth; how karma is real and why we need multiple lives to learn to become a person who radiates love in all circumstances. We learn that the concept of time is different in the spirit universe and about the basic building blocks of all matter.

In essence, the inquiries that you have had since you began questioning your place in this universe are answered by spirits interacting with the chosen few.

Learn what the spirit world is telling us. – The Spirit World Talks to Us.

I explore each of the seven tenets and how they have personally affected me and those around me. Giving yourself the seven tenets could be the best present of your life.

The 7 Tenets of Spiritism:

1. We are Immortal Souls

2. God and Jesus Love Us

3. We have Multiple Lives

4. During our Lives We Pay for Past Debts and Accumulate New Experiences

5. We Live and Learn in Close Family Groups

6. Our Destiny is Mostly Predetermined

7. We are Assisted in our Lives by Unseen Spirit Forces

Available at Amazon Kindle and in paperback, at *7 Tenets of Spiritism – How They Impact Your Daily Life.*

Explore Your Destiny – Since Your Life's Path is (mostly) Predetermined

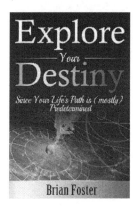

Explore Your Destiny is divided into four sections. Each section supplies one more piece of the puzzle for you to place, so you can look at your life's arc with new insights.

1. Why – Why are we here and why must we live what we are living through right now?

2. When – In what period along your souls timeline is all of this happening? Knowing your relative position in the path to perfection will guide you to understanding your current life.

3. How – How does all of this occur? How does the entire process affect your destiny and actions? What are the rules of the game?

4. Where – Where is this world that plans our destiny? Are there good places to be and are there bad?

Explore Your Destiny – Since Your Life's Path is (mostly) Predetermined.

The Case for Reincarnation – Your Path to Perfection

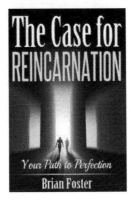

There is a realm, a universe greater than ours and it is filled with intelligences that we can only wonder at. There are spirits around the earth who are actively helping and guiding us in our planning and during our actual incarnations.

This book is here to answer your questions;

1. Why do we reincarnate?

2. How does the process work?

3. How many reincarnations must we have?

4. What memories do we retain from our previous lives?

5. Do we have control over our reincarnations?

6. Why must we suffer?

7. How may I insure my next life is better?

8. How may I progress to being a perfected spirit?

The Case for Reincarnation – Your Path to Perfection

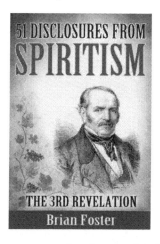

Spiritism has been presented to humankind for one reason, to enlighten us. To let us know the answers to questions that everyone has had since we started thinking about our place on earth, our destiny, why we are here, and is there life after death.

This book is divided into four sections, each categorizing a theme for the type of discoveries that you will make as you read:

1. Ourselves – What are we, why are we here, what do we have to do, what is our goal?

2. Spirit Realm – What is it, where is it, how does it work?

3. How to Ascend – What is the path to ascension, what is important to learn, why we must grow?

4. Prophecies – What do some past prophecies actually mean, what will happen to the world, how will it happen?

Learn what has been presented to the world, read the book, *51 Disclosures from Spiritism – The 3ʳᵈ Revelation.*

What Really Happens During Near Death Experiences, According to Spiritism

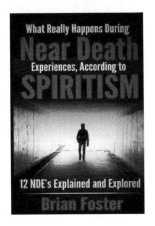

Why are we interested in Near Death Experiences (NDE)? With the advent of the internet, social media allows masses of people to more efficiently pool together shared experiences than at any other time in history.

Recollections from every country, culture, language and age group now reside in the great internet cloud. A mountain of data, which can no longer be wished away or ignored. The parallels and common themes from all corners of the world preclude everyone's account to be merely mass hysteria.

Spiritism explains why each person was chosen for their experience and what was presented to them. Find out what they were expected to learn from their life changing event.

What Really Happens During Near Death Experiences – 12 NDEs Explained and Explored is available at Amazon.

The Problem is the Solution

This book is different. Not that the others are bad or useless. Just that this book is different. It rests on an altered premise; life is a planned series of trials.

In this book your will learn to analyze why are you experiencing, or have been through, the following types of events:

1. Financial problems

2. Failed relationship(s) / marriage(s)

3. Family problems

4. Illnesses – physical and mental

5. Career setbacks

6. Addiction

7. Stress

And in doing so, you shall be able to make the first step in analyzing what you should have learned and how it will make you a better person.

The Problem is the Solution – 7 Life Complications Sent to Test and Teach You

This book presents information about Spiritism and how our lives are tethered to the spirit world and everyone else on this planet. I have divided my essays into three categories:

- What is Spiritism
- How the Spirit World Guides the Earth
- How the Spirit Realm Assists Us

All are interrelated. There are no hard dividing lines where our lives are unaffected by spirits around us. We literally walk in a sea of spirits. We hear and are unconsciously directed by suggestions from spirits. All types of spirits. Good, bad, indifferent, and foolish spirits.

Spiritism – Everything is Connected

Author

Stay in touch with the author via:

Spiritist Blog: http://www.nwspiritism.com

Facebook: https://www.facebook.com/nwspiritism

Facebook group to discuss Spiritism:
https://www.facebook.com/groups/Spiritist/

Twitter: https://twitter.com/nwspiritism

Author page on Amazon: https://www.amazon.com/Brian-Foster/e/B00O6JBO0G

If you liked *How we are Guided by Spirits – Book 3*, please post a review at Amazon.

Copyright

Bibliography

7th US Spiritist Symposium. (2015, August 2). *7th U.S. Spiritist Symposium - The Truth About Medium by Gary Schwartz, PhD* . Retrieved from YouTube: https://www.youtube.com/watch?v=_u7RqklxNnA

Amazon. (2014, May 14). *The Spirits Book*. Retrieved from Amazon Books: http://www.amazon.com/Spirits-Book-Spiritualist-Classics/dp/1907355987/ref=sr_1_1?s=books&ie=UTF8&qid=1399825900&sr=1-1&keywords=allan+kardec

Augustine, S. (2014). *The City of God*. Beloved Publishing.

Baker, M. M. (2016, July 15). *The Life of Jesus*. Retrieved from The Life of Jesus: https://lifeofjesus.wordpress.com

Bancarz, S. (2015, August 2). *Harvard Neurosurgeon Confirms The Afterlife Exists*. Retrieved from Spirit Science and Metaphysics: http://www.spiritscienceandmetaphysics.com/harvard-neurosurgeon-confirms-the-afterlife-exists/

Cayce, E. E. (1968). *Edgar Cayce On Atlantis*. New York: Grand Central Publishing.

Chriss. (2015). Collection of e-mails.

Christian Spiritualism. (2015, September 14). *The Life Beyond the Veil*. Retrieved from Christian Spiritualism: http://www.christianspiritualism.org/articles/lbtv.htm

Denis, L. (2012). *Life and Destiny*. Forgotten Books.

Dictionary.com. (2014, 03 02). *Dictionary Reference*. Retrieved from Dictionary.com: http://dictionary.reference.com/browse/didactic

Dictionary.com. (2015, May 22). *Dictionary.reference.com/obsession*. Retrieved from Dictionary.com: http://dictionary.reference.com/browse/obsession

Dryden, S. H. (1909). *Daisy Dryden - A Memoir*. Boston: Colonial Press.

EVFIT. (2014, December 22). *40,000 Years*. Retrieved from evfit.com: http://www.evfit.com/40,000ya.htm

Farnese, A. (1896). A Wanderer in the Spirit Lands (PDF version of the book). London.

Franco, D. (2016). *Planetary Transition*. Miami, Florida: Leal Publisher.

Franco, D. P. (unknown). *Understanding Spiritual and Mental Health*. unknown: unknown.

Honório, T. S. (2015, June 13). *Spiritual Contracts*. Retrieved from Kardec: http://www.kardec.com/Spiritual-Contracts.html

Hooper, R. (2007, 2012). *Jesus, Buddha, Krishna & Lao Tzu*. New York: Bristol Park Books.

Howard Ecklund, E. (2017, May 14). *Misconceptions of Science and Religion Found in New Study*. Retrieved from Rice University News and Media: http://news.rice.edu/2014/02/16/misconceptions-of-science-and-religion-found-in-new-study/

Jungian Center. (2015, July 3). *Art of Dying Well - Jungian Perspective of Death and Dying*. Retrieved from Jungian Center: http://jungiancenter.org/essay/art-dying-well-jungian-perspective-death-and-dying

Kardec, A. (2006). *Heaven and Hell*. Brasilia (DF), Brasil: International Spiritist Council.

Kardec, A. (2008). *The Gospel According to Spiritism*. Brasilia

(DF): International Spiritist Council.

Kardec, A. (2009). *Genesis - Miracles and Predictions according to Spiritism.* Brasilia (DF), Brasil: International Spiritist Council.

Kardec, A. (2010). *The Book on Mediums.* Guildford, England: White Crow Books.

Kardec, A. (2010). *The Spirits Book.* Guildford, UK: White Crow Books.

Kardec, A. (2015). *Spiritist Review, Journal of Psychological Studies - 1858.* United States Spiritist Council and IPEAK.

Kardec, A. (2015). *The Spiritist Review - Journal of Psychological Review - 1859.* United States Spiritist Council and the Spiritist Research Institute (IPEAK).

Katsman, D. A. (2015, June 28). *PHYSICAL MODEL OF THE PARALLEL ETHEREAL WORLD.* Retrieved from The Campaign for Philosophical Freedom: http://www.cfpf.org.uk/articles/rdp/physicalmodel.html

Limite, D. (2017, January 17). *Data Limite Segundo Chico Xavier.* Retrieved from YouTube: https://www.youtube.com/watch?v=4JxukHvGVzE

Live Science. (2015, July 10). *Japan 2011 Earthquake Tsunami Facts.* Retrieved from Live Science: http://www.livescience.com/39110-japan-2011-earthquake-tsunami-facts.html

Marshall, J. (2014, September 6). *My NDE.* Retrieved from NHNE Near Death: http://nhneneardeath.ning.com/profiles/blogs/my-nde-2

MIT. (2016, April 14). *Plato's Republic Book VII.* Retrieved from Classics MIT: http://classics.mit.edu/Plato/republic.8.vii.html

Near Death Experience Research Foundation. (2014, August 8).

Michael Joseph's NDE. Retrieved from NDERF.org: http://www.nderf.org/NDERF/NDE_Experiences/michael_j oseph_nde.htm

Near Death Experiences Research Foundation. (2016, January 23). *A Childs NDE*. Retrieved from nderf.org: http://www.nderf.org/NDERF/NDE_Experiences/achild's.h tm

Neto, G. L. (2013, June 15). *Remembering Chico Xavier and His Legacy*. Retrieved from YouTube: https://www.youtube.com/watch?v=wY5m3bk0AsY& list=TL01TkXUPh4dbuxLuFJq7Gmn-QZpLdKa5H

Owen, R. G. (1971). *The Outlands of Heaven.* London: The Greater World Association Trust.

Owen, R. G. (2012). *The Life Beyond the Veil.* Pahrump, NV: Square Circles Publishing.

Pereira, Y. A. (2012). *Memoirs of a Suicide.* Brasilia (DF), Brasil: International Spiritist Council (EDICEI).

Schwartz, D. G. (2015, August 2). *Dr. Gary Schwartz.* Retrieved from Demonstrations: http://www.drgaryschwartz.com/DEMONSTRATIONS.ht ml

Spiritism. (n.d.). *Wikipedia - Spiritism*. Retrieved September 18, 2014, from Wikipedia: http://en.wikipedia.org/wiki/Spiritism

Stanford Encyclopedia of Philosophy. (2015, August 8). *Descartes and the Pineal Gland*. Retrieved from Stanford Encyclopedia of Philosophy: http://plato.stanford.edu/entries/pineal-gland/#3.2

Steere, E. K. (2014, Oct. 6). *Research into Near Death Experiences Reveals Awareness May Continue even After the Brain Shutrs Down*. Retrieved from Daily Mail: http://www.dailymail.co.uk/health/article-

2783030/Research-near-death-experiences-reveals-awareness-continue-brain-shut-down.html

Swedenborg, E. (1758). *Heaven and Hell.* Europe: A Publice Domain Book.

Swedenborg, E. (2011). *A Swedenborg Sampler.* West Chester, PA: Swedenborg Foundation Press.

Unknown. (2017, January 23). *Channeled Messages from the Apostle Paul.* Retrieved from Channeled Messages from the Apostle Paul: http://messagesfromapostlepaul.zohosites.com/

Urantia Foundation. (1975). *The Urantia Book.* Chicago: Urantia Foundation.

Vale Owen, G. (1924). *Paul and Albert.* London: The Greater World Christian Spiritualist Association.

Wikipedia. (2014, March 7). *Chico Xavier.* Retrieved from Wikipedia: http://en.wikipedia.org/wiki/Chico_Xavier

Wikipedia. (2014, December 22). *Human Evolution.* Retrieved from Wikipedia: http://en.wikipedia.org/wiki/Human_evolution

Wikipedia. (2014, August 5). *Socrates.* Retrieved from Wikipedia: http://en.wikipedia.org/wiki/Socrates

Wikipedia. (2015, July 3). *Carl Jung.* Retrieved from Wikipedia: https://en.wikipedia.org/wiki/Carl_Jung#Thought

Wikipedia. (2015, August 8). *Descartes.* Retrieved from Wikipedia - Rene Descartes: https://en.wikipedia.org/wiki/Ren%C3%A9_Descartes

Wikipedia. (2015, October 15). *DNA.* Retrieved from Wikipedia: https://en.wikipedia.org/wiki/DNA

Wikipedia. (2015, August 2). *Dr. Gary Schwartz.* Retrieved from Wikipedia: https://en.wikipedia.org/wiki/Gary_Schwartz

Wikipedia. (2015, July 3). *Genetic Memory*. Retrieved from Wikipedia: https://en.wikipedia.org/wiki/Genetic_memory_(psycholog y)

Wikipedia. (2015, September 13). *George Vale Owen*. Retrieved from Wikipedia: https://en.wikipedia.org/wiki/George_Vale_Owen

Wikipedia. (2015, August 8). *Joan of Arc*. Retrieved from Wikipedia: https://en.wikipedia.org/wiki/Joan_of_Arc

Wikipedia. (2016, April 14). *Allegory of the Cave*. Retrieved from Wikipedia: https://en.wikipedia.org/wiki/Allegory_of_the_Cave

Wikipedia. (2016, March 20). *Fourth Dimensional Space*. Retrieved from Wikipedia: https://en.wikipedia.org/wiki/Four-dimensional_space

Wikipedia. (2016, Jan. 31). *String Theory*. Retrieved from Wikipedia: https://en.wikipedia.org/wiki/String_theory

Wikipedia. (2016, June 26). *Zoroastrianism*. Retrieved from Wikipedia: https://en.wikipedia.org/wiki/Zoroastrianism

Wikipedia. (2017, June 24). *French Revolution*. Retrieved from Wikipedia: https://en.wikipedia.org/wiki/French_Revolution

Wikipedia. (2017, April 22). *St Crispin's Day Speech*. Retrieved from Wikipedia: https://en.wikipedia.org/wiki/St_Crispin%27s_Day_Speech

Woolworth, T. (2011, February 6). *Thomas Edison's Telephone to the Dead: Myth or Fact?* Retrieved Sept. 20, 2014, from ITC Voices: http://itcvoices.org/thomas-edisons-telephone-to-the-dead-myth-or-fact/

Xavier, F. C. (1946). *Message from a Teen in the Spirit World.* Pedro Leopoldo, Brazil: International Spiritist Council.

Xavier, F. C. (2004). *In the Domain of Mediumship.* New York: Spiritist Alliance of Books, Inc.

Xavier, F. C. (2008). *The Messengers.* Philadelphia, PA: Allan Kardec Educational Society.

Xavier, F. C. (2008). *Workers of the Life Eternal.* Brasilia (DF) - Brazil: International Spiritist Council.

Xavier, F. C. (2009). *And Life Goes On.* Brasilia (DF), Brasil: International Spiritist Council.

Xavier, F. C. (2009). *In the Greater World.* Brasilia (DF), Brazil: International Spiritist Council.

Xavier, F. C. (2009). *Jesus in the Home.* Brasilia (DF), Brazil: EDICEI.

Xavier, F. C. (2009). *Missionaries of the Light.* Brasilia (DF), Brazil: International Spiritist Council.

Xavier, F. C. (2010). *Action and Reaction.* Brasilia (DF), Brazil: International Spiritist Council.

Xavier, F. C. (2010). *Nosso Lar.* Brasilia - (DF), Brazil: International Spiritist Council.

Xavier, F. C. (2010). *Our Daily Bread.* Brasilia (DF) - Brazil: EDICEI.

Xavier, F. C. (2011). *Between Heaven and Earth.* Brasilia (DF), Brazil: International Spiritist Council.

Xavier, F. C. (2011). *In the Realms of Mediumship.* Brasilia (DF), Brazil: EDICEI.

Xavier, F. C. (2011). *On the Way to the Light.* Brasilia (DF), Brazil: International Spiritist Council.

Xavier, F. C. (2012). *Hail Christ!* Brasilia (DF): EDICEI.

Xavier, F. C. (2013). *Liberation.* Brasilia (DF), Brazil: International Spiritist Council.

Xavier, F. C. (2013). *Sex and Destiny.* Miami, FL: EDICEI of America.

Xavier, F. C. (2013). *Voltei.* Brasilia (DF): FEB.

Xavier, F. C., & Pires, J. H. (2015). *Spiritual Wisdom: Missives of Hope.* New York: Spiritist Alliance for Books (SAB).

YouTube. (2016, September 1). *Geraldo Lemos Neto no Grupo Espírita Francisco Xavier - Porto Alegre | Parte 1 .* Retrieved from YouTube: https://www.youtube.com/watch?v=F-EsXDOYGsU

Footnotes

[1] Xavier, Francisco C. Voltei, FEB, p. 178

[2] Wikipedia, "George Vale Owen", n.d., https://en.wikipedia.org/wiki/George_Vale_Owen, (accessed Spetember 13, 2015)

[3] Christian Spiritualism, "Life Beyond the Veil", n.d., http://www.christianspiritualism.org/articles/lbtv.htm, (accessed September 14, 2015)

[4] Christian Spiritualism, "Life Beyond the Veil", n.d., http://www.christianspiritualism.org/articles/lbtv.htm, (accessed September 14, 2015)

[5] Christian Spiritualism, "Life Beyond the Veil", n.d., http://www.christianspiritualism.org/articles/lbtv.htm, (accessed September 14, 2015)

[6] Christian Spiritualism, "Life Beyond the Veil", n.d., http://www.christianspiritualism.org/articles/lbtv.htm, (accessed September 14, 2015)

[7] Owner, G. Vale, The Life Beyond the Veil, Square Circles Publishing, p. 4

[8] Owner, G. Vale, The Life Beyond the Veil, Square Circles Publishing, p. 33

[9] Owner, G. Vale, The Life Beyond the Veil, Square Circles Publishing, pp. 1ii-1iii

[10] Owner, G. Vale, The Life Beyond the Veil, Square Circles Publishing, pp. 178-179

[11] Owner, G. Vale, The Life Beyond the Veil, Square Circles Publishing, p. 262

[12] Christian Spiritualism, "Life Beyond the Veil", n.d., http://www.christianspiritualism.org/articles/lbtv.htm, (accessed September 14, 2015)

[13] Christian Spiritualism, "Life Beyond the Veil", n.d., http://www.christianspiritualism.org/articles/lbtv.htm, (accessed September 14, 2015)

[14] Owner, G. Vale, The Life Beyond the Veil, Square Circles Publishing, pp. xliv-xlv

[15] Owen, R. G. The Life Beyond the Veil, Square Circles Publishing, pp. 10-11

[16] Owen, R. G. The Life Beyond the Veil, Square Circles Publishing, p. 11

[17] Owen, R. G., The Life Beyond the Veil, Squares Circles Publishing, pp. 67-68

[18] Owen, R. G., The Life Beyond the Veil, Squares Circles Publishing, p. 68

[19] Owen R. G. Life Beyond the Veil, Squares Circles Publishing, p. 110

[20] Owen R. G. Life Beyond the Veil, Squares Circles Publishing, p. 118

[21] Owen R. G. Life Beyond the Veil, Squares Circles Publishing, p. 118

[22] Owen R. G. Life Beyond the Veil, Squares Circles Publishing, p. 118

[23] Owen R. G. Life Beyond the Veil, Squares Circles Publishing, p. 119

[24] Owen R. G. Life Beyond the Veil, Squares Circles Publishing, p. 119

[25] Owen R. G. Life Beyond the Veil, Squares Circles Publishing, p. 140

[26] Kardec, Allan, Spiritist Review, Journal of Psychological Studies – 1858, United States Spiritist Council, pp. 557-559

[27] Owen R. G. Life Beyond the Veil, Squares Circles Publishing, p. 140

[28] Owen R. G. Life Beyond the Veil, Squares Circles Publishing, p. 140

[29] Owen R. G. Life Beyond the Veil, Squares Circles Publishing, pp. 140-141

[30] Owen R. G. Life Beyond the Veil, Squares Circles Publishing, p. 141

[31] Wikipedia, "Fourth Dimensional Space", n.d., https://en.wikipedia.org/wiki/Four-dimensional_space, (accessed March 20, 2016)

[32] Owen R. G. Life Beyond the Veil, Squares Circles Publishing, p. 141

[33] Owen R. G. Life Beyond the Veil, Squares Circles Publishing, p. 152

[34] Owen R. G. Life Beyond the Veil, Squares Circles Publishing, p. 152

[35] Owen R. G. Life Beyond the Veil, Squares Circles Publishing, p. 153

[36] Owen R. G. Life Beyond the Veil, Squares Circles Publishing, p. 153

[37] Owen R. G. Life Beyond the Veil, Squares Circles Publishing, p. 154

[38] Owen R. G. Life Beyond the Veil, Squares Circles Publishing, pp. 154-155

[39] Owen R. G. Life Beyond the Veil, Squares Circles Publishing, p. 155

[40] Owen R. G. Life Beyond the Veil, Squares Circles Publishing, p. 155

[41] Owen R. G. Life Beyond the Veil, Squares Circles Publishing, pp. 166-167

[42] Owen R. G. Life Beyond the Veil, Squares Circles Publishing, p. 168

[43] Owen R. G. Life Beyond the Veil, Squares Circles Publishing, p. 168

[44] Owen R. G. Life Beyond the Veil, Squares Circles Publishing, p. 169

[45] Owen R. G. Life Beyond the Veil, Squares Circles Publishing, p. 174

[46] Owen R. G. Life Beyond the Veil, Squares Circles Publishing, pp. 174-175

[47] Owen R. G. Life Beyond the Veil, Squares Circles Publishing, p. 178

[48] Owen R. G. Life Beyond the Veil, Squares Circles Publishing, pp. 178-179

[49] Owen, G. Vale, The Life Beyond the Veil, Square Circles Publishing, p. 319

[50] Owen, G. Vale, The Life Beyond the Veil, Square Circles Publishing, p. 318

[51] Pereira, Y. A., Memoirs of a Suicide, EDICEI, p. 518

[52] Pereira, Y. A., Memoirs of a Suicide, EDICEI, p. 519

317

[53] Kardec, A, The Spiritist Review – Journal of Psychological Review – 1859, United States Spiritist Council and the Spiritist Research Institute (IPEAK), p. 218

[54] Kardec, A, The Spiritist Review – Journal of Psychological Review – 1859, United States Spiritist Council and the Spiritist Research Institute (IPEAK), p. 221

[55] Owen, G. Vale, The Life Beyond the Veil, Square Circles Publishing, pp. 319-320

[56] Owen, G. Vale, The Life Beyond the Veil, Square Circles Publishing, p. 320

[57] Owen R. G. Life Beyond the Veil, Squares Circles Publishing, pp. 378-379

[58] INADS NDE Radio, "Meeting with Jesus – Near Death Experience – Christian NDE", n.d., https://www.youtube.com/watch?v=57jA2Tl2NkU. (accessed July 30, 2016)

[59] INADS NDE Radio, "Meeting with Jesus – Near Death Experience – Christian NDE", n.d., https://www.youtube.com/watch?v=57jA2Tl2NkU. (accessed July 30, 2016)

[60] INADS NDE Radio, "Meeting with Jesus – Near Death Experience – Christian NDE", n.d., https://www.youtube.com/watch?v=57jA2Tl2NkU. (accessed July 30, 2016)

[61] INADS NDE Radio, "Meeting with Jesus – Near Death Experience – Christian NDE", n.d., https://www.youtube.com/watch?v=57jA2Tl2NkU. (accessed July 30, 2016)

[62] Xavier, Francisco C., In the Greater World, EDICEI, p. 158

[63] Xavier, Francisco C., In the Greater World, EDICEI, p. 158

[64] Xavier, Francisco C., In the Greater World, EDICEI, p. 158

[65] Xavier, Francisco C., In the Greater World, EDICEI, p. 159

[66] Owen R. G. Life Beyond the Veil, Squares Circles Publishing, pp. 374-375

[67] Owen R. G. Life Beyond the Veil, Squares Circles Publishing, p. 375

[68] Owen R. G. Life Beyond the Veil, Squares Circles Publishing, p. 376

[69] Owen R. G. Life Beyond the Veil, Squares Circles Publishing, p. 376

[70] Owen R. G. Life Beyond the Veil, Squares Circles Publishing, p. 390

[71] Owen R. G. Life Beyond the Veil, Squares Circles Publishing, pp. 390-391

[72] Owen R. G. Life Beyond the Veil, Squares Circles Publishing, pp. 391-392

[73] Owen R. G. Life Beyond the Veil, Squares Circles Publishing, p. 393

[74] Pereira, Yvonne A., Memoirs of a Suicide, EDICEI, p. 335

[75] Owen R. G. Life Beyond the Veil, Squares Circles Publishing, pp. 529-530

[76] Owen R. G. Life Beyond the Veil, Squares Circles Publishing, p. 530

[77] Xavier, F. C., Missionaries of the Light, EDICEI, pp. 219-220

[78] Owen R. G. Life Beyond the Veil, Squares Circles Publishing, pp. 530-531

[79] Owen, R. G., The Outlands of Heaven, The Greater World Association Trust, pp. 13-14

[80] Owen R. G. Life Beyond the Veil, Squares Circles Publishing, p. 40

[81] Owen R. G. Life Beyond the Veil, Squares Circles Publishing, pp. 40-41

[82] Xavier, Francisco C, Workers of the Life Eternal, EDICEI, pp. 304-305

[83] Owen R. G. Life Beyond the Veil, Squares Circles Publishing, pp. 41-42

[84] Owen, G. Vale, Outlands of Heaven, Greater World Association Trust, pp. 140-141

[85] Owen, G. Vale, Outlands of Heaven, Greater World Association Trust, p. 141

[86] NDERF.org, "A Child's NDE", n.d., http://www.nderf.org/NDERF/NDE_Experiences/achild's.htm, (accessed January 23, 2016)

[87] NDERF.org, "A Child's NDE", n.d., http://www.nderf.org/NDERF/NDE_Experiences/achild's.htm, (accessed January 23, 2016)

[88] Owen, G. Vale, Outlands of Heaven, Greater World Association Trust, p. 141

[89] Xavier, Francisco C. Message from a Teen in the Spirit World, International Spiritist Council, pp. 14-16

[90] Owen, G. Vale, Outlands of Heaven, Greater World Association Trust, p. 142

[91] Owen, G. Vale, Outlands of Heaven, Greater World Association Trust, p. 143

[92] Owen R. G. Life Beyond the Veil, Squares Circles Publishing, p. 97

[93] Owen R. G. Life Beyond the Veil, Squares Circles Publishing, pp. 97-98

[94] Owen R. G. Life Beyond the Veil, Squares Circles Publishing, p. 99

[95] Owen R. G. Life Beyond the Veil, Squares Circles Publishing, pp. 99-100

[96] Owen R. G. Life Beyond the Veil, Squares Circles Publishing, p. 103

[97] Kardec, Allan, The Spirits Book, White Crow Books, p. 153

[98] Owen R. G. Life Beyond the Veil, Squares Circles Publishing, p. 102

[99] Owen R. G. Life Beyond the Veil, Squares Circles Publishing, pp. 102-103

[100] Owen R. G. Life Beyond the Veil, Squares Circles Publishing, p. 111

[101] Owen R. G. Life Beyond the Veil, Squares Circles Publishing, p. 111

[102] Owen R. G. Life Beyond the Veil, Squares Circles Publishing, pp. 111-112

[103] Owen R. G. Life Beyond the Veil, Squares Circles Publishing, p. 112

[104] Owen R. G. Life Beyond the Veil, Squares Circles Publishing, pp. 113-114

[105] Owen R. G. Life Beyond the Veil, Squares Circles Publishing, pp. 114-115

[106] Owen R. G. Life Beyond the Veil, Squares Circles Publishing, p. 120

[107] Owen R. G. Life Beyond the Veil, Squares Circles Publishing, p. 120

[108] Owen R. G. Life Beyond the Veil, Squares Circles Publishing, pp. 120-121

[109] Owen R. G. Life Beyond the Veil, Squares Circles Publishing, p. 121

[110] Kardec, Allan, The Book on Mediums, White Crow Books, p.201

[111] Kardec, Allan, The Book on Mediums, White Crow Books, pp.201-202

[112] Kardec, Allan, The Book on Mediums, White Crow Books, p.203

[113] Owen, G. Vale, The Life Beyond the Veil, Square Circles Publishing, pp. 196-197

[114] Owen, G. Vale, The Life Beyond the Veil, Square Circles Publishing, p. 197

[115] Owen, G. Vale, The Life Beyond the Veil, Square Circles Publishing, p. 197

[116] Owen, G. Vale, The Life Beyond the Veil, Square Circles Publishing, p. 199

[117] Owen, G. Vale, The Life Beyond the Veil, Square Circles Publishing, p. 199

[118] Owen R. G. Life Beyond the Veil, Squares Circles Publishing, p. 205

[119] Owen R. G. Life Beyond the Veil, Squares Circles Publishing, p. 206

[120] Owen R. G. Life Beyond the Veil, Squares Circles Publishing, pp. 206-208

[121] Owen R. G. Life Beyond the Veil, Squares Circles Publishing, p. 209

[122] Owen R. G. Life Beyond the Veil, Squares Circles Publishing, p. 210

[123] Owen R. G. Life Beyond the Veil, Squares Circles Publishing, p. 210

[124] Kardec, Allan Spiritist Review, Journal of Psychological Studies – 1858, United States Spiritist Council and IPEAK, pp. 433-434

[125] Owen R. G. Life Beyond the Veil, Squares Circles Publishing, p. 210

[126] Owen R. G. Life Beyond the Veil, Squares Circles Publishing, p. 212

[127] Owen, G. Vale, The Life Beyond the Veil, Square Circles Publishing, pp. 239-240

[128] Owen, G. Vale, The Life Beyond the Veil, Square Circles Publishing, p. 240

[129] Owen, G. Vale, The Life Beyond the Veil, Square Circles Publishing, p. 240

[130] Owen, G. Vale, The Life Beyond the Veil, Square Circles Publishing, pp. 240-241

[131] Owen, G. Vale, The Life Beyond the Veil, Square Circles Publishing, p. 241

[132] NDERF.org, "My NDE", n.d., http://nhneneardeath.ning.com/profiles/blogs/my-nde-2, (accessed Sept. 6, 2014)

[133] NDERF.org, "My NDE", n.d., http://nhneneardeath.ning.com/profiles/blogs/my-nde-2, (accessed Sept. 6, 2014)

[134] Owen, G. Vale, The Life Beyond the Veil, Square Circles Publishing, p. 242

[135] Owen, G. Vale, The Life Beyond the Veil, Square Circles Publishing, p. 267

[136] Xavier, Francisco C., Nosso Lar, EDICEI, p. 70

[137] Owen, G. Vale, The Life Beyond the Veil, Square Circles Publishing, pp. 267-268

[138] Owen, G. Vale, The Life Beyond the Veil, Square Circles Publishing, pp. 268-269

[139] Owen, G. Vale, The Life Beyond the Veil, Square Circles Publishing, pp. 269-270

[140] Owen, G. Vale, The Life Beyond the Veil, Square Circles Publishing, p. 315

[141] Xavier, F. C. Workers of the Life Eternal, EDICEI, p. 61

[142] Xavier, F. C. Workers of the Life Eternal, EDICEI, p. 63

[143] Owen, G. Vale, The Life Beyond the Veil, Square Circles Publishing, pp. 315-316

[144] Owen, G. Vale, The Life Beyond the Veil, Square Circles Publishing, p. 316

[145] Owen, G. Vale, The Life Beyond the Veil, Square Circles Publishing, p. 316

[146] Owen, G. Vale, The Life Beyond the Veil, Square Circles Publishing, pp. 425-426

[147] Owen, G. Vale, The Life Beyond the Veil, Square Circles Publishing, pp. 426-427

[148] Owen, G. Vale, The Life Beyond the Veil, Square Circles Publishing, p. 428

[149] Owen, G. Vale, The Life Beyond the Veil, Square Circles Publishing, p. 428

[150] Owen, G. Vale, The Life Beyond the Veil, Square Circles Publishing, p. 429

[151] Owen, G. Vale, The Life Beyond the Veil, Square Circles Publishing, p. 335

[152] Kardec, Allen, The Spiritist Review – Journal of Psychological Review – 1859, United States Spiritist Council and the Spiritist Research Institute (IPEAK), pp. 210-211

[153] Owen, G. Vale, The Life Beyond the Veil, Square Circles Publishing, pp. 339-340

[154] Owen, G. Vale, The Life Beyond the Veil, Square Circles Publishing, pp. 338-339

[155] Owen, G. Vale, The Life Beyond the Veil, Square Circles Publishing, pp. 341-342

[156] Owen, G. Vale, The Life Beyond the Veil, Square Circles Publishing, p. 321

[157] Owen, G. Vale, The Life Beyond the Veil, Square Circles Publishing, p. 322

[158] Owen, G. Vale, The Life Beyond the Veil, Square Circles Publishing, p. 322

[159] Owen, G. Vale, The Life Beyond the Veil, Square Circles Publishing, pp. 322-323

[160] Owen, G. Vale, The Life Beyond the Veil, Square Circles Publishing, p. 323

[161] Owen, G. Vale, The Life Beyond the Veil, Square Circles Publishing, pp. 563-564

[162] Owen, G. Vale, The Life Beyond the Veil, Square Circles Publishing, p. 565

[163] Owen, G. Vale, The Life Beyond the Veil, Square Circles Publishing, p. 565

[164] Owen, G. Vale, The Life Beyond the Veil, Square Circles Publishing, p. 566

[165] Xavier, F. C., On the Way to the Light, EDICEI, pp.116-117

[166] Xavier, F. C., On the Way to the Light, EDICEI, p.210

[167] Xavier, F. C., In the Greater World, EDICEI, pp.24-25

[168] Xavier, F. C., In the Greater World, EDICEI, p.27

[169] Xavier, F. C., On the Way to the Light, EDICEI, p. 167

[170] Owen, G. Vale, The Life Beyond the Veil, Square Circles Publishing, p. 593

[171] Owen, G. Vale, The Life Beyond the Veil, Square Circles Publishing, p. 593

[172] Owen, G. Vale, The Life Beyond the Veil, Square Circles Publishing, p. 594

[173] Owen, G. Vale, The Life Beyond the Veil, Square Circles Publishing, p. 595

[174] Owen, G. Vale, The Life Beyond the Veil, Square Circles Publishing, p. 599

[175] Owen R. G. Life Beyond the Veil, Squares Circles Publishing, p. 159

[176] Owen R. G. Life Beyond the Veil, Squares Circles Publishing, p. 160

[177] Owen R. G. Life Beyond the Veil, Squares Circles Publishing, pp. 160-161

[178] Owen R. G. Life Beyond the Veil, Squares Circles Publishing, p. 161

[179] Owen R. G. Life Beyond the Veil, Squares Circles Publishing, pp. 161-162

[180] Owen R. G. Life Beyond the Veil, Squares Circles Publishing, p. 184

[181] Owen R. G. Life Beyond the Veil, Squares Circles Publishing, p. 184

[182] Owen R. G. Life Beyond the Veil, Squares Circles Publishing, p. 184

[183] Xavier, Francisco C. On the Way to the Light, EDICEI, pp. 44-45

[184] Owen R. G. Life Beyond the Veil, Squares Circles Publishing, pp. 185-186

[185] Owen R. G. Life Beyond the Veil, Squares Circles Publishing, p. 186

[186] Owen R. G. Life Beyond the Veil, Squares Circles Publishing, pp. 186-187

[187] Owen, G. Vale, The Life Beyond the Veil, Square Circles Publishing, p. 187

[188] Farnese, A., A Wanderer in the Spirit Lands, W.J. Sinkins, PDF, p. 116

[189] Xavier, Francisco C. In the Greater World, EDICEI, p. 240

[190] NDERF.org, "Michael Joseph NDE", n.d., http://www.nderf.org/NDERF/NDE_Experiences/michael_joseph_nde.htm, (accessed Aug. 8, 2014)

[191] NDERF.org, "Michael Joseph NDE", n.d., http://www.nderf.org/NDERF/NDE_Experiences/michael_joseph_nde.htm, (accessed Aug. 8, 2014)

[192] NDERF.org, "Michael Joseph NDE", n.d., http://www.nderf.org/NDERF/NDE_Experiences/michael_joseph_nde.htm, (accessed Aug. 8, 2014)

[193] Owen, G. Vale, The Life Beyond the Veil, Square Circles Publishing, p. 188

[194] Owen, G. Vale, The Life Beyond the Veil, Square Circles Publishing, p. 188

[195] Owen, G. Vale, The Life Beyond the Veil, Square Circles Publishing, p. 188

[196] Owen, G. Vale, The Life Beyond the Veil, Square Circles Publishing, p. 337

[197] Owen, G. Vale, The Life Beyond the Veil, Square Circles Publishing, p. 337

[198] Owen, G. Vale, The Life Beyond the Veil, Square Circles Publishing, p. 642

[199] Owen, G. Vale, The Life Beyond the Veil, Square Circles Publishing, pp. 642-643

[200] Owen, G. Vale, The Life Beyond the Veil, Square Circles Publishing, p. 643

[201] Owen, G. Vale, The Life Beyond the Veil, Square Circles Publishing, pp. 643-644

[202] Owen, G. Vale, The Life Beyond the Veil, Square Circles Publishing, pp. 644-645

[203] Owen, G. Vale, The Life Beyond the Veil, Square Circles Publishing, p. 558

[204] Owen, G. Vale, The Life Beyond the Veil, Square Circles Publishing, p. 559

[205] Owen, G. Vale, The Life Beyond the Veil, Square Circles Publishing, p. 560

[206] Owen, G. Vale, The Life Beyond the Veil, Square Circles Publishing, p. 560

[207] Limite, D., "Data Limite Segundo Chico Xavier", n.d., https://www.youtube.com/watch?v=4JxukHvGVzE, (accessed January 17, 2017)

[208] Xavier, F. C., On the Way to the Light, EDICEI, p. 205

[209] Owen, G. Vale, The Life Beyond the Veil, Square Circles Publishing, pp. 560-561

[210] Owen, G. Vale, The Life Beyond the Veil, Square Circles Publishing, p. 621

[211] Cayce, E.E., Edgar Cayce On Atlantis, Grand Central Publishing, pp. 79-81

[212] Cayce, E.E., Edgar Cayce On Atlantis, Grand Central Publishing, p. 115

[213] Xavier, Francisco C., Liberation, EDICEI, p. 17

[214] Wikipedia, "Human Evolution", n.d., http://en.wikipedia.org/wiki/Human_evolution, (accessed December 22, 2014)

[215] Wikipedia, "EVFIT", n.d., evfit.com: http://www.evfit.com/40,000ya.htm, (accessed December 22, 2014)

[216] Owen, G. Vale, The Life Beyond the Veil, Square Circles Publishing, p. 621

[217] Rice University News and Media, "Misconceptions of Science and Religion Found in New Study", n.d., http://news.rice.edu/2014/02/16/misconceptions-of-science-and-religion-found-in-new-study/ , (accessed May 14, 2017)

[218] Owen, G. Vale, The Life Beyond the Veil, Square Circles Publishing, p. 630

[219] Owen, G. Vale, The Life Beyond the Veil, Square Circles Publishing, pp. 633-634

[220] XAVIER, Francisco C. In the Greater World, EDICEI, p. 16

[221] XAVIER, Francisco C. In the Greater World, EDICEI, p. 17

[222] XAVIER, Francisco C. In the Greater World, EDICEI, p. 23

[223] XAVIER, Francisco C. In the Greater World, EDICEI, p. 27

[224] XAVIER, Francisco C. In the Greater World, EDICEI, p. 30

[225] XAVIER, Francisco C. In the Greater World, EDICEI, p. 31

[226] XAVIER, Francisco C. In the Greater World, EDICEI, p. 31

[227] Kardec, Allan, Genesis, EDICEI, p. 428

[228] Kardec, Allan, Genesis, EDICEI, p. 429

[229] XAVIER, Francisco C. In the Greater World, EDICEI, p. 31

[230] XAVIER, Francisco C. In the Greater World, EDICEI, p. 33

[231] XAVIER, Francisco C. In the Greater World, EDICEI, p. 32

[232] XAVIER, Francisco C. In the Greater World, EDICEI, p. 201

[233] XAVIER, Francisco C. In the Greater World, EDICEI, p. 204

[234] XAVIER, Francisco C. In the Greater World, EDICEI, p. 205

[235] XAVIER, Francisco C. In the Greater World, EDICEI, p. 208

[236] Xavier, Francisco C., Missionaries of the Light, EDICEI, p. 87

[237] Xavier, Francisco C., Missionaries of the Light, EDICEI, p. 87

[238] Owen, G. Vale, The Life Beyond the Veil, Square Circles Publishing, pp. 658-659

[239] Xavier, F. C., On the Way to the Light, EDICEI, pp. 123-124

[240] Goldennuggetswebs, "Revelation", n.d., http://www.goldnuggetwebs.com/revelation/revelation-p2.html, (accessed September 7, 2014)

[241] Xavier, F. C., On the Way to the Light, EDICEI, pp. 124-125

[242] Xavier, F. C., On the Way to the Light, EDICEI, p. 125

[243] Kardec, A., The Spirits Book, White Crow Books, Ques. 1019, p. 522

[244] Kardec, A., The Spirits Book, White Crow Books, Ques. 1019, p. 523

[245] Kardec, Allan. Genesis, EDICEI Cap. 18, item 27

[246] Kardec, A., The Gospel According to Spiritism, EDICEI, p. 327

[247] Owen, G. Vale, The Life Beyond the Veil, Square Circles Publishing, p. 662

[248] Owen, G. Vale, The Life Beyond the Veil, Square Circles Publishing, p. 663

[249] Owen, G. Vale, The Life Beyond the Veil, Square Circles Publishing, pp. 665-666

[250] Owen, G. Vale, The Life Beyond the Veil, Square Circles Publishing, pp. 667-668

[251] Owen, G. Vale, The Life Beyond the Veil, Square Circles Publishing, p. 669

[252] Owen, G. Vale, The Outlands of Heaven, The Greater World Association Trust, p. 207

Made in the USA
Columbia, SC
02 March 2019